W9-CDK-213

The Spy in Hitler's Inner Circle

Hans-Thilo Schmidt and the Intelligence Network that Decoded Enigma

Paul Paillole

Translated by
Curtis Key and Hannah McAdams

CASEMATE
Oxford & Philadelphia

Published in Great Britain and
the United States of America in 2016 by
CASEMATE PUBLISHERS
10 Hythe Bridge Street, Oxford OX1 2EW, UK

and

1950 Lawrence Road, Havertown PA 19083, USA

Notre espion chez Hitler © Nouveau Monde éditions 2011
English translation © Casemate UK Ltd 2016

Hardcover Edition: ISBN 978-1-61200-371-9
Digital Edition: ISBN 978-1-61200-372-6 (epub)

A CIP record for this book is available from the British Library

Printed and bound in the United States of America

For a complete list of Casemate titles, please contact:

CASEMATE PUBLISHERS (UK)
Telephone (01865) 241249
Fax (01865) 794449
Email: casemate-uk@casematepublishers.co.uk
www.casematepublishers.co.uk

CASEMATE PUBLISHERS (US)
Telephone (610) 853-9131
Fax (610) 853-9146
Email: casemate@casematepublishers.com
www.casematepublishers.com

Contents

Glossary

The Deuxième Bureau was the French external military intelligence agency until 1940, but the term is used more broadly as a term for French military intelligence services. Palliole also uses a variety of terms and acronyms for the sections of the French military intelligence services.

B.C.R.A.   *Bureau Central de Renseignements et d'Action.* De Gaulle's intelligence agency.

C.E.   *Service de centralization des renseignements.* French central intelligence service from 1936 until the fall of France.

F.A.   *Forschungsamt.* special service created by Goering for interceptions, wiretapping, and decoding.

G.C. & C.S.   Government Code and Cipher School. British Organization for intercepting and decrypting messages. Became G.C.H.Q. in 1939.

Gestapo   *Geheime Staatspolizei.* Reich secret police.

G.F.P.   *Geheimfeldpolizei.* Secret military police of the Wehrmacht.

III.F   Counterintelligence research group, a section of the Abwehr.

N.S.B.D.   Organization of the National Socialist Party in the business sector.

N.S.D.A.P.   *Nationalsozialistische Deutsche Arbeiterpartei.* National Socialist German Workers' Party, the Nazi party.

O.K.H.   *Oberkommando der Heeres.* High Command of the German Army.

O.K.W.   *Oberkommando der Wehrmacht.* German High Command (of the armed forces).

O.S.S.   *Office of Strategic Services:* American intelligence agency.

P.T.T.   *Postes, Télécommunications et Télédiffusion.* The post office and telecommunications service.

R.S.H.A.   *Reichssicherheitshauptamt.* Central Office of Reich Security.

S.A.   *Sturmabteilung.* Assault sections of the N.S.D.A.P.

S.R-S.C.R.	*Deuxième Bureau.* Intelligence agency of the French Army General Staff, comprising the S.R. and the S.C.R.
S.C.R.	*Service de centralisation des reseignements.* A section within the Deuxième Bureau charged with counter-espionage.
S.D.	*Sicherheitsdienst.* German security service within the S.S.
S.H.A.E.F.	Supreme Headquarters Allied Expeditionary Force.
S.I.P.O.	*Sicherheitspolizei.* Nazi security police.
S.I.M.	*Servizio Informazione Military.* The Italian intelligence agency.
S.I.S.	Secret Intelligence Service. The British intelligence agency for foreign intelligence (MI6).
S.R.	*Service de reseignement.* A section within the Deuxième Bureau charged with foreign intelligence.
S.S.	*Schutzstaffeln.* Elite troops of the Nazi Party and Hitler's private guard.
S.T.O.	*Service de Travail Obligatoire.* German war work imposed on the French populace.
V.M.	*Vertrauen Männer.* Secret agents.

Code names and aliases

Hans-Thilo Schmidt	Asché/H.E.
André Perruche	Alison
Rodolphe Lemoine (Rudolf Stallman)	Rex, von Koenig, Verdier
Guy Schlesser	St. George
Gustave Bertrand	Barsac

Preface

Notre espion chez Hitler, written by Paul Paillole in 1985, has continued to attract readers for over thirty years since its original publication in France. The reasons for its enduring appeal are twofold. First, the author: Paul Paillole had a central role in the secret war between France and Germany, before and for the duration of World War II. Louis Rivet wrote about his war service in 1945: "The counterespionage service, which he autonomously directed from the beginning of 1942, was able to engage the Gestapo in a thankless struggle and confront the wrath of those French members partnered with it; this unexpected result was obtained by the clear intelligence, the steel-like energy, and the incomparable and uncompromising patriotism of Commander Paillole…" The second reason, of course, concerns the content of the book. After publishing *Services Spéciaux (1935–1945),*[1] Paul Paillole invited us to discover the crucial moments that mark the most, shall we say *enigmatic*, aspects of the war—those of the "code war."

Through a three-pronged approach—human, technical, and operational—we are reminded that history is never written, and that men of character can alter its course in one direction or another. The most influential players in this story include Gustave Bertrand, Rodolphe Lemoine, Hans-Thilo Schmidt, Marian Rejewski… and Paul Paillole. He delivers a great history lesson, and offers us a document which retains all its interest and topicality, especially given how much historians have relied upon his archival studies for their own work, supporting and confirming Paillole's research much more frequently than criticizing it.

Let's look at the man first. Paul Paillole was born in November 1905 in Rennes. Twenty years later, he joined the ranks of the Saint-

Cyr Special Military Academy on a scholarship; his father, an artillery lieutenant, Knight of the Legion of Honor, had died "for France, as a result of his injuries." Promoted to lieutenant, young Paillole chose to join what was known at the time as l'armée d'Afrique (the Army of Africa). He served as a young officer in the 17th and then 21st Regiments of the Algerian Fusiliers. When he asked, in 1930, for authorization to take the entrance examination to the officers' school for the Versailles Gendarmerie, its directors, who had great esteem for Paillole, offered him their full support, noting his energy and "étoffe" (meaning that he had the right attributes to be a leader).

In 1931, at the end of his training, he joined the 3rd Legion of the Republican Mobile Guard in Lyon. There he was universally admired due to "his natural authority, his enlightened zeal and methodical work ethic," recorded by Colonel Ripault, who held the command of the legion. The following year, Paillole received two laudatory testimonials highlighting his brilliance and gallant conduct in the difficult situations he had faced. In 1935, on the eve of his departure for the Deuxième Bureau, Colonel Garnier described him as "spunky, loved and admired by his subordinates."

On December 1, 1935, Paillole's career—and life—changed direction. Officially transferred to the personal staff of the gendarmerie in Paris, in reality he was moved to the Deuxième Bureau of the *Section de renseignements*—the French Intelligence Department—and assigned to the Central Intelligence Section of the Army General Staff. During the months that followed he was personally selected and promoted to captain, which his new chief, Lieutenant Colonel Rivet, head of both the S.R. and S.C.R. (Central Intelligence Section), considered as "just reward for his achievements and services rendered."

Employing the innate energy and methodical nature that his former chiefs had noticed and described, he began to revive and reform a department that had become routine and even obsolete. Paillole's enterprising initiatives led Rivet to consider him an "unrivaled innovator and architect of counterespionage techniques which were unprecedented in suppressing the enemy spy."

When war broke out in 1939,[2] Paillole joined the Cinquième Bureau, a natural growth and extension of the Deuxième Bureau. There, he redoubled his efforts in the fight against espionage, predominantly German efforts. After France's defeat, the struggle continued for the Cinquième Bureau despite the fact that the armistice agreements imposed on France forced it to dissolve its intelligence services.

Though officially closed, the Cinquième Bureau continued to operate under Louis Rivet, with the support of General Weygand, in the guise of the very official-sounding Bureau of Anti-National Activities (B.M.A.).[3] As for counterintelligence activities, Paul Paillole transformed the department into an "agricultural organization" known as the Rural Works (TR), headquartered in Marseilles.[4] From this city HQ and the ten offices created between 1940 and 1941, the fight against German espionage continued in secret under the leadership of Paillole, the "backbone" of the organization. Placed on official Armistice leave in December 1942, he departed surreptitiously for North Africa via Spain,[5] and in April 1943 he became the director of military security, a position he would hold until November 1944. In this station he gained the respect and admiration of Jacques Soustelle, who ran the Special Services Branch (D.G.H.S.) and the Department of General of Studies and Research successively. Admitted into the reserves under the rank of colonel in 1955, he was to take on the assignment of "national liquidator of the S.S.M.F./T.R.", which he himself had created in 1940.[6]

Paillole was one of a rare few who, throughout all those years, was a participant in—or, moreover, a privileged witness to—one of the biggest espionage cases of the war, that of the Enigma machine. He experienced every day of the operation, from Rodolphe Lemoine's recruitment of Hans-Thilo Schmidt, also known as "H.E.," through the epic period when Polish, French and British cryptologists used the intelligence to decipher the Enigma messages, until Schmidt's death and the arrest of Rodolphe Lemoine, first by the Germans and then by the French, and his death in 1946. Above all, Paillole was one of the few in France to write about this little known and undervalued episode in French military history, justifying the reissue of this book.[7] Though a true eyewitness account and document of great importance for the history of World War II (and that of the French intelligence services), his work reads like a novel due to its lucid style and compelling "characters."

When, ten years after writing *Services Spéciaux (1935–1945)*, Paul Paillole decided to take up his pen once more, it was to write about the critical issue of the infiltration of German agencies by French military counterintelligence, specifically through the recruitment of a man at the very heart of the German "code", Hans-Thilo Schmidt. Furthermore, it was also Paillole's goal to shed new light on the cooperation between the French, British and Polish agencies, most notably surrounding the history of the Enigma machine. In doing so, Paul Paillole brings one of the most important espionage affairs of the war back into focus, and setting the role of the French, from the early 1930s right up to 1946 into the context of the existing Anglo-Saxon and Polish historiography.

The reception of the book has, however, led many to forget that the history of the French secret services,[8] had not only been almost entirely forgotten prior to its publication, except by those who had been involved with the resistance, but had also been impossible to piece together because the archives had been seized, first by the Germans in 1942, and then by the Soviets in 1945.[9]

Notre espion chez Hitler is a rare retrospective testimony which, when it was first published in 1985, brought back into the spotlight the little that civilians knew about the Enigma machine from the books of David Kahn,[10] Gustave Bertrand,[11] Gordon Welchman,[12] Sir Francis Harry Hinsley,[13] and Władysław Kozaczuk.[14] Since then, historians have continued to present their research, and witnesses to tell their stories. Our knowledge of Enigma—from the research done by the Polish to the return of Hans-Thilo Schmidt—and the actions of Rex and the French services has greatly improved. For the most part, it hasn't contradicted the initial contributions of Paul Paillole, even if at times—restrained by his modesty and his obvious desire to speak out about facts that he felt should remain hidden or secret, he stayed his pen.

Among the journals offering more in-depth analysis, the quarterly publication *Cryptologia*,[15] founded in 1977 by a group of historians and passionate cryptologists organized around founding editor David Kahn, offers reference articles on this general theme. The articles dedicated to Enigma complete the cryptologic dimension of the human stories told by Bertrand and Paillole.[16] In Krakow, Poland, Zdzisław Jan Kapera has since 1990 been the editor of a remarkable and well-documented newsletter, with the majority of articles written in English or German: *The Enigma Bulletin*.[17] Much the same may be said for the many articles published over the years in two international journals: *Intelligence and National Security*[18] and *The Journal of Intelligence History*.[19]

The British journalist and historian Hugh Sebag-Montefiore offers a broader perspective in his book *Enigma, The Battle for the Code*, one of most meticulous and best-researched works on the issue since Colonel Paillole's work.[20] Sebag-Montefiore is, to the best of our knowledge, the only author who has recently worked on all of the aspects of decryption and the use of the Enigma machine from three perspectives: first human, then technical, and finally operational. While many historians have primarily addressed the technical dimension (breaching the mode of operation, constructing the machine and utilizing it), or its operational aspects (operations in the Mediterranean, Norway, France, in the Atlantic, etc.), Sebag-Montefiore is the primary researcher to have, in an extension of Paul Paillole's reflections, devoted special attention to the men who participated in this adventure. His work on Hans-Thilo Schmidt, a.k.a. H.E., a.k.a. Asché (which is the sound made when the letters 'H' and 'E' are pronounced together in French), is as remarkable and thorough as it is nuanced. For example, Schmidt, probably considered at the time of his death in a Berlin prison in 1943 as a "traitor through-and-through" by the Allies as much as by the Germans, wrote three messages to his wife and children just before he died. It was Hugh Sebag-Montefiore who found and cited them in his work. One note in particular deserves attention, because it is so far removed from preconceived ideas, and ends with these words: "Goodbye, from a free and peaceful Germany."

The author dwells rather less on Gustave Bertrand and Rodolphe Lemoine a.k.a. Rex, who was the largest recruiter for the *Deuxième Bureau* during the inter-war period and the agent assigned to Hans-Thilo Schmidt. This is not the case, however, concerning the Mitrokine[21] archives, which provide us with valuable details on the "Soviet track."

In Chapter IV, Paul Paillole mentions a certain "de Ry," writing: "At the end of September 1942, Rex received an urgent call from the doorman of the Splendid [...] One of his Swiss friends, named de Ry, absolutely wanted to meet him." de Ry was clearly a "friend" of Lemoine, and "a code trafficker like him" with whom he had been in business since the 1920s. But what Paillole disregards, or at least feigns to disregard, is the fact that de Ry was also, as the Soviet archives revealed, in communication with the Parisian resident of the O.G.P.U. (Soviet All-Union State Political Administration), Vladimir Voïnovitch, to whom he sold diplomatic ciphers, primarily Italian. Another agent of the O.G.P.U., an outlaw at this time, Dimitri Bystroletov, received orders to contact Lemoine through the intermediary of de Ry and "to entrust to another illegal O.G.P.U. agent in Paris, Ignatius Reiss."[22] The latter, posing, according to Christopher Andrew, as a "U.S. intelligence officer," attempted to recruit Lemoine. Did he succeed? Most unlikely, as Lemoine had the good sense to inform the French, who were then able to identify Reiss.

In November 1933, Gustave Bertrand arrived on the scene. From then on, since everyone knew each other, the three men meet on multiple occasions and negotiate the "Italian, Czechoslovakian and Hungarian ciphers."[23] This triple encounter, which at first sight might appear commonplace or trivial, is in fact quite interesting. It allows us, thanks to information provided by Paul Paillole and complemented by the K.G.B. archives, if not to understand then at least to question the conditions surrounding the detention of Rodolphe Lemoine by the Germans: it has been claimed, at one point, that the meeting was facilitated by a "multi-card agent" working for the Soviets.

The Polish perspective, already presented through the work of Władysław Kozaczuk, opportunely reappeared in 2005 to mark the centenary of the birth of Marian Rejewski. In this year, the Polish Defense Ministry published a special issue of its *Przegl d Historyczno-Wojskowy* (Military History Review),[24] focused on the *in extenso* reproduction of two fundamental texts written by Marian Rejewski in 1967 and in 1974 in Polish and English. The first text offers an essentially scientific and technical approach to the Enigma machine by the agent who broke the code. The second records his memories of the Polish participation in the deciphering of the machine and the period surrounding it, from initial contacts with the office of the Polish cipher bureau in Poznan during the late 1920s through his involvement with the Polish Army in Britain, passing through France between 1940 and 1943. These texts, deposited in the Polish historic service archives, had only previously been accessed by Władysław Kozaczuk[25] and David Kahn, making their full publication that much more interesting. Finally, the publication of the excellent work by Jean Medrala,[26] again in 2005, shows, among other things, how the Polish Enigma team, concealed in the region of Uzès, France after the defeat of June 1940, resumed its activities and managed to work for both its French leaders, in the case of Bertrand, and the Polish government in exile without the French ever realizing it. This explains, for example, how the number of Enigma messages decoded by the team (P.C. Cadix for the French, Ekspozytura 300 for the Poles), can vary dramatically between French and Polish sources.

In France, during the same period, Olivier Forcade began to compare the existing historiography, which included Paul Paillole's work, with the archives of the French intelligence services and the Committee of General Security returned to France by Russia between 1993 and 2000. After having conducted a methodical examination, he wrote *La République secrète. Histoire des services spéciaux français de 1918 à 1939*,[27] the outcome of ten years of research. The exploration of these archives systematically confirms what was written by Paillole. It demonstrates the absolutely uncompromising character of the information he provides about intelligence gathered in the years 1935–44, and most notably about the pre-war period and the establishment of an offensive counterintelligence tool. It is a page of history often swept aside by the 1940 defeat; only that military debacle is remembered, while the role of intelligence provided by the secret apparatus is overlooked. Examined and exposed, the Moscow archives shed new light on the book by Paul Paillole, who had not had access to them. The treatment of the 1936 Rhineland crisis in this work and the studies that have resulted from it by Peter Jackson, R. Gerald Hughes, Scott and Len Olivier Forcade,[28] in hand with the archives of the Deuxième Bureau and Moscow, leave no doubt that Paillole's book is a major contribution to the history of the secret services in the 1930s.

This is confirmed by the recent publication *Carnets du chef des services secrets, 1936–1944*.[29] Paul Paillole mentions these diaries several times in his writing, even going so far as to include an extract from the day of June 9, 1939. The entry, which ends with the words "*June 9, 1939*: Letter from H.E. Pay attention to the end of August," entices one to jump right into Olivier Forcade's and Sébastien Laurent's fully annotated work on the diaries.

It also shows us, from the pen of Paul Paillole, that H.E.—that is to say, Hans-Thilo Schmidt—predicted the invasion of Poland with remarkable accuracy—only three days out.

Frédéric Guelton

Foreword

1933–1940: The French intelligence service was at the heart of the Third Reich. Hitler had been betrayed.

Yet despite this, France was defeated.

And thanks to this, England was saved.

The Allied victory was safeguarded.

You must judge for yourself whether these simple sentences accurately reflect the real-life events related in these pages.

At times reason is forced to deal with gaps in documentation, the demands of discretion, obligations to secrets still classified, and the missing testimonies of those who were too committed to the cause.

Never has my imagination replaced what I believe to have been reality.

I have done this work without complacency for my country.

Without complacency for my old Bureau, of which I keep a precious memory, due to its honesty and desire to serve.

By doing this I aim to help its cause, so often mistreated by history.

PAUL PAILLOLE

Introduction

On Saturday June 2, 1973, I returned to 2bis, avenue de Tourville to walk once more along the route I used to take thirty-eight years before in 1935 when, as a young officer, I had just been assigned to the Bureaus of Intelligence and Counterespionage of the Army General Staff, Deuxième Bureau (S.R.-S.C.R.).

With a heavy heart, I looked for the last time on the dilapidated premises that we had had to abandon in a panic on June 11, 1940. These ruins were to be handed over to architects and prepared for demolition. Les Invalides, its inner court stripped of these additional buildings constructed at the beginning of the twentieth century, would be returned to the state of historic purity intended by Louvois.

General Thozet, director of the Military Security Service and the building superintendent, albeit for only a short period, received us— General Henri Navarre, about a hundred comrades, and myself. He was surrounded by his general staff: Jeannou Lacaze, research director at the S.D.E.C.E.,[30] and Charles Chenevier, president of the *Fédération des Réseaux de la France Combattante*.

For the 'elders', 2bis represented the pre-war Bureau where we scrutinized our adversaries in order to uncover their objectives and neutralize their efforts. For those who joined us after 1940, it was the *temple mystérieux* they had heard about on so many occasions, which we had taught them to respect by involving them in our fight against the aggressor. For the new recruits enlisted after the Liberation, it was a place charged with history, to which they would have to bid farewell after this ultimate reminder of the past.

The Last Post was sounded. Frozen at attention in front of the monument erected in memory of Colonel André Sérot, our thoughts went out to them, to him. If ever there were a representative figure of the spirit that prevailed in our services, it would certainly be found in this soldier, a volunteer combatant in World War II, chief intelligence officer of the Air Force in Belfort from 1930 to 1940, my adjutant from 1941 to 1944, and himself director of Military Security from 1946 to 1947. Hunted in vain by the enemy for more than ten years, he lived through the ordeal of his wife being arrested and deported in retaliation to Buchenwald. Modest, efficient, Sérot never stopped serving until his assassination in Jerusalem on September 17, 1948, alongside the Count Folke-Bernadotte. Both men, mandated by the U.N., were attempting to restore peace in the Middle East.

In this moment of recollection, my memories were drawn to the offices of 2bis, which had been a symbol of French intelligence that was for us all were, again and for just a short time; the old walls that had witnessed so many vicissitudes, so many sacrifices.

Was this masterpiece, quietly accomplished by the legendary Deuxième Bureau, to be buried forever beneath the rubble of our old buildings?

As a final witness and tribute to the work that inspired such an extraordinary notion of defense and roused the purest patriotism, I felt compelled, to preserve the honor of our Bureau and in the interests of history, to disclose our largest research venture into Nazi Germany: the case of H.E (also known as Asché).[31]

Judged on the quantity and quality of information gathered between 1931 and 1940, its effect on the course and outcome of the war, and its dramatic and human aspects, the H.E. case is undoubtedly the most characteristic and important example of espionage in World War II. Furthermore, it is a perfect example of the activity of the French Military Special Services at that time.

To expose the nature of this case, which surpasses in scientific, strategic and tactical significance that of the German Sorge, a Soviet spy at the heart of the German embassy in Japan, I have included along with my own recollections those of the privileged and undercover participants.

From 1935 onward, I lived through all those gripping adventures with them. It was my job to ensure their safety and maintain the strict secrecy of the case. I gained the trust of Rodolphe Lemoine, a.k.a. Rex, the experienced agent and recruiter and later a senile old man. The recruiter of our intelligence services and jack-of-all-trades of the Bureau since 1920, was the most notorious French spy of the time, feared and admired in equal measures and sought after by intelligence services all over the world. I also had in my possession the logbooks of our chief, General Louis Rivet. I researched the German archives and the minutes of the Nuremberg court hearings for war criminals, which served to complement and confirm what we knew. I was finally able to benefit from the assistance of my fellow Polish and British special service colleagues, as well as Gilbert Bloch's patient and meticulous research on the Enigma machine. Some details, however, remain in the shadows and will probably never be revealed; archives have been destroyed or forever buried in the well of special service secrets of allies and enemies alike. In any case, discretion or common decency has stopped me pursuing some sensitive areas of research.

It is now well established that the decoded messages, thanks to the reconstruction by the Allies of that mysterious code-generating machine, had a considerable, if not decisive, role in the successful resolution of World War II.

Thanks to the Deuxième Bureau, its informant H.E and the fundamental information he gathered, the decoding process was able to commence in 1933, just in time for it to become operational at the beginning of World War II and a decisive moment for the future of the Western world, known as the Battle of Britain.

Through the lens of our computer age, one might be surprised at the length of time it took for us arrive at a method of exploiting such a discovery. This of course would be to misunderstand the realities of the time and scale of problems that had to be resolved.

Our reproduction would have remained stubbornly silent had it not been for the successful concordance of its configuration[32] and alignment with the German machines in operation, and without the reconstruction of specific ciphers used in each message.

It was a gigantic task—and a disheartening one—to have to adapt to the ceaseless changes and variations imposed by the enemy. Without owning the original machine themselves, none of the Allies had dared to tackle its intricacies.

Particular credit must go to the Polish intelligence services for attempting the impossible in 1926, when the first mechanically encrypted messages by the German army started to appear. And recognition goes to the French Intelligence Bureau, which, from 1931, provided the Polish with the data—available thanks to H.E. —essential to the solution of the major issue at hand, constructing a replica Enigma machine. With the continued support of the French Intelligence Bureau and at the cost of long mathematical analyses, done quietly in isolation, the Polish managed to develop scientific methods that could rapidly penetrate the secrets that spilled from the Enigma machines, their transformations, their settings, and their ciphers.

Yet Germany, confident in the reliability of its encrypting devices, multiplied the number of messages they sent by the thousands.[33] With a wide variety of settings and diverse characteristics, the Enigma machine endowed the Reichswehr and the O.K.W., the Wehrmacht, the Abwehr, the police, the S.S., and the large administrations with the ability to convey encrypted communications. In 1939, crushed by the ever-increasing difficulties involved in breaking the code-generating machine, the Poles offered their work over the French and British, who had both been until that point strangely remote from the research of their Polish allies.

An incomprehensible aberration of our intelligence offices once again left it to others to continue the work. From 1940 it was British cryptologists and scientists, with abilities on a scale commensurate with their exceptional interest in the penetration of the most secret transmissions of the Third Reich, who completed and masterfully developed the work of the Polish pioneers. It was thus at Bletchley Park, some seventy kilometers from London, that the revolutionary era of calculators and computers began.

The Enigma machines reproduced by the Allies would henceforth begin to speak more and more. Throughout the war, it would offer the

Allied secret services the means to gather intelligence on Germany in the most profound and secure way—the most private as well, because no one, except the decoders and a few V.I.P.s under oath of secrecy, knew the origin of the intelligence gathered for analysis.[34] It will never be possible to completely and accurately assess the extent of Enigma's use. However, the history of the secret code war, obscure, perplexing and with staggering consequences, brings to light Enigma's contribution during the decisive phases of World War II:

- The Battle of France, whereupon the successful replication of the Enigma machine revealed its possibilities as well as its limitations.
- The Battle of Britain, 1940–41, about which we will most likely never know the exact role of the machine albeit that it was a considerable one, later resulting in victory over the Luftwaffe.
- The Battle of the Atlantic that the British Admiralty successfully defended from 1941 to 1945, especially in May 1943 when, among the thousands of messages captured and decoded, the secrets of Admiral Doenitz's submarine projects were found.
- The Battle of Libya in March 1943, where three of Rommel's panzer divisions, tracked every day by Enigma, were destroyed by Montgomery, ultimately resulting in the definitive defeat of the Wehrmacht in North Africa.
- The Battle of Normandy where, in August 1944, secret enemy radio messages were breached, permitting the Americans to successfully resist Hitler's powerful armored counteroffensive in the region of Mortain, and to pave the way for the Liberation.
- The Battle of Alsace, where the Allied replica of the Enigma, previously unable to reveal the preparations of the German Ardennes offensive in December 1944, successfully captured communications and warned US Command on January 1, 1945 of the impending Wehrmacht attacks in the northern Vosges and on recently liberated Strasbourg.

These successes, among others (including most notably that in the Pacific on June 4, 1942 during the naval battle of Midway), thus have their origins in the espionage work of the French Intelligence Bureau which had begun in 1931, and in particular the exceptional quality of information that H.E. was able to offer. Paradoxically, the intelligence was met with poor a response in France.

The same could be said for the stunningly precise and varied intelligence gathered by H.E. between 1932 and 1940 on the Nazi party, the rearmament of Germany, the organization of its military, administration and police, on the activities of the Wehrmacht High Command and the Abwehr, the mysterious work being done by the Research Office of the Reich Ministry of Aviation (Forschungsamt),[35] on Hitler's intentions captured from the very source of the Reich Chancellery... It was our agent alone who combed through the bulk of our intelligence requirements on Germany.

The extent of his immense resources was revealed to me during one of the secretive weekly meetings held on Monday mornings where various department heads gathered around the boss, discussed the current situation, and formed our work plans for the week. Despite being something of a novice, I was admitted for the first time into this inner circle on January 26, 1936. Commander de Robien, leader of our German section of Counterintelligence (E.C.), and whose position I would later take over, was ill, and had requested that I stand in for him at the meeting. Among these experienced experts and lacking in confidence, I remained silent. In his deep voice, Rivet focused our discussion on the research in Germany. Perruche[36] had just returned from Basel, where he had met with the mysterious H.E.

"Our informant is sure," the head of the research section affirmed very clearly. "A military operation on the left bank of the Rhine is being studied in the greatest secrecy. His brother, Colonel of the General Staff of the Army High Command, is taking part in its preparation, which must be completed by the end of February. Approximately forty battalions will be allocated. The entire forty will only be called upon if the launching of the operation does not create too many waves. H.E. will provide further details in invisible ink."

On February 18, 1936, H.E. confirmed in writing that the operation was imminent and specified the nature of the units that were to be involved. After having captured the bridgeheads of Cologne, Koblenz, and Mainz, they would push a few symbolic detachments all the way to Saarbrücken, Trier and Aix-la-Chapelle.

"This is very serious," Rivet commented at the closure of our meeting. "I will be going to Boulevard Saint-Germain in order to notify Gauché[37] and the Command."[38]

Six weeks later, on March 7, 1936 at 5.00 a.m., detachments of the Reichswehr would penetrate the Rhineland demilitarized zone. Shock and disbelief reverberated throughout Paris and London.

"We will not allow Strasbourg to remain under the threat of German guns," stated Albert Sarraut, President of the Council of Ministers.

Well, we all know what happened... the incredulous and careless France was inexorably on its way to defeat.

At the same time, the German Richard Sorge, who had been posted into the very heart of the German Embassy in Tokyo since 1933, extracted information, on behalf of the Soviets, from his friend General Ott, military attaché and then ambassador of the Third Reich to Japan. In May 1941, he warned his masters at the Kremlin of the next attack by the Wehrmacht.

Like those in the West who were unaccepting of the warnings divulged by Hans-Thilo Schmidt, the skeptical and paranoid Stalin likewise neglected those of Sorge. And so, just a month later, the Germans rushed the gates of Moscow. However, through two decisive circumstances, the two spy masters would each play a vital role in preventing their homeland from bringing victory within her reach.

Late 1940: Hitler loses the Battle of Britain, defeated by the RAF, whose efforts were deftly guided and oriented by "Ultra-Enigma."

Late 1941: Hitler loses the Battle of Moscow, defeated by the Soviet reinforcements brought in from Siberia. On October 15, 1941, Sorge made it clear to Stalin about Japan's conduct, thus relieving the troops stationed in the Far East of their duties. On October 18, 1941 he was arrested by the Japanese Kempetai[39] and on October 7, 1944, at the conclusion of a momentous trial in Tokyo, Sorge was hanged. Twenty years later, he was awarded the supreme honor of being made a Hero of the Soviet Union.

On March 23, 1943 Hans-Thilo Schmidt was arrested by the Abwehr. He disappeared from the world of the living. Unknown and ignored by the general public, he is hardly mentioned by those who have examined the crucial role that codebreaking played in the war and the military and scientific consequences that resulted from it.

What a curious destiny for the Third Reich, whose police organization spread terror throughout the continent, and was doomed to collapse by the actions of two of its very own citizens.

CHAPTER I

Enigma's Secrets Revealed

The Verviers rendezvous • Rex, the S.R.'s jack-of-all-trades • The unveiling of the Enigma • H.E.'s work begins to take shape • Rex in Berlin • Breaching the Enigma • H.E. at the heart of the Nazi intelligence services • The strange discretion of the Poles and the infancy of the computer

The Verviers rendezvous

Verviers, Sunday November 1, 1931—All Saints Day—10.30 a.m. An anxious traveler descended from a train that had arrived from Berlin two hours late.

Of average build, wrapped in a dark, unassuming overcoat, and with a black hat drawn down over his eyes, the man left the station, stopping briefly to ask for directions to the Grand Hotel.

Minutes later, the hotel concierge gave him the key to a room that had been reserved by phone, along with a letter delivered the previous evening, labeled: "Deliver to Hans-Thilo Schmidt upon his arrival."

Schmidt rushed into the elevator. A man in his sixties[40] was sitting on the couch in the lobby, observing him closely from behind a newspaper. Schmidt dropped his heavy black leather bag and frantically tore open the envelope. His face, puffy from lack of sleep, began to turn red as he read the brief message hand-written in German: "You are expected in suite 31, first floor, at 12 noon."

That left an hour to clean up, take a short rest, go through some papers, and reread a few notes he had pulled from an inner pocket of his bag.

At noon, Schmidt knocked on the door of suite 31. To his surprise, a distinguished woman with white hair opened the door and invited him to sit in an armchair before disappearing into an adjoining room. In the background music softly plays on a radio. The living room was cozy; the atmosphere warm. On the small bar stood a few bottles of aperitifs and elegant crystal glasses next to several cigar boxes.

"Guten Morgen, Herr Schmidt! Hatten sie eine gute Reise?"

The sexagenarian entering the room was immense. His strange light blue eyes, framed by large glasses, were staring at Schmidt, who immediately jumped to his feet, looking intimidated.

"Sit down, please. How are Madame Schmidt and your two children?"

The question was kindly asked, in a very pure German without any regional accent. Caught off guard by the question, Schmidt replied that, for the moment and due to the economy, he was living alone in a furnished room in Berlin on 17 Lorenzstrasse. His family were living with his in-laws in Bavaria.

"I know," his host interrupted. "You will want to bring your family back together soon and resume a pleasant life. That, of course, depends on you. We will assist you if your cooperation proves fruitful to us. Whiskey? Port, sherry? Would you like a cigar?"

Schmidt, confused, sank further into his chair, a big glass in his hands.

"Your resourcefulness last June in Berlin was quite exceptional and effective, Mr. Schmidt. Quite fortunately you happened upon an official of the French Embassy who had been previously notified about you and was inconspicuous… What would you have done if he had thought you were an agent provocateur and had called the police?"

The question was blunt and brutal. Schmidt suddenly became conscious of the strangeness of his situation. His future could well depend on his response. All of a sudden he became a different man, confident, defiant, ready to challenge his interrogator:

"I thought you would understand. If you feel this way, my only option is to withdraw. Others will know how to interpret my motivations and the rationale of my propositions."

"Easy now, Mr. Schmidt. It is not common for an official of your standing, who holds such an important position in a secret organization, to provide such services to a foreign power. We appreciate your initiative and the benefit we can gain from it. However, it is still necessary to maintain a level of trust between us and that our reports be free of suspicion.

"Let me be frank. My name is Lemoine, and I represent the French Intelligence Bureau. Here is your letter dated July 1, 1931 from Prague to the War Ministry, Deuxième Bureau, 75, rue de l'Université in Paris. As I promised in my response, I will reimburse you for your travel and hotel expenses. You shall even receive a substantial bonus if, at the end of our interview, we are all satisfied.

"You must have undoubtedly understood that we would have already performed a background check on you. Tell me in detail who you are, what you do and why you are turning to us. I will listen… but first, would you like another glass of whiskey? We can have lunch together a little later."

Lemoine said all of this without raising his voice, though with a firm and reassuring authority.

Schmidt sat with a freshly topped-up glass and lit his cigar as if he were a connoisseur. In silence he pulled his identity card out of his wallet and a German *Ausweis* card crossed through in red. Lemoine, a.k.a. Rex, was able to read on the first document: Schmidt, Hans-Thilo, born May 13, 1888 in Berlin, residing in Berlin Lorenzstrasse 17—Occupation: civil service employ. The second document was a permanent pass issued by the War Ministry[41] in the name of Reserve Lieutenant Schmidt, Hans-Thilo, *Beamter im höheren Dienst* at the Chiffrierstelle (civil servant posted within the intelligence office).

"How on earth were you able to gain access to such a secure position?"

More relaxed after his whiskey, the German said: "I have an older brother, a lieutenant colonel, currently head of the transmissions bureau for the Reichswehrministerium. From 1925 to 1928 he was the chief of the Chiffrierstelle. As for me, after working in a soap factory, I was unemployed along with more than 6,000,000 of my compatriots. This has been the case for the past two years. It has been impossible for me to find any work despite my high school studies, despite my certification as a chemical technician, despite my soldier status, and even despite my family situation and my two children. I've been desperate."

Schmidt's demeanor became more impassioned. He stared straight into Lemoine's eyes: "How can one live on 75 marks[42] unemployment allowance per month? You have to admit it's rather degrading. Rudolf, my brother, realized that I could not go on like that any more. Miraculously, his successor to the Chiffrierstelle, Major Oschmann,[43] was looking for a trusted colleague. He recommended me."

Lemoine listened, his face revealing no emotion. Unperturbed, Schmidt continued: "Oh, it's far from being an ideal situation! With what they give me I still won't be able to repay my debts… The work, however, is interesting. We must provide the Reichswehr with the means and methods to produce secret and impenetrable ciphers."

Schmidt hesitated. Rex moved closer to him, inquiring, pressing him to continue. Schmidt resumed his story, resolute and full of information: "The technicians responsible for identifying the material to be adopted for the army began with a commercial machine intended to encrypt and decipher codes called Enigma. The modifications they've made to it allow for an infinite number of possible encryption combinations."

"As for the Chiffrierstelle, it establishes the rubrics for operating the machine. They vary the rubrics each day depending on the ciphers we secretly broadcast every month. Furthermore, each message has a specific key.

"When the message is encrypted, it is assigned to a transmission unit who sends it by radio to the recipient. The receiver possesses a machine set with the same rubrics as the one that produced the code, which he then uses to decrypt the code."

Schmidt paused again. He observed Rex, whose face reflected an air of puzzlement, and smiled, pleased at the effect his revelations had had on the Frenchman: "Believe me, Mr. Lemoine, the reliability of our Enigma is total, absolute. Your cryptologists will never manage to decrypt its messages unless they have help."

"Is this what you are proposing?"

"Of course. That's what I tried to explain to the foolish official at your embassy."

"Not so foolish, as I am here! How is your relationship with your brother?"

"Excellent. I repeat: it was he who pulled me out of the rut I was in. As a signals and encryption specialist, he ended the war as a captain in the General Staff of 4th Army and was awarded the Iron Cross First and Second Class. He is very interested in armored warfare, and says that it's the future. He took his General Staff training from 1928 to 1930. I believe he is destined for the highest ranks of the military."

At that very moment, the blue eyes of the German toughened: "See how fate is unjust and how ungrateful my country is. I too was in the war, second lieutenant, then lieutenant. I also won the Iron Cross. I had the misfortune of being gassed and disabled several years after the armistice. While my brother pursued a successful career, I was struggling to make ends meet. I am appalled when I think about the past, about my origins—my father a history professor with a doctorate in philology; my mother, whose family is of Prussian nobility; about my privileged childhood. I've had enough of my miserable life! This has to change!"

With an expert eye Lemoine flipped through and inspected the pages of the booklet stamped *GEHEIM* ("SECRET"). Its authenticity and timeliness were obvious. His conviction was set. The case was huge. Urgent. This must be achieved without further delay.

"Return here next Sunday with as much intelligence you're able to provide about this. I'll tell you exactly what we will pay. How much do you earn now?

"Five hundred Reichsmarks a month,[44] sometimes working night and day."

"Here is triple that amount to compensate you for this first assignment, and to assist you with getting back here on Sunday. But beware! You are taking an enormous risk crossing the border with secret documents. How did you manage it?"

"That is my problem, my dear sir; could I trouble you for another whiskey?"

*

Waxing eloquently, Lemoine recounted to me his first interview with Hans-Thilo Schmidt, the number one agent of our Intelligence Service. It was Saturday, January 17, 1936, around 8.00 p.m. I had gone to his home, rue de Lisbonne, at the request of Commander Perruche, head of the research section. A letter posted in Berlin on January 15, 1936 had arrived at one of the mailboxes in Paris specifically dedicated to this agent's correspondence, listed in our special file under the code "H.E."[45] Orders stated that such correspondence was always to be handled with urgency and priority.

Lemoine carefully opened the envelope and pulled out the letter. The contents revealed nothing more than some small talk about the severe cold that paralyzed the capital of the Reich and the health of a cousin. Lemoine carefully moistened the paper with a cotton cloth soaked in a solution of silver nitrate before ironing it with a hot iron.

"It is simple and relatively reliable," he said. "H.E. did this intentionally. He has a good background as chemist. He writes to us between the lines with a simple solution of sodium chloride (salt), holding the letter over steam for about 30 seconds and then covering the contents with a starch solution."

Together we read the message that appeared, written in German: "Rendezvous on January 24, 1936 at 9 p.m. at the agreed location stop—Attendance of Alison and Rex essential." Alison was the alias of Perruche, and Rex that of Lemoine.

What a unique character that Rex was! Of German origin, he became a naturalized French citizen in 1900 and served, without making a big deal of it, our country for over twenty years. His loyalty was demonstrated on many occasions and his effectiveness proven by his masterful ability to resolve the most varied and ambiguous problems in a thorough and trustworthy manner. Thus initial contacts with those who were viewed as being potentially useful to our Intelligence Bureau were generally delegated to him. He performed wonders through his key role as recruiter of agents, his interpersonal skills and psychology, his knowledge of other countries, especially Germany, his language skills and understanding of dialects. His height and his piercing and domineering stare added to the prestige conferred upon him by the label Deuxième Bureau and by his financial security, the origin of which never appeared entirely clear to me. The variety and lavishness of his personal activities, often on the very limit of what was considered acceptable, provided him effective cover and resources, the ostentation of which demonstrated his importance.

In around mid-August 1931, Captain Lacape brought to him on behalf of the chief of our Military Secret Service the famous letter of July 1, 1931 by Hans-Thilo Schmidt, addressed to 75 rue de l'Université.[46] What did he think of it?

"Believe me, sir, everyone sensed that a provocation was imminent. Of course, Germany in 1931 was in complete disarray, but still the nerve of this man was unbelievable. Listen and I will translate for you the gist of what he wrote:

> I confirm what I said to your representative from Pariser Platz[47] on June 8, 1931 who gave me your address. I am able to transmit documents that are of the highest importance. To convince you of the seriousness of my offer, below I am offering you some references. Your specialists will know what they are worth. Please answer me by October 1, 1931 at the following address: Hans-Thilo Schmidt, 2 Kaufhausgasse—Basel—Switzerland. If this goes unanswered and the date passes, I will take my intelligence elsewhere. If you are able to provide me with an appointment, make sure that it is on a Sunday and preferably in Belgium or Holland, near the German border.
> Salutations."

As a postscript, Schmidt indicated that he was in a position to deliver two documents: the instructions for both the use and the encryption process for the machine that had been in service since June 1, 1930.

Lemoine then shared with me the response to this letter: "I went to see Commander Perruche, chief of the Intelligence Bureau (S.R.)

and Captain Bertrand, head of Section D responsible for encryption research."

Both men were aware of this unique offer, and though immensely interested by it, they were, however, perplexed—especially Bertrand. He had not yet received any indication of such new mechanical ciphers created by the German Army. Messages intercepted up to this point had remained impenetrable to the Cipher Section of the Army General Staff, which had been deemed one of the best in the world. The unique opportunity to finally unlock the secrets of the Chiffrierstelle and consequently those of the German army might just be within reach.

"For my part," affirmed Lemoine, "I was determined to take every risk in order to be sure. Together, we convinced the boss[48] to give me carte blanche."

We asked Maurice Dejean, our representative in Berlin, to do a quick background check on Schmidt and his origins. The response was swift; he had received the German on June 8 and caught wind of the deal of the century, and was already well informed on the German. Schmidt and his brother, a senior officer, were indeed listed with the Reichswehr. Their parents, recently deceased, were known among Berlin high society. Their father had managed a higher education institution. The mother, née von Könitz, was from a great Prussian family.

"I knew well enough that I should meet Schmidt and establish my own opinion. You know how the rest played out."

Lemoine moved closer to me and continued in a lower, somewhat professorial, tone: "We are paying dearly not only for services rendered and the risk that is involved, but also for the personality of the man and his social origins. Never treat informants of this caliber with the slightest appearance of contempt. Schmidt deliberately turned his back on his family, his traditions, his homeland. Whatever you think of his motives, he came over to our side. Totally. Loyally. Rest assured, it could not be any other way!"

Lemoine finished his statement by forcefully driving home this assertion. It was an act of faith. It was also an indication of the terrible threat that a ruthless blackmailer could pose. Was there a parallel between his own destiny and that of the German he had recruited? Both were irrevocably linked to the cause of a country they had chosen all while betraying their own. The extent of their commitment cemented their sincerity. Rex's brutality quickly laid bare the dramatic human aspects of our business.

Rex, the S.R.'s jack-of-all-trades

This was my third meeting with Rex.

Commander de Robien, whom I was to replace in 1936 as the head of the German section of counterespionage, had been anxious to introduce him to me a few weeks before, as soon as I arrived at the Intelligence Bureau. One of our missions, the protection of our research bodies, included, most notably, the monitoring of their agents. Without question, Rex was one of the most important.

"You are going to encounter a curious character," de Robien had informed me. "Espionage is as much in his nature as alcohol is to a drunkard. He is the son of a wealthy Berlin jeweler named Stallman. He was to succeed his father, but as he was wealthy, he spent his time traveling around France, Italy, England, Africa, Chile, Argentina… when in Spain, during the 1914–1918 war he was infected by the espionage virus, to France's advantage. It should be said that during this time he married a charming French women, whose surname he took. She usually accompanies him on his travels.

"The gentleman has great taste… He has maintained a certain amount of liberty regarding the source of his financial affairs. I do not know too much about what the Bureau provides him. What I do know is that until recently, living in Paris, at 27 rue de Madrid, he was the head of a small office from where he kept as much an eye on Guyana as the Indies, and where he took advantage of certain concessions granted by the French government in recognition of the services rendered.

"Since Hitler came to power in 1933, we have had to increase our recruitment and our research on Germany. He thus moved over to rue Lisbon where he was able to devote even more resources to his work with the Intelligence Bureau, assisted by another German hiding out in France, named Drach.

"My dear friend," de Robien concluded with a half-smile, "He is an amazing person who knows as much about how to compromise a minister as he does recruiting a general. He's as much able to get his hands on a safe as acquire a Yugoslavian passport for you in twenty-four hours, or secure a seat in a sleeping car that the Cook agency refuses to give you. That is to say that you must keep your eyes open and ensure you are not ensnared by the undeniable charm of the man."

This, my first contact with the Lemoine Bureau, had a worldly air about it. Presentations, general considerations, promises of friendly collaboration, a certain condescension directed at me as the newcomer.

Our second meeting was more professional. It was Christmas Eve 1935. I have always kept a vivid memory of it, for it had revealed to me the resources that the Bureau could gain from this singularly unique character.

In late December 1935, during a traditional New Year's reception at the Foreign Ministry, an official of the Austrian Embassy named Bodo had revealed to de Robien's brother, a plenipotentiary minister, his strong apprehensions regarding Nazi conduct in his country. We, along with de Robien, thought that without compromising his position, Bodo might be useful. Perruche agreed.

Before attempting to approach him, it was essential for us to learn more about his personal circumstances and his innermost feelings regarding France and Hitler's Germany.

The problem presented to Lemoine on December 24, 1935 was resolved on January 2, 1936. Bodo, who was anti-Nazi, agreed to work with us in defense of his country against the expansionist threat conducted by the Third Reich. On December 30, the P.T.T., generously incentivized by Lemoine, had installed in his home a telephone line that a diplomat in a modest position, with family responsibilities and limited funds from his embassy, would not have been able to acquire for himself.

Within a few days, our man had mustered the resolve to contact Bodo, to convince him of the importance of a permanent liaison with the Deuxième Bureau, and to provide him the means to fulfill his responsibilities, which would include an effective staff bureau worthy of recognition.

"A great nobleman, you see!" Perruche said ironically. A nobleman indeed, especially since he was able to offer us additional intelligence channels.

"I know that you're worried about Japanese activities in the area of aviation," Lemoine confided to us. "I think I can offer you a solution. While speaking with Mr. Bodo, I learned that an Austrian aviator officer named Koser works with him at the embassy, and is in one hundred percent agreement with regard to the threat Hitler represents to his country.

"The three of us had lunch at Drouant the day before yesterday. It was very relaxed, Koser is very friendly. He is even more anti-Nazi than Bodo! I learned that his wife is employed as an interpreter at the Japanese Embassy. Would you authorize me to meet her? I'm pretty sure she would agree to help us."

De Robien left it for me to answer, undoubtedly wanting to verify how well I was assimilating into my new profession:

"In principle, we agree, Mr. Lemoine. Nevertheless, permit us a few days of reflection before giving you the green light. I'll call you."

I gave him my answer, in the affirmative, a week later, after a discreet and favorable investigation into the Koser household.

Madame Koser was to become our best informant on the Japanese Embassy. In 1939, she was responsible for the arrest of two diplomatic couriers who were transporting full plans and secrets of a new aircraft engine being tested at Gnome and Rhône to Marseilles for delivery to a Japanese ship. As for her husband, opposed to the Anschluss, he succeeded, through the efforts of his wife, in being hired in June 1938 by the Japanese. Because of his specialty, they gave him the responsibility of scouting out aircraft construction firms in Italy and Germany who were willing to work with Japan. Thus he delivered to

France the plans of the latest German and Italian civil and military aircraft models being developed.

At the time of our meeting on January 17, 1936, it was therefore the third time that I had encountered Lemoine, which prompted the story of his initial meeting with Hans-Thilo Schmidt. I was thoroughly captivated. I would have liked to learn even more.

But it was getting late. I realized that my interlocutor preferred to leave the rest of the story for my comrades to tell. He respected their acute sense of discretion, their fervent passion of their mission and Bertrand's touchy disposition.

I retrieved Schmidt's letter informing Perruche about the rendezvous of January 24, 1936 in Basel and thanked him. In the street, I could not stop thinking about the strange tandem that Rex and H.E. formed. Their audacity, their complicit amorality, their intuitive intelligence in the business of espionage was incredible. The fate of this amazing matter, so beneficial to our Bureau and my country was paradoxically linked to these two Germans. Such a destiny appeared to be at the mercy of the slightest mistake, the slightest carelessness, the first failure. Our responsibilities seemed very grave to me, but what an exciting venture!

The unveiling of the Enigma

As for the rest of Lemoine's tale, Bertrand would reveal it to me after one of the Monday morning conferences where, under the direction of the department head, the heads of intelligence and counterintelligence would assess their knowledge and debate the meaning and methods of research going on in Germany.

In early 1936, our informants, agents (among whom Perruche placed H.E. in the top ranks), and honorable correspondents were achieving good results. We were following the stages of the administrative and police reorganization of our neighbors, as well as that of their rearmament. But a major component still lay in the shadows: their intentions. We knew they were dependent upon the impulsive decisions of the Führer. Certainly, our front-line agents were infiltrating themselves better and better into the rapidly expanding Abwehr. They were providing good information about the concerns and research of the German command. But their information was far from representative of Hitler's thought process and projects at any particular time. If it were possible to decode the growing number of messages seized from the Wehrmacht, the Abwehr, the Administration, the SS and the Police Reich, a major step would be taken towards a solution of this important problem.

Irritated by the constant repetition of this obvious fact which placed into question the performance of his section and aggravated his hypersensitive nature, Bertrand pulled me into his office. With his customary reserve, he confided in me at length his moods and the results of his work with Asché:[49]

> Deputy Captain Louis and I established Section D in 1930. Our role is to acquire from abroad, with the assistance of the S.R. and the E.C., the current decoding methods in use and to facilitate the task of our decoders of the Cipher Service of the Army General Staff. It is not easy. The Bureau's new research orientation seems to have become even more urgent and necessary since between 1926 and 1930 the German military have generalized the use of the mechanical encryption. Even our best specialists admit that they unable to unlock the secrets.
>
> I've used the good relationships our Bureau has with allied bureaus in London, Prague and Warsaw to comparing our level of knowledge with theirs and work to share our intelligence efforts. The British know less than us. They show a faint interest in the research in Germany and cryptography. The only ones who are truly passionate about these problems are the Poles. For them it is a question of 'vital' security, stuck as they are between the ambitions and threats of the U.S.S.R. and the Third Reich.
>
> In March 1931, during my first mission to Poland, I was graciously welcomed by Colonel Mayer, head of the Deuxième Bureau, and Lieutenant Colonel Guido Langer, head of the Secret Service. They were, like us, faced with the insoluble problem of the mechanical encryption adopted by the German Army.
>
> They showed me the encryption machine, commercially available under the name Enigma, precisely the one Asché had discussed with Rex when they first met in Verviers. They were convinced that after modifications and improvements, it served as the basis for encrypting machines used by the Navy since 1926 and since 1928 by the Army. But what were the changes? What were the improvements?

On the outside this commercial machine had the appearance of a kind of typewriter. Typing a character to encrypt triggered an electric current, which then flowed through internal mechanisms—in this case three drums (rotors). The result was that each time a key was hit, the machine produced a different substituted character.

Attentive to my reaction, Bertrand filled in his explanations by providing a sketch of the current flow. He continued:

Conversely, on the same machine, typing in the encrypted letter caused to reappear, by way of reversing the path, the original unencrypted letter. The decoding of such an encrypted message was only possible with a machine meticulously modeled after the encryption machine.

For over two years, the Poles researched the codes that made the captured German messages impervious to their best cryptographers. In vain. No path to a solution. Not a single clue that could provide a direction to their research despite the impressive accumulation of encrypted texts they had intercepted over several years.

Revealing to them the goals of Section D convinced them to work with us and we thus decided to exchange information.

The months passed without finding a solution when, thanks to Lemoine, to whom we owe the credit, I made the acquaintance of Schmidt at Verviers on November 8, 1931. A true miracle! I must tell you the story of that first and decisive interview.

The history captivated me, but as I looked at my watch I noticed how much time had already passed.

"Let's go to a restaurant, I will tell you the rest of it over lunch. We won't waste any time."

Once the two of us were seated in a corner of the second floor at Le Tourville,[50] Bertrand resumed his narrative:

We had arrived at Verviers the day before. According to the scenario planned by Rex, we—Bintz, the photographer of 2bis, and myself—set ourselves up in two rooms of the Grand Hotel. We spent part of the night busy ensuring that the electricity was functioning properly in my bathroom, and conducting tests of our Leica camera. We adjusted the lighting with portable lamps and set the appropriate exposure time.

From 9.00 a.m. on Sunday, November 8, 1931 we were expecting a call from Lemoine, who was settled in like a prince, as usual, in suite 31. Baron Schenk, his bodyguard, kept a close watch in the hotel's lobby. Alert, invisible.

Around 10.00 a.m. Rex rang: "We apologize for the delay. Can you come down?"

Alone, I rushed down, impatient and anxious. The prospects Lemoine had given us a glimpse of were so important that I could hardly contain my emotions.

In the cigar smoke-filled lobby fluttered the blare of a radio,[51] Lemoine introduced me to his man. Schmidt was standing, a glass of whiskey in hand. A smile lit up his face. He bowed before me, heels together. His dark gray suit was poor, his shoes worn out, yet his ease and courtesy denoted a real distinction. His blue eyes were beautiful, they shone with intelligence.

"Mr. Barsac (my alias), you are, I believe, going to be satisfied. Mr. Schmidt did not hesitate to entrust us with a few documents. He will need them back by no later than 3 p.m. in order to catch the train back to Berlin."

Schmidt then took out of his black bag an enormous file. He handed it to me and, stunned, I pulled the following out of it:

- a diagram of the German Chiffrierstelle;
- a radio service code, since Enigma encrypted messages are then transmitted through radio waves;
- a set of instructions for manual coding with an accompanying cipher for the Army General Staff;
- a study by the Reichswehrministerium on toxic gases (usage and protection) that he claimed to have procured from his brother;
- a short technical manual on the variable connection machine Enigma I currently in service (derived from the Enigma G machine);
- a numbered manual of the Enigma machine I (Gebrauchsanweisung H. Dv. g. 13 H. E. L. Dv. g. 13);
- a numbered encryption manual for the Enigma I machine (Schlüsselanleitung. H. Dv. g. 14, L. Dv. g. 14 H. E. M. Dv. g. 168);

All of these documents bore the stamp *Geheim*—secret.

The last two records were essential to the physical reconstruction of the machine in service. Their possession was of paramount interest. A sort of panic seized me as I was presented with the scope and importance of the documents offered here: at least a hundred papers, some printed on both sides with drawings and photographs. It would take at least a few hours to examine the contents, photograph everything and return the file.

Schmidt, satisfaction radiating from his face despite his best efforts, took a shot of whiskey and discreetly consulted Lemoine on the amount he could expect. Taken aback, the latter stalled: "I'll take care of you later!" He added, cynically: "Too bad you did not bring the rubric of daily ciphers for this month.[52] You had promised it. You would have had a lot more!"

"Exactly. Usually that document is within my reach, but my chief left it with one of my colleagues for binding and I did not dare ask for it."

Asché then paused for a moment. His mood grew somber. Was he hesitating about his future participation? Would he stop at this point? Would he settle for the considerable sum that his voluminous offering was worth? Would he disappear with that lifeline and resume a harmless, bourgeois existence? On our part it would have been an unforgivable mistake to leave without having secured such a promising contact for the future.

I observed Lemoine. He understood my concern, but remained calmer. No doubt he already had his own ideas on how events would unfold. I pulled him aside for a brief moment. I proposed an amount of 5,000 marks and invited him to stay with Schmidt to probe his intentions while we photographed the documents.

"We must hold firmly on to him and without delay," he said to me quietly, in an urgent tone. "Let me give him twice the amount, 10,000 marks."[53] "I want to promise him that much so that he will continue to help us," adding in a cynical and threatening voice: "He is too engaged, he has no other choice…"

"I couldn't agree more."

I climbed back up to my floor three stairs at a time. The photographic equipment was ready and with Bintz, we set to work. That day we did not eat lunch. At 3 p.m., I found Asché smoking cigar after cigar, sipping on cognac and chatting chirpily with Lemoine. The cheerful expression of both men reassured me of the positive outcome of their interview. Rex's persuasiveness was equal to his ability to resist fatigue and alcohol. I congratulated Schmidt and handed back his file. In bad German, I asked if he was satisfied with his conversation with Lemoine, and if all steps had been taken between the two to establish the terms of another appointment.

"*Ja wohl, meine Herren. Besten Dank! Alles ist in Ordnung!*"

He bowed, snapped his heels together, and disappeared. I assure you, my old Paillole, I was staggered! We finally had the thread that would permit us to get to the heart of the Enigma mystery.

Back in Paris, I rushed to see the boss. He could not believe his eyes. I went the next day to see my colleagues at the Intelligence Bureau of the Army General Staff. Without revealing the origins, nor displaying all my treasures, I presented the findings that we could use to attempt to reconstruct the military machine called Enigma and the decoding of the numerous messages captured over the air.

"Mechanical encryption is impenetrable," one responded in a peremptory tone and after much discussion. "Why waste any time on it?"

I insisted. I suggested the acquisition of a commercial Enigma in order to study and research the mechanism with the aid of the Asché documents and its various transformations. I returned later with all the samples that Schmidt had supplied.

The head of the Intelligence Bureau, Colonel Bassières, whom I knew well, listened and accepted my documentation. I met him on November 20, 1931 to learn the results of his own expertise and that of his cryptographic services. Alas, I was all too aware of their great skill. It was a sad day for me as he gave his conclusion:

"Impossible to extract anything useful from your documentation. Too many elements are missing in order for us to successfully reproduce the machine. Even if we assumed that we could get there, it would then force upon us a monumental amount of work setting the controls and ciphers. We simply do not have the means."

That was their final judgment; there would be no appeal. Agreeing with my bosses who were as disappointed as I was, I decided to consult our British allies.

In Paris, I entrusted the photographs of the two encryption and usage manuals for the Enigma machine to the representative of the Secret Intelligence Service, Commander Wilfred Dunderdale. I begged him to inform his superiors of the opportunities that were available to us. I proposed to go to London to discuss with British specialists the common direction we should take for our research.

If my approach were to succeed, I had secretly hoped that it would encourage the interest of French decoding services. Naturally enthusiastic, Dunderdale, convinced of the importance of the documents I possessed, immediately went to England. It was November 23, 1931. On the 26th, he was back. From the look of dismay on his face, I knew that he had been hardly any more successful than I had been in France.

It was hopeless. On the advice of the boss, who was just as convinced as I was that we should fully exploit the Asché resources, I petitioned, via the Polish Embassy, for an urgent meeting with Lieutenant Colonel Langer, head of the Cipher Bureau (Biuro Szyfrow).

Twenty-four hours later, the Polish military attaché gave me the green light. I sent the photographs of my precious portfolio by diplomatic valise and retrieved them at the French Embassy in Warsaw on December 7, 1931.

My comrade fell silent. The waiter was hovering around our table. Our lunch long finished. The dining room was empty. We were so engrossed in the story that we had not even noticed. We took our time returning to 2bis, at which point Bertrand was finally able to tell me what was on his mind:

On December 8, at 9.00 a.m., I was at Langer's. Our local in-house representative in Poland, alerted by radio, had prepared my accommodation and set the time for our meeting.

There was an explosion of amazement and joy at the examination of the initial documents, namely the operating instructions and usage of the Enigma machine.

Langer disappeared for quite a long time. Imagine my state of mind! I was anxious, impatient. He finally returned with Colonel Mayer and the head of the German Cipher Bureau, Major Ciezki.

Mayer congratulated me, and thanked me warmly: "This is extraordinary and unexpected. Permit us forty-eight hours in order to better study your documentation and tell you what conclusions we are able to reach in that time."

As agreed, on December 10 at 4.00 p.m., I was in the office of the Bureau chief. Mayer and Langer were waiting for me. They were radiant.

"Thanks to your documents, we now know the description and operating instructions for the machine. This is crucial for the future of our research. The adjustments made to the inner workings of the commercial device appear numerous, especially to the construction of the mobile and return drums. But the modification that is particularly sensational is the introduction of a wiring board which, with the moving panels controlled by the operator, ensures the supplemental substitution of one letter with another at the entry and exit points of the electric current. The number of possible combinations is thus astronomical. It is not surprising that we have never yet been able to reconstruct the process and decode messages encrypted in such a manner. We cannot express enough our gratitude."

Langer, at this point in his observations, paused to reflect and temper our enthusiasm: "If we are able to reconstitute the Enigma machine, about which I have no more doubt, there still remain many unknowns: the internal wiring within each of the three drums and the return drum, the daily rubrics of the various mobile elements (drums, wiring board), the specific keys for each message. All of these could undoubtedly be reconstituted by process of calculation. It would be a long process! Very long! If we had access to one or more of the monthly tables reporting the daily modifications—even if they were obsolete—we would progress much further and save years of work. This is evidence of how valuable your informant's contributions can be to us and the sharing of our knowledge with that of the French cryptographic services who have benefited from this invaluable documentation."

I was perplexed! How was I, Bertrand, to respond to such an invitation, when I knew the failures of our Bureau? I rationalized my decision by affirming that the research in France, as in Britain moreover, appeared to me much less advanced.

"You do not have the same motivations as we do," observed Langer generously, noticing my embarrassment.

And so Bertrand, resolutely optimistic, concluded his story:

Thus we commenced our close collaboration with the Polish. Our difficulties though, haven't yet ended. Since 1932, each time our allies think they have just about succeeded, the Germans launch new changes to their machine and their ciphers.

Fortunately, Asché was still in the picture.

H.E.'s work begins to take shape

What Bertrand did not reveal to me, but which I learned from Lemoine and Perruche, were Asché's working conditions and the magnitude of his production on other essential subjects.

On November 8, 1931 at Verviers, while for three hours Bertrand and Bintz took snapshot after snapshot, Rex and Schmidt discussed the future while sharing a meal, with Moselle wine flowing freely.

Lemoine's highly persuasive arguments, as much as the lure of financial gain, had quickly convinced Asché that he had no other choice but to continue on the path he had started down. Concerned for the safety of his young colt, Rex forced him to think about his new location in Berlin in terms of the unique resources it could provide him.

During the week preceding the meeting, already certain of its positive outcome, he had taken the time to note two 'mailboxes' available in Paris. Schmidt was to address his messages there, written in invisible ink. He agreed to limit his movements, especially with such incriminating documents on his person. When such documents were deemed indispensable, Rex explored solutions that would avoid the constant danger of crossing the border, even if surveillance from the German side appeared to be sparse and somewhat sloppy.

In collaboration with another one of our 'honorable correspondents' (H.C.), Father Vorage, priest of a small parish near Versailles, Rex developed a scenario which presented incontestable security guarantees. The priest, a native of Dutch Limburg, had offered his services to France in August 1914. This was a boon for the Deuxième Bureau. His knowledge of Germany and its language, the ease of movement which his neutral nationality offered him, his robe and the Kerkrade seminary along the border where he finished his theological studies, made him an invaluable intelligence officer. In 1917, wanted by the German Police and with a substantial reward offered for his capture, Father Vorage was forced to retreat to France. There, he nevertheless continued to serve the Bureau with boundless dedication. The many outside contacts he had preserved, including those in the Netherlands where his family resided, made him a permanent collaborator of our Intelligence Service. He had no equal when it came to discreetly crossing borders—in September 1935, the priest escorted a funeral procession from Cologne to Paris with an enormous set of documentation on the order of battle and mobilization of the sixth Wehrkreis (military district) of Münster.

Rex and Vorage were familiar with one another even though they did not see each other very often. They resembled one another, if not in their ideas on morality, at least in their relentless ingenuity, constant alertness, and their height: both were close to two meters tall.

Limburg, which Vorage knew inside out, was a crowded Dutch enclave, sandwiched between Belgium and Germany. Its borders were artificially created. The roads wound through an incredible tangle of fields, gardens, and houses. Some buildings had their entries in one country and one or more exits in another. During times of peace, the comings and goings between the borders of the three states were frequent, ongoing, uncontrollable.

Vorage had given Rex a sketch of the route to follow, starting from the Aix-la-Chapelle station, in order to arrive safely at Kerkrade in the Netherlands: ten short kilometers by tram and foot. From Kerkrade, Schmidt would arrive in Maastricht via Liège and Verviers.

"It's a bit complicated," Asché had observed, "but it seems good to me."

With the 10,000 marks handed over, we were left in a state of complete euphoria. The sensational harvest brought in on November 9, 1931 by Bertrand and Lemoine had earned the admiration of even the skeptical Perruche. What he had learned from Asché persuaded him that this agent offered far greater possibilities than just technical details from the Chiffrierstelle.

An unsolicited delivery of the secret report on toxic gases had further confirmed this conviction. A meeting between the two men appeared to be essential in order to obtain the maximum return from the informant. Although he had only recently been assigned to the Intelligence Bureau, Perruche had the boss's full attention and especially that of his future assistant, Colonel Louis Rivet.[54] Supported by an enthusiastic Bertrand returning from Poland, he obtained rather easily on December 16, 1931 the funds to reward Schmidt generously. The latter had set an appointment for Sunday, December 20, 1931 in Verviers.

"At this rate," observed the boss, "H.E. will cost us as much as all of our other informants put together!"

On December 19, Rex, Bertrand and Perruche arrived separately at the Grand Hotel in Verviers. Bertrand, carrier of the Leica, had become an expert in photographic reproduction, and replaced Bintz as photographer of the documents delivered by Schmidt. These were numerous and of great value:

- a note on the mobilization of the Chiffrierstelle;
- a secret note on the use of pigeons "drafted" into intelligence transmission service which his brother manages;
- The keys for manual encryption for the Army for November and December 1931;
- a bundle of technical documents on various types of Enigma machines studied since 1928;
- and above all, the table of keys (one key per day) Heeres-M. for December 1931. This document would fulfill the wishes of Poles since it provides the daily Enigma settings for the end of the year.

Upon his return to Paris, Bertrand would forward the documents by diplomatic valise and through the intermediary of our representative in Warsaw. While he worked on the reproduction of these precious documents, Alison (a.k.a. Perruche) and Lemoine had lunch with H.E., who had not arrived in Verviers until around noon.

"Your route is impeccable," he said to Rex, "but it's so long."

This time H.E. was properly dressed and quite at ease. He bowed respectfully before Alison. Tall, svelte, with a receding hairline, fine features and a look of intelligence, Perruche spoke with a manner that was both lively and reflective. Forty-five years old, single, quite cultivated, a music lover and collector of rare objects, he selected his friends carefully and observed an unwavering discretion with regard to his craft. He was passionate about it.

"The next time, Mr. Schmidt, we will shorten your route if you wish!"

At his request, Schmidt once again disclosed his personal circumstances, his mission within the ministry, his relationship with his brother, and his motives. It was all clear, without any contradiction with his earlier statements. In a casual manner, he took from his wallet a card for the N.S.D.A.P. (National Socialist Party) No. 738736, dated December 1, 1931.

"I thought that this would provide a good cover for the future. I am sure that in less than a year, the Nazis will have the majority in the Reichstag. They have had 107 deputies since September 14, 1930."

Schmidt painted a remarkably precise tableau of the internal situation of his country. Debt-ridden Germany was the victim of a tragic economic crisis. It faced permanent social unrest resulting from an unprecedented level of unemployment.

"The head of state, the old Marshal Hindenburg, will not be able to withstand the pressure exerted by the Nazis for very long," said H.E. "After the rally of September 6, 1931 at Gera in Thüringer where the Nazi leader was hailed by the S.A.[55] and the people, Hindenburg gave him an audience on October 10. Hitler did not hesitate to repeat to the president that which he had continued to proclaim everywhere: 'I am ready to take down the evils that burden the German people by assuming the responsibilities of power.'"

Schmidt concluded his report by emphasizing how important his membership in a party called to lead Germany was for the Deuxième Bureau.

"The machine is running! Look, my membership card has the number 738736. Do you know a political party that has a membership number as high as this, in France or elsewhere?"

Throughout lunch, and after the inevitable drinks, Alison did not stop listening to, questioning and observing Schmidt. His nerve, this kind of reckless bragging that drove him to expose and sell the secrets of his country just as a wine merchant would recruit his clientele by having him taste his best wines, made him feel ill at ease. Nevertheless, he could not stop himself from feeling a true admiration when considering the significant benefit that the Bureau should be able to draw from this singular character.

He was insistent that Schmidt cultivate his relationship with his brother. In addition to the encryption secrets, those of the German command relating to the clandestine rearmament and the political and military developments in Germany were of considerable interest.

"I was not disappointed," confided Perruche while reporting to me one day about his impressions of his first interview with Schmidt. "His brother is very interested in armored infantry, so since the beginning of 1932 we have received whole pages written in invisible ink describing the Reichswehr's attention to tanks and motorization. We learned in a similar fashion the secret directives given for the management of automobile and train troops in order to proceed with officer training and to organize maneuvers with simulated armored equipment.

"He revealed to us the secret agreements signed with the Soviets that would permit, beginning in 1932, future armored divisions to perfect their skills inside Russia. And that's not all!"

On Sunday, May 8, 1932, the trio of Rex, Alison and Barsac once again met with Schmidt at Verviers. In addition to a comprehensive report produced from details provided by his brother on the situation of the Reichswehr, Schmidt was the bearer of a new Enigma provision.

The intelligence was sufficiently interesting that Bertrand decided to seize the opportunity to go to Warsaw the very next day, May 9. In the diplomatic valise entrusted to him, he was carrying, among other instructions and codes, photographs of cipher tables from May 1932. After the dispatch of the December 1931 cipher table and the technical notes on the Enigma machine, our comrade had been somewhat disappointed not to have had any indication as to how much our friends benefited had from it.

"This is wonderful!" exclaimed Lieutenant Colonel Langer, receiving Bertrand with great affability as always. "But unfortunately we are not able yet to re-establish the internal circuitry of the drums and thus reconstitute a complete replica of the transmitting machines."

Bertrand, surprised, rather wished he could discuss this with the Polish researchers, and take stock of their work and knowledge. Discreetly, he simply asked the chief of the Cipher Bureau what he needed. It was Major Ciezki, the official in charge of the work on the Enigma who responded:

"The ideal situation would be access to the internal wiring diagrams for the three mobile drums and for the return drum. In the absence of such plans, examples of their encoded messages with their translations would be invaluable."

Bertrand returned to Paris. He certainly understood the desire of his Polish allies. What he understood less was being kept at a distance from the results achieved; he suspected they were important given the Poles' enthusiasm upon receiving his documentation.

The weekly meeting of department heads on the following Monday was going to be stormy. In the absence of concrete results regarding the decoding of Enigma messages captured in France and Poland, some might suggest a hiatus of research in this direction.

Perruche, for his part, wished to take a break, hence limiting the risk to H.E. He proposed that they direct their work exclusively, at least for a time, to the gathering of more traditional political and military intelligence.

"It is not prudent to let our agent spread himself so thinly, and moreover to force him to cross the border so frequently carrying terribly incriminating documents. The Enigma intelligence that the Poles still desire does not seem essential to the success of their research.

"On the other hand, the disruption caused by Hitler, his claim to power, the program he outlined in *Mein Kampf*—all of this imposes on us a priority: to follow, if not be in advance of, the development of events across the Rhine."

The irritated tone of Bertrand's response threw a chill across the room: "We are far from having exhausted the secrets of the Chiffrierstelle. If our French specialists had truly wanted to grant the intellectual effort over to the Polish cryptographers, all we would have to do is simply ask for their help and to await the outcome of their work. We have taken the first steps toward them, the matter is too serious to retreat now and not support their efforts."

At that point the debate turned sour. Colonel Louis Rivet,[56] who was presiding over the meeting for the first time put an end to it. His long experience had instilled in him an authority that reinforced his advice, which was in any case always full of good sense and delivered with courtesy.

"It is high time we go to Berlin. We have to see H.E., see how he's doing over there, if he's living up to his potential, and how he is making use of the enormous funds being delivered to him. It is also necessary to provide him with the means to correspond with us in a way other than traveling abroad or by writing in invisible ink. In case of emergencies, we should put him in contact with our representative at the French Embassy, Maurice Dejean—that is if the latter does not fear being compromised. This solution would have the advantage of not leaving our ambassador, André François-Poncet, in the dark about what essential matters we are able to learn at a time when significant events could happen in Germany soon and at short notice."

I imagine that at this moment Perruche and Bertrand saw an exciting new task dawning for them... but Rivet cut in: "Summon Rex! Each of you will tell him everything he wishes to know. I will then see him along with both of you to clarify his mission and ensure the logistics of his operation. He's an old enough fox to sniff out any decisions that need to be made on the spot. He will know how to give the necessary instructions to H.E. in order to ensure his effectiveness and safety."

There were several motivations behind Rivet's decision. The exceptional importance of the H.E. case deserved better than the current conditions, which Rivet considered hazardous. He must discipline and restrain the enthusiasm of the two attending officers. Despite their qualities, Perruche and Bertrand were relatively new to the business: twenty-four and eighteen months respectively. As soldiers in active service and holders of crucial secrets, they could not be engaged in a risky operation abroad. Rex was the one with wide experience of this type of mission, well aware of the level of caution that must be the driving force behind a spy and his employers. He had the advantage of speaking German, of knowing Berlin, and of being a friend of Maurice Dejean, whom he had met in Paris or in the parish of Father Vorage on numerous occasions to play bridge or discuss a scandalous affair across the Rhine. Moreover, his dominance over Schmidt would allow him to impose a rigorous working method on the German.

Rex in Berlin

Berlin, Sunday July 31, 1932, 10 p.m.

As the Paris Express pulled into the station, a green-clad porter approached the platform edge. From the first-class carriage stepped Mr. von Koenig, an Austrian businessman on a tour of the European capitals. The porter rushed to take his bags, and with long strides led von Koenig through the labyrinthine station. Outside, the Friedrichstrasse was already lit up, full of gaudy advertisements, gleaming with lights. The blare of car horns and the shouts of newspaper vendors was deafening. Windows bedecked in colorful flags and a thick mess of pamphlets on the road, in the gutters and littering the sidewalks alerted any newcomers that the Reichstag elections had just taken place. The future of Germany was uncertain as the country held its breath, waiting anxiously for the next day's announcement.

The porter hailed a black and white checkered taxi and the client rushed into it, eager to be on his way. Minutes later, von Koenig arrived at the Hotel Adlon. A besplendent doorman stepped forward to open the door and carry Mr. von Koenig's bags to reception. They had been expecting him.

An obsequious concierge dressed in a sharp tuxedo led him to suite number 12. Von Koenig slipped a 10-mark note into his hand and passed him a letter.

"Deliver this tomorrow morning."

On the envelope was the address of a mailbox used by Schmidt. Von Koenig, a.k.a. Rex, had not wanted to inform Schmidt in advance of his visit to Berlin. Was this caution, a tactical move, or a desire to reserve a little time for his own personal business?

Rex spent the next day with Maurice Dejean at the French Embassy. Dejean had met with Schmidt on June 8, 1931 at the time of his first contact. In accordance with the rules surrounding French diplomatic and consular representations at the time, Dejean had appeared to dismiss Schmidt, while secretly providing him with both the means to go to Paris and the address he should visit. His discreet inquiries had confirmed Schmidt's profession, revealed his origins and also established the existence of his brother, a senior officer.

Intelligent, slim, yet far from delicate, Dejean, a future ambassador of France after World War II,[57] graduated with honors from the Center for Advanced Germanic Studies in Strasbourg, a veritable breeding ground for staff members of the French Special Services. Following an internship at 2bis, avenue de Tourville, he was assigned to the Ministry of Foreign Affairs and at the request of the Bureau, seconded to the French Embassy in Berlin. The unremitting assistance that he brought to the Bureau satisfied his taste for secret research and adventure. His activity, simultaneously passionate and prudent, worked wonders.

Rex and Dejean got on exceedingly well together, appreciating each other's qualities and commitment, which made their negotiations regarding Schmidt's espionage activities go smoothly. The decisions they made were inspired by concern for both efficiency and security.

In the future, Schmidt would be paid in cash (marks) in Berlin itself. The clippings would be placed in a briefcase or bag and sent to Dejean by diplomatic valise. The latter would then deposit the bag at the luggage room of one of the stations in Berlin, and the deposit slip would be addressed to a *poste restante* on Tiergartenstrasse, in an envelope for one Mr. Ernst Rau. In readiness for this, Schmidt crafted a false identity card for Rex under that name. It was understood that the station, the *poste restante* and the alias used would be changed regularly. A simple letter sent by Dejean to one of the informant mailboxes would serve as notification to Rex about the deposit. Similarly, though only in exceptional circumstances, urgent and important intelligence gathered by H.E. could be deposited in another *poste restante* in Berlin. Dejean, alerted by an ordinary postcard addressed to one of the mailboxes he controls, would then collect the mail and forward it to Paris after reading the contents and extracting any intelligence he deemed useful. The Bureau had complete confidence in François-Poncet, who was overseeing to the best of his ability Dejean's Intelligence Bureau mission.

On Tuesday, August 2, 1932 at around 8.00 p.m. Rex found Schmidt in one of the lounges of the Hotel Adlon, the very one in which Laval and Briand had liked to relax, smoke, and converse just over a year before during their meetings with Marshal Hindenburg and his ministers Brüning and Curtius. Everything was embellished in gold, which gave the room a warm glow in the low light. A muffled silence instilled a certain sense of confidence.

While recounting this meeting to me four years later, Lemoine's eyes still reflected the pride of his destiny. The details he gave were meant as much to convince me of the importance of his role as to impress the informant of the effectiveness of his method and to confirm his superiority over him:

> Schmidt arrived radiant, dressed elegantly in light flannel. He did not seem surprised by my presence in Berlin. After we congratulated one another, he described to me at length the extent of the recent success of the Nazi party. His comments clearly demonstrated his satisfaction at having been able to predict so accurately several months in advance the rise of Hitler.
>
> "It's not over", he added, "In a few months we will have the power."
>
> I let him talk.
>
> He was involved with Goering himself and the team of the N.S.D.A.P. responsible for the Brandenburg sector in the election campaign and for the fights with the Berlin communists.
>
> I called his attention to the need not to flaunt his occasional militancy.
>
> "I know," he said, "that our boss von Schleicher[58] is not a friend of the Führer, yet he shares many of his opinions on the future of Germany. But don't worry, I am careful. Besides, my comrades at the Chiffrierstelle are even more active in the party than me—especially my friend Gottfried Schapper. He's been closely linked to Goering ever since the Great War—a specialist in radio interceptions. During the war he organized this radio intelligence for the benefit of the General Headquarters, then developed it in several major units, including the air force. And so this is how he knew Goering.

"He is a Nazi through and through, and has been from the very beginning. He joined the Chiffrierstelle in 1927 and occupies a higher position than me. It is he who leads the section that centralizes and operates the encrypted interceptions. Much of his work was focused on the Abwehr. He has frequent and friendly relations with this branch and its leader, Captain Patzig.

"He's always talking about the unease felt as much in the Abwehr as in the Chiffrierstelle due to the chaotic organization of the research and analysis of the intelligence. Everyone gets involved, military and civilian, sailors, airmen, police, foreign affairs, postal, customs and so on.

"Schapper's idea, in line with that of Patzig and the many specialists in the Abwehr, is to create a 'Central Intelligence Office'. This organization would be directly dependent on the Chancellor, and would centralize and coordinate research, and would oversee its analysis."

"The main aspects of this project were submitted by Schapper to Goering. If the Führer approves in turn, and if the Nazis take power, it is likely that this reform will happen. Schapper will then occupy an important place and surely ask me to take a place next to him."

"Easy, easy," I said. "Hitler is not yet Chancellor and you haven't finished your work in the Chiffrierstelle."

Time was ticking.

"Shall we celebrate this victory?" Schmidt proposed. I nodded, eager to get a better understanding of H.E.'s thoughts and his way of life. It was 9 p.m.

Outside everything was lit and swarming with people strolling, hungry for some fresh air. An army of prostitutes was parading on Friedrichstrasse and Kurfurstendam. A ribald Schmidt tried to tickle some of them along the path. In Potsdam Square, he led me into a monumental café, a real cathedral with marble pillars.

"You will see Berlin's joie de vivre!" he exclaimed.

In the smoke-filled crowd we found a corner table amongst the tourists, the bourgeois and the flirtatious girls mingling around and had a pint of beer fortified with a small glass of alcohol. At the back of the room, an orchestra roared. Unable to hear one another and getting hungry, we got a taxi to Charlottenburg, to an ultra-chic cabaret with an inconspicuous entrance surrounded by plush curtains. A stylish maître d' and friend of Schmidt welcomed us in as regulars and led us to a booth upholstered with ruby-red velvet and adorned with gold tassels. In the richly decorated room, couples dined to the sound of violins discreetly playing in the background. At the dimly lit bar a few pretty girls were drinking champagne. After ordering, Schmidt excused himself for a moment to greet the ladies and to most likely make a few dates. I was transfixed. Our man finally had the life of his dreams.

It was past midnight when we left, but we would see each other again very soon, as I'd invited him to a working dinner in my suite at the Hotel

Adlon. Elegant and precise, he arrived at 7 p.m. exactly. He readily accepted the *modus vivendi* order with Dejean, of whom I revealed neither his name nor his function. I asked him questions supplied by Perruche and Bertrand, and gave him a Leica and its accessories for the reproduction of documents.

"If you stay for a few more days," he told me, "I will give you the ciphers currently in use and those planned for the coming months. I also hope to have the blueprint of the internal circuitry of the Enigma. I am on duty on Sunday and my chief has left the keys to the safe with me. Next Saturday, I will spend a good part of the day with my brother, as I do most Saturdays. I'll see what I can learn from him."

"My dear captain," continued Rex, hammering out his words and moving closer to me, "I left Berlin on August 16, 1932 after passing to Dejean a large package containing crucial secrets that was to be sent to Paris by valise…"

Among other items there was the following:
- the daily ciphers scheduled for September and those in preparation for October 1932;
- a plain text message and its corresponding code encrypted by the Enigma machine in operation at the Reichswehr headquarters;
- various new training materials sent to the Army and the Luftwaffe about the Enigma;
- a 1931 study on the German officers' corps (*Das deutsche Offizierkorps*);
- a confidential report of some twenty pages on the official and secret resources of Germany. It had been created on July 20, 1932 by the Reichswehrministerium at the request of the Minister von Schleicher. Schmidt's brother had been involved in its drafting.

As far as I can remember, it was emphasized that in addition to 100,000 men[59] authorized by the Treaty of Versailles, the Reich could make use of 4,000,000 educated N.C.O.s and soldiers and 60,000 reserve officers. This workforce was discreetly maintained at the Reichswehrministerium Pension Service, 38 Königin-Augustastrasse, and included the Gendarmerie, the Police, Customs and above all paramilitary associations (Stahlhelm, Sturmabteilung, Reichsbanner Schwarz-Rot-Gold, Eiserne Front, etc.).

In terms of aviation, the report took stock of German manufacturing plants transferred to Switzerland, Sweden and Denmark: nearly 1,500 airplanes could be converted into military aircraft with an arsenal of materials in reserve. The report estimated that 8,000 young people were currently learning how to fly in the gliding schools.

As for the Navy, the report stated that under agreements negotiated with Spain by Captain Canaris[60] a prototype submarine of 750 tonnes and

53-centimeter torpedoes were being designed and manufactured in Cadiz. Finally, the report revealed the existence of laboratories specializing in chemical warfare in an annex of the Badische Anilin located in Gatersleben."

"I am not able to recall," added Rex, "everything else that was in this important document."

Important, indeed. It would serve as the basis for several studies of the Deuxième Bureau of the Army General Staff sent to Commander-in-Chief General Weygand and War Minister Paul Boncour to emphasize the dangers of Germany's clandestine rearmament.

By submitting all this intelligence to Lemoine, Schmidt had explained what he knew of Hitler's plans. On August 13, 1932, the Führer, accompanied by two of his top aides—the S.A. chief of staff Ernst Röhm, and Wilhelm Frick, the future minister of the interior of the Reich—met President Hindenburg, Chancellor von Papen and Secretary of State Maissner. He re-affirmed his will to rise to power, stressing his electoral success of July 31 (230 MPs instead of 107). The rupture was complete. Driven by his minister of war, General von Schleicher, the old marshal was tough and secured von Papen at the head of his government.

On the same day in Pirmasens, ten kilometers from the French border, 100,000 former German soldiers were shouting their determination to ensure the return of large territories lost in the east and west to the great state of Germany.

"Make this clear in Paris," H.E. insisted, apparently more concerned with the interests of France than with the future of his own country. "In under six months there will be more to come here!" He explained: "The N.S.D.A.P. is overflowing with money, banks, large industrial complexes, employee contributions… and moreover, at every meeting (there is one every day), a minimum contribution of one mark is imposed on the participants. The activists are becoming more numerous—young people, those who are unemployed, those who are simply unhappy… Our managers are former officers obsessed with the idea of revenge.

"Remember our combat objectives: The Treaty of Versailles, Jews, Marxism, and capitalism."

Schmidt had used the Leica to take a mass of photographs of documents from the Chiffrierstelle. Some had been extracted from the trunk of Major Oschmann.[61] He apologized for not having dared to open two large sealed envelopes, one of which which contained an overview diagram (Ubersichts-Schaltbild), and the other the assembly diagram (Montage-Schaltbild) for the Enigma machine in service.

As for the secret report of July 20, 1932, he more or less stole an original from the office of his brother, whom he had visited at the War Ministry on Saturday morning. It was one of the twenty-five mimeographed copies intended to be numbered and circulated in principal bureaus at headquarters.

"One more or one less, no one will notice that a copy is missing," commented Schmidt, casually and unconcerned about putting his brother in a bind.

"I did not want to leave Berlin," Rex continued:

> … without having examined again with H.E. the *modus vivendi* and the use of funds that we provided him in cash. The behavior he exhibited, his all-too-apparent existence as a bachelor playboy, would draw attention sooner or later, despite the licentious manners that the Berlin of 1932 audaciously displayed as a sort of challenge to the economic crisis and misery of the city. I was worried. I noted with satisfaction that he too had thought about it:
>
> "My wish is to live on the outskirts of Berlin, to start a business successful enough to allow me to retire, not too late, from administration and find a job more consistent with my original training as a chemist. I will seek out a bank loan and help from my brother to assist me with buying a nice property in the suburbs. In addition to my family I'll also bring back with me a fellow who is also an unemployed chemist like me, I'd like to start a small soap factory, as I had tried to do in 1926. The opportunities are enormous at present and I have some experience in this kind of business.
>
> "I have enough freedom at the Chiffrierstelle to able to handle it. Everyone knows that I am a member of the Nazi party. No one would want to mess with them! The prosperity of this business will fully justify my lifestyle and my trips abroad."
>
> He emphasized this last sentence with a wink that spoke volumes about his determination to continue his lucrative work with us and maintain his access to the pleasures and luxuries he could not enjoy in his own country.
>
> The best trips, luxury hotels, good food, women… I assure you, Captain, that since 1933, he has not been deprived.

Breaching the Enigma

Armed with new intelligence on the Enigma, which arrived in Paris on August 19, 1932 by diplomatic valise, Bertrand attempted once more to rouse the interest of the Cipher Section of the Army General Staff in the decoding of mechanically encrypted messages. His welcome from Colonel Bassières was polite, even friendly. The documents were examined with curiosity, and promises made to examine how to take advantage of them. The offer to provide what the Intelligence Bureau had, or would have, in possession was, of course, recognized. It always helps to enrich the documentation one already has on hand.

Two weeks passed. No response or reaction. The disappointment was tough to accept.

On September 17, 1932 with the consent of the boss, Bertrand returned to Poland. As always, he deposited Asché's findings into the diplomatic valise, which this time included the monthly reports from the Army (Heeres M.) providing the daily Enigma rubrics for the months of September and October 1932, and the plain-text message with its corresponding encrypted code.

Lieutenant Colonel Langer and Major Ciezki accepted it with the same cordiality. The document examination lasted four days, during which, under the guidance of an officer from the Biuro Szyfrow,[62] Bertrand visited Krakow and Wilno, before returning for a stroll around old Warsaw. On September 22, the eve of his departure for Paris, Bertrand was summoned by the head of the Bureau, Colonel Mayer, to appear at 4 p.m. before the head of the General Staff of the Polish Army. He was congratulated, thanked. His assistance was required more than ever, they said—but there was still nothing on where the progress of the research stood.

This prolonged silence infuriated the Frenchman. When he raised his concern with Langer, he was told: "Be patient! The work is very complex. I assure you that we will succeed, and when we do, you will be the very first to know."

Langer would keep this promise, but after a long delay, as we shall see later in this story.

Despite their best efforts, by late summer 1932 the military technicians of the Biuro Szyfrow had failed to overcome the remaining problems that stood in the way of the Enigma's reconstruction. These two obstacles were of a structural nature, and concerned 1) the internal wiring of the drums, and 2) the regulatory nature regarding the daily settings of the machine.

However, on September 17 the French Intelligence Bureau was able to provide information that could potentially brush aside these impediments: the daily configuration tables for the months of September and October 1932.[63]

For thirty long days, Major Ciezki's military team, conscientious and stubborn in equal proportions, strove to resolve these remaining problems. It was a wasted effort. Pushed by his bosses, Ciezki had to concede that they had failed. Swallowing his pride, he entrusted the uncrackable file to a young mathematician, an expert in cryptology who had been assigned to his service on September 1, 1932: Marian Rejewski.

Convinced of the vital importance of decoding, in 1929 the Polish General Staff created a chair of cryptology at the University of Poznan. Only the most talented students in mathematics were admitted after being put through their paces in a rigorous selection process. In 1930, three of the most brilliant of them, Zygalski, Rosicki and Rejewski, had been chosen to participate in the work conducted at the Biuro Szyfrow.

*

We have now reached October 17, 1932. After a miracle performed by the Intelligence Bureau, we would finally achieve the scientific feat that had been eluding us for months. Between Christmas 1932 and New Year's Day 1933, Rejewski would deliver to his boss the results of his scientific calculations. The technical data he provided was so accurate that it was finally possible to construct of an exact replica of the machine in service in the Reichswehr.

The work was executed in Warsaw before being handed over to the engineer Palluth of the firm A.V.A., a specialist in electromechanical and radio equipment.

In April 1933, the first prototype of a complete reproduction of the Enigma Type I was completed. Additional copies were to follow—but the Deuxième Bureau would not be informed about them.

*

Having returned from his trip to Warsaw in September without useful results, Bertrand, disappointed and bitter, summoned Asché to Liège. He wanted to confirm the value of the documents delivered to the Polish and to restore his confidence in his relationship with the informant.

The meeting took place on October 29 and 30, 1932 in the Hotel d'Angleterre.

Perruche and Lemoine accompanied him.

Always efficient and very attentive to those around him, the informant, having arrived at the hotel the day before, came bearing valuable documents:

- a secret report from the Reichswehr Chief of Staff, dated October 20, 1932, presenting the findings of maneuvers that took place in late September in the Frankfurt-Oder region before Marshal Hindenburg and a Soviet military delegation headed by Marshal Tukhachevsky.
- ("Well, well!" Perruche exclaimed, reading the document and surprised by the detail.)
- the monthly Heeres M. ciphers for November and December 1932.

"Mr. Barsac," Schmidt commented kindly, "I intend on delivering the daily ciphers to you every two or three months. With these you shouldn't have too much difficulty with the decoding."

Bertrand, dismissive, avoided the question and abruptly posed one of his own, which had been weighing heavily on his mind for some time:

"Are you sure that the documents you provided us, and the ones you are delivering to me now, are those for the machine currently in service?"

Schmidt flinched. He raised his eyebrows, his gaze stiffened. He shifted his focus between Bertrand and Rex, who both understood the underlying threat behind the question.

"I am not a crook. If you have any doubts, they should be that your own cryptologists are completely incapable."

The conversation had taken a sour turn. Conciliatory, Lemoine attempted to satisfy Bertrand by guaranteeing the relevance of Schmidt's information.

Perruche, who had been following the conversation, rapidly came to a conclusion: "Gentlemen, it is high time for you to eat!" He and Bertrand left for his room to photograph the documents brought by H.E.

Alone with Rex in a discreet corner of the restaurant of the Hotel d'Angleterre, H.E. returned to Bertrand's unusual question:

"Is it to hide the results of your research? Is it to test me?"

Lemoine reassured him. As a testament to his total trust of H.E.'s service, he slid under his napkin the usual envelope containing 5,000 marks.

Relaxed, Schmidt plunged into a story about his personal circumstances:

"I am in talks to acquire a building where I will be able to set up my soap factory. It is a few kilometers from Berlin, on the banks of the River Spree in Ketschendorf. Before I commit, though, I want to make sure my friend will be free and agrees to operate the business with me. My participation in the party is intense at the moment. Beginning on October 1 the Orstgruppe of Berlin has entrusted to me the responsibility of the section of the N.S.B.D.[64] at the Chiffrierstelle. My role as militant and propagandist takes up much of my time. We have to prepare for the Reichstag elections, which will be held next week, on November 6. Hitler is increasingly determined to take power."

Rex urged caution. He advised using connections in Berlin or communicating by post. Schmidt must avoid any movements that might ultimately appear suspicious.

Schmidt agreed, adding: "Thank you for sparing me from having to going all the way to Verviers. This detour via Holland and Kerkrade is still very long, though. Why not change location? My family and I spent a few days on vacation in late August and early September in Czechoslovakia, in Spindlermühle in the Sudetenland, some two or three kilometers from the German border. It's a charming tourist resort at eight hundred meters—'the pearl of Giant Mountains'! The Davidsbaude hotel is perfect. It's discreet, access is just as easy from Berlin as it is from Prague—no border controls. The population is German, and very welcoming. I think this place would be ideal for an upcoming rendezvous."

Rex agreed, promising to propose it to the boss.

Meanwhile, Bertrand and Perruche worked through the night photographing the documents H.E. had brought them. Before leaving on October 30, Perruche pulled H.E. to one side:

"In the long report that you brought, I noticed some information that could only come from a high level of command—the recommendation for the transformation of the horse-drawn carriages into motorized units and the train car, including that of the General Staff at Döberitz, into combat units, achieved by using both actual equipment (armored cars, anti-tank weapons, etc.) and fictitious (*Attrapen*), consisting of carcasses mounted on various types of vehicles. Such efforts can only be the work of armored infantry specialists. Can you give me the source?"

H.E. smiled. "I's my brother. Since July 1, he has been the director of the Kriegsakademie.[65] He was involved with the preparation of this report and he has learned things that would truly shock you. He provided me with this copy of the document addressed to the minister. I have to return it to him tomorrow.

"Rudolf is aware of my position of responsibility in the Nazi party. He is keeping me informed of the *Stimmung*[66] within military circles by design. Many of his ideas are in alignment with those of Hitler. One day I will arrange a meeting with him and the Führer so that they can discuss their views."

On the train back to Paris, Bertrand and Perruche congratulated each other on the results of their harvest. Bertrand, with a certain sadness, could not help noting the exceptional value of the informant, the risks he was taking and the scant amount of decoding intelligence they had only been able to gather up to this point for the Bureau and France. H.E.'s intelligence would serve as a basis for a report from the Deuxième Bureau of the Army General Staff which, at the end of 1932 would force the French military and the government to confront their responsibilities while disarmament negotiations were taking place in Geneva.

"One sees included in their drills a squadron, heavy artillery groups, a battalion of simulated tanks, fake armored squadrons [...] a few 'civil' aircraft gliding over the troops [...] undoubtedly certain weapons, certain resources, are missing from the German divisions of 1932, but the framework is there [...] passionately displaying their fake equipment as reality..."

The report put forward a chilling prophecy: "The Reichswehr will not be happy for very long with just a few samples of weapons and materials..."

H.E. at the heart of the Nazi intelligence services

On January 30, 1933, aware of the inability of the current government to assert its authority and tired of political and social crises that followed one after another, the old President Marshal Hindenburg handed power over to Hitler. Von Papen became Vice Chancellor, von Blomberg Minister of the Reichswehr, and Goering held the combined functions of Reichstag President, Minister of the Interior of the Reich, Aviation Commissioner, and President of the Prussian Council. The enthusiasm of the Nazis was deluded by ambition. Determined to strengthen his popular base, the new Chancellor, with Goering's support, immediately dissolved the Reichstag and set elections for March 5. The only realistic opposition to the regime? The Communists.

During the night of February 27/28, 1933 a fire of questionable origin destroyed the Reichstag. Shrewd and aggressive propaganda surrounded the event, denouncing and placing responsibility for the fire on the Communists, and as a result a series of drastic measures were implemented. A state of emergency was declared. Communist and socialist meetings were prohibited and their newspapers suspended during the election campaign. The swastika was presented as the symbol of order and security.

An aggressive speech given by the Führer at Koenigsberg, East Prussia, redefined the Nazis' objectives. It was also a challenge to Poland, as he announced the occupation of Danzig and the Corridor. In brief, Hitler's speech was an impassioned appeal for the fight against Communism.

And it was heard loud and clear. March 5 was a triumph for the Nazis. Approximately 17,200,000 people came out to vote (compared to the 11,700,000 on November 6, 1932) giving them 44 percent of the seats in the Reichstag. With the appointment of a few deputies from the far right, it was an absolute majority.

At an equally important event in the Länder,[67] the Nazis took control of municipal buildings and raised the swastika flag. It marked the end of federalism and German particularism. Wherever the local government was not yet in the hands of the N.S.D.A.P., Hitler and Goering assigned Reich commissioners as supreme leaders: this was the case in Bavaria, Württemberg, Baden, Hamburg, and Bremen. Goering reigned supreme in Prussia.

On March 23, 1933, the new assembly met at the Kroll Opera House, opposite the ruins of the Reichstag at the entrance to the Tiergarten. By a vote of 441 to 94, the election gave total power to Hitler. Eighty-three Communist deputies were excluded from the vote and a dozen of their socialist comrades were in prison. Even before the vote took place, the first round of measures adopted by the Führer was already underway. These included:

- standardization of Nazi policies throughout Germany;
- fierce repression of political crimes;
- a complete purge of the administration and the police (as for the army, we will see that later);
- an anti-Semitic campaign so frenzied that it provokes furious indignation of Western democratic countries. In Britain and the United States protests were accompanied by the boycott of German products.

Such dramatic steps were underpinned by significant decisions made in secret. Their immediate effect was to transform Germany into a police state, giving the Third Reich unparalleled powers in both its domestic dominance and its expansionist policy.

There was no doubt that this was what H.E. urgently wanted to communicate to his "friends".

On March 15, 1933, a brief message let Perruche know that Asché was unable to travel. He had serious matters to discuss and requested that Rex come to Berlin.

On March 31, Mr. von Koenig returned to the Hotel Adlon.

"You're arriving at a difficult time," the toadying head of reception confided in him. "Tomorrow, Saturday April 1 is a national day of protest against the anti-German campaign incited by the Jews abroad."

Rex shrugged. "We'll see."

The next morning at 8 a.m., he was awakened by a cacophonous concert of fifes, trumpets, and drums. Perched on a truck, a group of young SA members were holding up signs insulting the Jews; following them was a motley crowd screaming threatening slogans and brandishing anti-Semitic banners.

When Rex ventured outside a few hours later to join Maurice Dejean in an inconspicuous Charlottenburg restaurant, a strange atmosphere hung in the air. The Jewish shopkeepers had pulled their curtains and locked their doors. During the night, posters had been pasted onto their shop fronts: *Deutsche! Kauftnicht beim Juden*" ("Germans, do not buy from Jews"). On the front of the clothing store Heitinger, the word "*JUDE*" had been written several times in big white letters. A little further down, another store window was shattered under the impassive eye of a policeman and the indifference of onlookers.

"This is how it is across Germany," Dejean informed him. "Consuls are phoning to tell us that these vindictive demonstrations are spreading. Sometimes it gets violent. It's a reaction against the boycott of German products in England and the United States; the Nazis are placing responsibility on the Jews.

"Certainly the persecutions are starting to spread throughout the Reich. In many places Jews have been excluded from administrations, universities, hospitals… Soon they will not be permitted to go abroad without special passports."

Vividly and accurately, Dejean painted a portrait of the shifting of policy in Germany.

"All on the same day, you will see an amorphous mass—sensitive beings, pleasant beings, flowery processions, good-natured people, '*gemütlich*' even. And then, right next to them, thousands of troublemakers disguised as soldiers, threatening figures, shouting curses and slogans. Next to the indifference of others, they impose their brutal determination… this is Germany, with its simple, docile masses, all perfectly willing to be led. Heaven knows the Nazis assert this to us. Here, you see, the ignorant and the stupid have the privilege of being modest and subordinating themselves to those they believe are superior."

"This is very serious," Rex whispered after a long silence. "Have you any news of Schmidt?"

"Nothing. So all is well. Our delivery system by *poste restante* is working well. However, because of the situation this country is in and events that may occur at any time, I ask you to provide Schmidt with a faster way to reach me in an emergency without compromising the embassy."

Dejean handed him a card on which was written the phone number of Georges Blun, the Berlin correspondent of the Paris newspaper *Le Journal*.

"Blun is a highly regarded journalist well connected in all the German circles. He is discreet. He is clever. During my last trip to Paris, I met his boss Paul Gerar-Dubot, editor-in-chief and for quite some time honorary correspondent of the Bureau. With Rivet's agreement, he has given us authorization to request the services of his colleague. In anticipation of your visit, I saw him the day before yesterday. He agreed that Schmidt, whom he knows nothing about, can telephone him, meet him, and include him in the transmission of messages. It is understood that this method of communication will be only be used in cases of extreme emergency. It does not change our usual approach."

At 5 p.m. in the corner lounge of the Hotel Adlon, Rex met Schmidt.

"Events are moving more quickly than I had expected," said H.E., who was in a rush to get to the heart of his subject.

"Today especially I feel that there will be a reckoning with the Jews," observed Lemoine, still reeling from the disorder and brutality that he had witnessed on the street.

"That is only one aspect of it! Besides, these reprisals against the Jews will not last too long—Hitler and Goering have given orders at Hindenburg's request.

"What I want to speak to you about is top secret and no one is to talk about it. It's about carefully taking decisive steps to establish the regime, silencing opponents, researching what is happening and being said in the Reich, including the embassies. Do you recall the plans to create a 'Central Intelligence Office,' which I discussed with you in August 1932?"

Rex nodded in agreement.

"The project resurfaced in February, at Goering's request. Under his presidency, and sometimes in the presence of Hitler, a group of specially handpicked department heads and leading figures of the N.S.D.A.P., including Heinrich Himmler, Reinhard Heydrich and my friend Paul Körner, who has become the private secretary to Goering, and my comrade Gottfried Schapper met secretly at the Reich Chancellery for several weeks.

"The Führer only has limited confidence in the Gestapo and the

Abwehr. The idea that emerged was to create something new by appointing affirmed Nazis to key positions: the 'S.S.'"[68]

"It's good politics," Rex commented wryly. "Competence is sacrificed on the altar of militancy."

"Don't believe it!" replied H.E. "In this case, competence and activism—I would say fanaticism—go hand in hand. This is what caused the failure, at least until now, of the grand Central Office project.

"Himmler's adjutant, Reinhard Heydrich, is a Nazi of exceptional class and is terribly ambitious. At the end of 1931, he founded a branch of the S.S. for surveillance and intelligence: the Sicherheitsdienst (S.D.), which provides a multitude of services to the party and its leader. He intends to move to Berlin[69] as quickly as possible and take under his purview the internal and external security of the entire Reich. His arguments particularly impressed Hitler given the growing opposition against the S.A. chief Ernst Roehm.[70] He's a thug. He rules a revolutionary army of over one million boors. You've seen them at work today? Do you know they have opened concentration camps where they systematically imprison anyone whom they don't like?

"More than ever the Führer needs the S.S. to protect him and bring about order. There is no question of opposing Himmler and Heydrich. Nor is there any question, for the moment, of interfering with the Abwehr against the will of its chief, von Blomberg, minister of the Reichswehr.

"The outcome of all this is that the Führer has instructed Goering to organize—in secret and outside of the Chancellery so as not to offend anyone—intelligence services essential to the safety of the Reich. Remember, Mr. Lemoine, there are in Germany around 8,000,000 unemployed; this is a record, 5,000,000 voters who voted for the Communist Party and 7,000,000 who voted for the Social Democrats, many of whom are hostile to the Nazis. Do not forget that other nations are observing us and criticizing us.

"Two initiatives are in preparation and will come to light in the days that follow.[71] 1) Creation of the Forschungsamt (F.A.), a camouflaged secret organization within the Reich Ministry of Aviation. It will have a monopoly over all kinds of interceptions and wiretapping, both in Germany and abroad. The best way to be informed is to know what is written and said at all times and everywhere. The head of this service will be a friend of Goering, Lieutenant Commander Hans Schimpf, who currently acts as liaison between the Navy and the Abwehr. Schapper will be his adjutant. Both have asked for me to come over to this new organization. What do you think? How do you think Paris will react?"

Rex jumped.

"Please, continue. I'll tell you once I've heard more. The second decision was…?"

"2) Creation of a Secret State Police: the Geheime Staatspolizei (Gestapo) in Prussia, of which Goering is minister of the interior and president. This Gestapo, once broken in, will be extended throughout the Reich. It will be in Goering's hands, and he will take with him my friend Körner[72] who will serve as liaison between the Gestapo and Forschungsamt."

"As I understand it," said Rex, "with the Forschungsamt, the Nazis are going to eavesdrop, open letters, and penetrate the secrets of the embassies. With the Gestapo and the concentration camps, all opposition will disappear…"

"This is more or less the case," H.E. agreed, smiling. "But the role of Forschungsamt should be paramount, since in Hitler's mind—as in that of Goering—it must be at the source of the most private intelligence, inside and outside the Reich. It will work in constant liaison with the Gestapo, the Abwehr and especially the Chiffrierstelle for the deciphering of intercepted encrypted messages. It is expected that the basic recruitment will be here and Schapper is offering me an important position."

H.E. paused expectantly. Rex hesitated, then said: "For now, do not go anywhere. Observe what happens and stay in touch with Schapper. Until further notice be sure to remain in your current position. The Forschungsamt will not be operational for a long time and we still have much to learn about Enigma. I will report everything to the bosses. I'll let you know as soon as I return to Paris if they are of the same opinion."

"Hurry," insists H.E. "My comrade is impatiently awaiting a response. Tomorrow is Sunday. I will photograph the daily Enigma keys for March and April and hand them over to you."

"Understood," Rex concluded. "Let's have dinner. Any idea of where you'd like to dine?"

The evening pleasantly ended at The Tavern, on Friedrichstrasse. Lemoine informed Schmidt of the emergency backup communication plan using George Brun as a contact. A rendezvous was made for the next day at 5 p.m., before Rex's departure to Paris. Precise and always serious in his work, Schmidt carried the Enigma documents and the news of his brother's next promotion to the rank of colonel.

Three days later, he received from Paris this simple message written in invisible ink: "STAY AT YOUR POST."

The strange discretion of the Poles, and the infancy of the computer

Before leaving Lemoine on the evening of April 2, H.E. informed him about some significant intelligence that had been collected that day by his brother. The day before, the Führer had decided to initiate a complete overhaul of the Reichswehr. On December 10, 1932 the Allies, ignoring the warnings from France, had left a sizable opening for the Reichswehr, one that granted Germany equal rights with regards to armaments, and Germany was no longer adhering to Article V of the Treaty of Versailles.

By the time Hitler rose to power and the veil shrouding the Enigma machine began to lift, Franco-Polish diplomatic relations were at best lukewarm. Paris wanted to integrate the 1921 Franco-Polish alliance into the League of Nations. Minister of War Marshal Pilsudski, and his close colleague, Minister of Foreign Affairs Colonel Beck, both rejected this organization, which they judged to be spineless. They categorically rejected the French proposal.

In parallel with this conflicting situation, a policy of good relations was established with Poland's two powerful neighbors. The policy was, or would be, implemented by non-aggression pacts with the U.S.S.R. in 1932, and with the Third Reich on January 26, 1934. Hitler would prove the hypocrisy of the pact on October 2, 1938 by forcing Czechoslovakia to cede Teschen to Poland.

Having been kept informed about the evolution of research on the German encryption machine, Pilsudski and Beck (former head of the Polish Intelligence Service in 1920) ordered absolute secrecy. The slightest indiscretion, the least imprudence might jeopardize the *modus vivendi* reached with Germany and annihilate any benefit that Poland could gain from its peacetime work, if war were to break out. No-one could share in this secret, not even the Deuxième Bureau.

If by some unfortunate chance, Bertrand's informant was to be held accountable before his country, it would be too dangerous for him to have any knowledge of Rejewski's successes.

Such drastic measures alarmed Mayer, Langer, and Ciezski since it forced them to deprive Bertrand of his due share of the satisfaction. They would scrupulously respect their orders all the while increasing their show of trust and friendship toward the French officer. Perhaps they also considered that France, herself failing to commit to a level of scientific effort similar to theirs, could afford to wait for better times.

And so, determined to maintain good relations with the French Special Services, Lieutenant Colonel Langer invited Bertrand to come to Poland in order to attend the drills that the Polish interception and decoding group was conducting between May 9 and 15, 1933. The purpose of the exercise was to capture and decipher as many messages as possible, and to observe the maneuvers of the German army along the Polish border facing the Danzig corridor.

Major Ciezki received Bertrand respectfully and accompanied him to where the operations were taking place.

"You see, sir, it is from this area that a war could begin. The Germans do not admit to the existence of this corridor, nor to the Free City of Danzig. It is vital for us to identify at any instant the threat and to track its developments."

In fact, even without the French having access to the inner workings of the mobile group based around Thorn, he was aware of the messages exchanged and captured between the major German units in operation. Some may have been encrypted by the Enigma I machine and read by the Poles with relative rapidity. No secret was revealed to him regarding this point.

"During such maneuvers," Ciezki observed, "the Germans have committed monumental errors, for example by mixing unencrypted and encrypted messages. Our work on classic decoding has been greatly facilitated by their mistakes.

"The possession of a replica Enigma machine will certainly be a decisive step toward unlocking the secrets of their messages, but it will be only one step. It will next be necessary to develop a scientific method in order to discover, as quickly as the appropriate analysis of decrypted messages demands it, the daily Enigma configurations, i.e. the settings according to the day's ciphers. In this final phase, your informant's contribution is indispensable."

"Perhaps he could also help us to learn about Hitler's intentions with regards to our country and especially about the corridor and Danzig," added Lieutenant Colonel Langer who joined Bertrand and Ciezki on 14 May.

The question was certainly a valid one. Bertrand, satisfied with his trip, promised to ask.

Yet on 15 May 1933 he once again left Warsaw without any details on the progress of the work on Enigma. Langer assured Bertrand that he would travel to Paris before the end of the year "to take stock of the situation."

At the end of 1932, Perruche's research section received an excellent reinforcement: Commander Guy Schlesser, trained by the General Staff and the Centre for Advanced Germanic Studies. He was assigned to the German section. Tall, slim, and stylish, he was a thoroughbred rider—a go-getter. Five years later, I would have the opportunity of having him as the leader of our counterespionage service.

His keen intelligence convinced him that Hitler's Germany was engaged in a process of irreversible political and military expansion.

He gauged the dangers of this in the face of a powerless League of Nations, a Europe divided and lax, and an indifferent and pacifist[73] France, which had surrendered to the games of "party politics." He quickly understood the extent of H.E.'s resources and the benefit that the Bureau could draw from his intelligence. He had one immediate desire: to meet the informant, form an opinion of him and direct his research accordingly.

His opportunity soon arrived.

On his return from Warsaw, Bertrand presented the question posed by the Poles about the Third Reich's policy toward Poland to H.E., who responded at the end of August: "rendezvous on September 16 at Spindlermühle."

Rex was on vacation, but as Schlesser was fluent in German, he agreed to attend, and the proposition was accepted.

In Prague, the French representative, a deputy military attaché, put a car at the disposal of 'St. George' (Schlesser's alias) and Barsac. On the night of the 15th, they checked into the Hotel Davidsbaude, as instructed by H.E. A little out of the way, overlooking Spindlermühle, it was surrounded by thick forests that extended into nearby Germany. This was a vast mountain-style chalet: two storeys with sloping ceilings on the upper storey. A large tiled stove heated the large living room, which was furnished with heavy seats. Four customers were playing cards noisily in a corner—but there was no sign of Schmidt.

The next morning, the two officers found themselves on a rocky path that slowly climbed through the forest toward the German border. Schlesser later told me what happened:

> Bertrand demanded that we each take a revolver. For my first mission of this kind, Barsac undoubtedly wanted to impress me. We were only 1,500 meters from the German border, but now that I knew Schmidt, I can say that he was capable of sniffing out all the traps.
>
> Around 11 a.m., we saw the silhouette of a climber descending briskly toward us.
>
> "That's Asché," Barsac revealed. "I'll introduce you as Alison's assistant."
>
> Right away, I was struck by the strength of his clear gaze, his conduct, his ease. He wore woolen leggings, his knees bare, embroidered suede pants, heavy

studded shoes, a dark green wool jacket and his felted badger hat completed his Bavarian figure. He was carrying a huge rucksack. The sun was hot. A small stream ran alongside the road and separated us from the deep forest.

"Isn't it beautiful?" H.E. exclaimed, inviting us to enter the forest to take a break. He had come by road via Dresden and Hirschberg, but left his car near the border and finished the few kilometers on foot in order to reach us.

"That was imprudent!" scolded Barsac.

"In the unlikely event that our papers are checked, the party card is sovereign here."

It was true that since February 1933 the Nazi Henlein exalted the German population of the Sudetenland and was persuading it to demand its incorporation into the Reich.

What Schmidt was carrying in his rucksack was unbelievable, my dear Paillole, absolutely incredible. It contained nothing but secret documents, authentic and up to date. Right there, on the patch of moss where we had stopped, I took a quick inventory: papers for Bertrand including the daily Enigma keys for September and October, a huge study of the German General Staff in the corridor and Danzig entitled *Deutschland und der Korridor*, which provided a detailed description of places and peoples, orders of battle, supporting maps, Polish and German troops, air and sea threats that Poland exerted (or was able to exert) over the Reich... I kept a few photos of these documents, which I am passing to you!

There was still more, from his brother—the Kriegsakademie work program for 1934, a program established according to the guidelines set by Hitler which consisted of creating twenty-one infantry divisions instead of seven (three times more) and providing these units with new equipment.

I was amazed. I have never seen another informant who could provide so many secret documents worth so much. What more could I add to my thanks? I could barely dare, because of the depth of H.E.'s perceptiveness and sense of intelligence, to ask him to indicate to us, at the appropriate time, when each of the stages of the program were achieved.[74] Everything he did, of course, he did with precise regularity and flawless precision.

We returned to the hotel at around 1 p.m. The restaurant was nearly empty. I let Bertrand go to his room to photograph the documents that Schmidt was expecting to retrieve the same evening. He wanted to sleep in Dresden where he probably had some rendezvous or other. Our lunch was nice as hell! It's true, with several whiskeys, two bottles of burgundy and a glass of cognac, H.E. let down his guard and was completely uninhibited, even though I was still a stranger to him.

I wanted, with the two of us alone, to discuss the Forschungsamt, confirm the importance of his liaison mission with the organization. He talked at length with me about the Nazi motivations for the creation of this top-secret intelligence service, their obsessive desire to know the opposition and defeat it.

"It is essential," I said to him, "that you obtain an organizational diagram of the new service, its working methods and of course the results it expects to achieve."

"It's still a little early," H.E. replied, not in the least surprised by my request. "I see Schapper almost every day; the organization is up and running, inconspicuously administered on Behrenstrasse from the premises of the Reich Aviation Ministry.[75] In my view, it will be barely functional before the end of the year. In addition to the consolidation of the material, financial and personal resources—which takes some time—don't forget that we must overcome the reluctance of those both near and far who take part in the interceptions and whom we're going to bypass." (He was saying "we" so that I clearly understood that he was at the very heart of the F.A.) "Also do not forget that we have to go about this quietly and always with Goering's agreement."

Around 5 p.m., Bertrand, his stomach growling, came downstairs with the rucksack tightly closed.

"It's heavier than when I arrived," he told H.E. in broken German, giving me a wink. Later, he whispered to me "I gave him 10,000 marks!" It was a big fee, but the contents of the rucksack were priceless. We accompanied him on the way to the border toward Hirschberg. The sun was low in the sky. It was cool outside. We watched it set for a long time, in silence…

As agreed, Lieutenant Colonel Langer came to Paris in late September 1933. The intelligence collected by H.E. about the work of the Abwehr in Poland and the intentions of the German command with respect to the Danzig corridor caused quite a stir, as did the settings for the daily Enigma keys for the months of September and October 1933.

The head of the Polish Cipher Bureau delivered to Perruche intelligence on the Soviet military and economic situation, along with a report on the relationship between the Reichswehr and the Soviet Army. To Bertrand, he delivered diplomatic codes recovered in Hungary, though I am not too sure how he did this.

There was, however, nothing new regarding the work of the Biuro Szyfrow. In Warsaw, however, great strides were being made. After the physical reconstruction of the encryption machine, Rejewski, joined by Rozicki and Zygalski and with the help of the monthly rubrics provided by Asché, had managed to decipher, through endless calculations,[76] a number of messages. It took too long; they had to look for another way—without the unpredictable help of the miraculous French source.

And so the team embarked on the search for mechanical methods which could enable the faster discovery of the ciphers and the daily settings of the Enigma in service. The firm A.V.A. had put seventeen machines into production, along with a certain number of parts (notably the mobile drums), for the requirements of the scientific work being completed by Rejewski and his comrades. Between 1934 and 1936, they would develop various methods, all unsatisfactory. It wouldn't be until 1937 and 1938 that they would come close to reaching our goal.

Two methods would be tested: one manual, the other electromechanical. The manual process, the work of Zygalski, would consist of a number of perforated sheets based on the characteristics of the intercepted messages and the possible configurations of the transmitting machine. Arranged on a lit table, those perforations through which light passed formed the basis of complicated calculations, which in turn permitted one to define the settings.

The electromechanical process, heavier but faster and also more reliable, would consist of a kind of calculating machine composed of several Enigma drums designed in accordance with the possibilities of their arrangement in the transmitting machine. This would be called the "Bomba" and it would bring with it the seeds of the revolutionary principles of the computer that British scientists would later develop.

"We used to decipher codes every day, often in record time," Rejewski would write, "without the French ever being informed and without the Germans ever suspecting such a feat."

CHAPTER II

Inside the Reich

The Mürren rendezvous: H.E.'s activities take on a new dimension • The secret transformation of the Reichswehr • The Forschungsamt • Revealing the Third Reich's plans • The secret conference • Canaris' search for the leak • The Anschluss • A serious warning for Rex • The end of Czechoslovakia • H.E. announces the Nazi plan for Poland

The Mürren rendezvous: H.E.'s activities take on a new dimension

The journey from Interlaken to Mürren in the Bernese Alps takes just an hour and a half by Bernese Oberland cog rail. At over 1,600 meters, the village was almost buried in snow when our story takes us there in January 1934. A muffled silence enveloped the town. Its exclusive and cosmopolitan inhabitants gently meandered through the streets, where narrow trenches had been shoveled and cleared by snowplows. Occasionally a group of skiers came bolting down from a dizzying steep slope and disappeared around a bend.

It was getting late on Thursday, January 4—the façade of the Hotel Mürren was already illuminated. It was a solid, comfortable palace of about one hundred rooms overlooking the Lauterbrunnen Valley nearly a thousand meters below. It feels like it should be possible to almost touch the snowy peaks and glaciers of the Jungfrau, the Mönch and the Eiger on the opposite side of the valley as they sparkle in the last rays of the day's sun. Sitting by a large window, Rex and his wife were transfixed by this grandiose fairyland. Sunken cozily into their armchairs in the hotel's lounge, they listened to the Viennese waltzes that a seemingly invisible pianist was playing for customers at tea time.

A wood fire crackled in a large stone fireplace. Two new guests approached, discreet and cautious. They each took turns warming their hands and backs. One was tall, thin, a bit flashy in style. The other was of medium height, more bulky in build, dressed in dark clothing. Schlesser and Bertrand had just arrived in Mürren for a long weekend.

*

Out of the corner of his eye, Rex noted their presence. He had spent Christmas and New Year with his family in this busy resort. It was Schmidt himself who, through a cryptic message, had requested this rendezvous in Switzerland, abandoning, it would seem, any solution that involved clandestine border crossings. He was expected on the evening of Friday, January 5.

The Hotel Mürren, designed in the style of a Middle Eastern caravansary, was particularly well suited for this kind of meeting. It had a mostly foreign clientele, which changed as regularly as the weather. Indifferent and selfish, the guests came and went under the tired, jaded eyes of the staff.

It was agreed in Paris that, once they were all at the hotel, Rex would recognize H.E. as a friend and invite him to his table. Schlesser and Bertrand, coming back from a day of skiing and trekking, would join the two men in the evening in the living room of Lemoine's private suite.

Schmidt, ever punctual, was among the last of the passengers to board the funicular on January 5. Wearing an astrakhan hat, a loose fur-lined coat, après-ski suede shoes, and carrying a big brown leather bag, he arrived on a fashionable sled, much to the amusement of the habitants of the hotel lobby. Watching him arrive in such a manner, Rex thought back to the tormented man—now almost unrecognizable—he had welcomed in Verviers not too long ago.

The reunion was warm. After a few minutes spent in his room, H.E.

joined Rex in a discreet corner of the bar, while Madame Lemoine slipped away quietly. Further down, at one of the few tables available during the swanky cocktail hour, Schlesser and Bertrand conversed, satisfied. Everything was unfolding as planned.

What a memorable meeting! How many times have I heard this story—Rex jaded yet infatuated with the situation, Schlesser enthusiastic, talkative, Bertrand mysterious and enigmatic.

Their circumstances, in terms of location and activity, were strange ones, comfortable yet full of risk. Neutral Switzerland, a gracious host of course, was nevertheless rigorous in its opposition to any espionage activity taking place in its territory. The Social Democratic Party was still new but already awakening curiosity; the Abwehr was rapidly expanding its presence among its neighbors. Indeed, having discovered *a posteriori* the scope of Schmidt's resources and his ingenious methods for producing intelligence, and having measured, fifty years later, the strategic, tactical and scientific consequences thereof, I am more impressed now by the outstanding value of the agent than my colleagues could ever have been in 1934. Undoubtedly, my training, my experience of the secret war and my knowledge of the investigative procedures deployed from 1935 to 1944 by our opponents—all affect my assessment of our older methods.

In any case, H.E., familiar with illegal border crossings, had taken stock of the risks. At forty-six, well positioned in the Nazi hierarchy, holding a superior civil post, now frequenting—thanks to the fame of his parents and his brother—the upper milieus of the Berlin military and civil societies, he had decided to be done with the ways of low-class spies.

Rex could not believe his ears:

"Since December 1, 1933," says Schmidt, "I have been the one responsible to act as liaison between the Chiffrierstelle and the Forschungsamt. I am responsible for the analysis of the interceptions and decoded intelligence captured from intercepted messages in Western Europe. From this, I have drawn one important initial conclusion: The Stuttgart listening station is overwhelmed, inadequate. The geographic position of Switzerland should allow the installation of an additional listening station. Schimpf and Schapper[77] jumped on my proposal and gave me carte blanche to study its implementation. And so I went to Bern the day before yesterday to discuss the issue with our officials at the embassy. As I am carrying confidential documentation…"

"How confidential?" Rex interrupted.

"Very confidential," continued H.E., laughing. "I made clear to Schimpf that I did not want any problems at the border. He gave me a mission approved by the Ministry of Aviation, and which also had Goering's signature; moreover, he provided me with a diplomatic passport."

"What a thing!" Schlesser whispered into Bertrand's ear. It was nearly midnight: the champagne was flowing, and the noise was deafening, as joyful yelps occasionally rose from the large living room. A gypsy orchestra had enticed a few couples to dance late into the night.

Unaffected, H.E. removed from his briefcase a large number of files. Bertrand, the first to be served, slipped away to photograph (on the floor of his bathroom) the table of secret radio transmissions for the first trimester of 1934, the monthly rubrics of the Enigma keys for January and February, and the Army's mobilization codes.

Schlesser industriously took notes in shorthand as Schmidt reported on the Nazis' immediate projects: Himmler taking control of all police headquarters of the Reich,[78] Heydrich appointed as head of the Gestapo and the S.D.,[79] the overhaul of the penal code with new punitive measures up to death in order to protect the regime and to punish traitors,[80] and the organization (or, more accurately, reorganization) of the Dachau Oranienburg concentration camps near Berlin to accommodate Jews and political opponents discovered through the Forschungsamt's wiretapping.

"Well, this is all very promising!" exclaimed Schlesser.

His well of information inexhaustible, Schmidt continued, commenting on a document prepared by Schimpf with Goering's agreement: The Forschungsamt's breviary, *Guidelines for the collection of intelligence by means of transmission.*

"You can keep that," he said. "I have another copy."

Schlesser and Rex leant over the document and noticed "*GEHEIME REICHSSACHE*" (STATE SECRET) marked upon it. Its relevance and authenticity was undeniable. It had eight parts and some thirty pages: radio transmissions, telephone interceptions, radio compasses, microphones, interceptions from traffic control and wire communications, analyses, advised precautions and safety measures.

"I'll examine everything," concluded an impressed Schlesser. "We will speak more about it tomorrow. It is high time for bed."

The hotel was silent as they returned to their rooms.

On Saturday, January 6, at 11 p.m., the group of spies convened once more in Rex's room—champagne and cigars included, of course.

H.E. answered all of my colleagues' questions, always obliging, always accurate. Schlesser gave him a long questionnaire prepared with the Deuxième Bureau of the Army General Staff, which inquired about the position of the new units of the Reichswehr and the industrial facilities involved in the manufacture of tanks, assessing their production capacity and so on.[81] Rex, ever mindful of the personal situation of the informant and his safety, asked about his soap factory plans.

"I am just about ready," Schmidt replied happily. "I've found a suitable building in Ketschendorf on the Spree, close to Fürstenwalde, not far from Berlin. I am waiting now for authorization from the landlord permitting me to make the necessary changes in the annex of a local house. I want to do something simple but modern, to treat pork fat in such a way that my costs are kept to a minimum, though I will have to acquire a minimum amount of equipment. If all goes well, I hope to move in this spring. Then I'll bring my wife, son and daughter. All three will help run the factory with me until my comrade, who's still unemployed, is able to come. But all this is expensive, very expensive…" punctuated H.E., staring pointedly at his companions. It was an unsubtle plea for funding even by his standards.

"Here's your envelope," said Schlesser. "It contains 10,000 marks. You'll have to make do with what you receive each month from Berlin. If that is not enough, tell me. The key now is to help us track Hitler's military policy. I count on you to contact us as soon as possible when you have any further intelligence on it."

*

The year 1934, which Schmidt would tackle with a tenfold passion compared to Schlesser, represented a turning point in H.E.'s espionage activities. Since 1931, he had been endeavoring to gather as much intelligence as possible on the work of the Chiffrierstelle and Enigma. Although Bertrand had not revealed anything to him about the state of research on the machine itself, and on the decoding of its messages (and for good reason), H.E. knew that the documentation he'd submitted from late 1931 to 1933 was sufficient to allow for the physical reconstruction of the Enigma in service. He also knew that the intelligence he had delivered had permitted the secret services to make use of the daily settings. The few questions he had quietly asked Bertrand in order to establish "whether he was satisfied" were met, in recent months, with only evasive answers. After the explosions of joy in 1931 and 1932, his regular deliveries, particularly those of the monthly cipher settings, now prompted no more than a routine "Thank you."

Since his Spindlermühle rendezvous with a determined and ardent Schlesser, H.E. was well aware of the passionate and growing interest that such intelligence on the situation of Germany, its rearmament, its clandestine activities and especially on the intentions and plans of the Nazis provoked. His privileged position in the party, the rise of his brother in the military high command, his extensive responsibilities in the Forschungsamt—all offered daily opportunities.

While continuing to supply Bertrand's cryptology service, H.E. would henceforth give priority to intelligence research on military and political developments of the Third Reich. H.E. would devote himself to this mission with even more passion than previously seen.

Rex—due to his age, his experience, his knowledge of Germany, his indifference bordering on cynicism, his stature—still inspired in H.E. the sort of respect in which admiration and fear mingle in equal parts.

He had total confidence in Schlesser, whose resemblance to his brother Rudolf was striking. His eyes were clear, his hands strong, his passion for his craft ringing loud in everything he said. He was courteous and familiar, attentive to the smallest details of his relationship with Schmidt: "Thanks to his incomparable personal talents dominated by an innate flair for research, he has modernized the methods of the French S.R. [...] In 1934 our S.R. was embedded into the very heart of the German General Staff. An unprecedented success with the majority of the credit going to him!"

Such was the scale of the appreciation that Rivet, the boss, had for Schlesser[82] in 1935, recognizing the successful leadership he had given to the "H.E. formation." It is true that the rapport of the case officer with his agent demonstrated certain admirable psychological and humanitarian qualities.

On Sunday, January 6, 1934, Schmidt left Mürren on the first cog rail. He was determined to do his best to respond to all the requests of the French officer.

The secret transformation of the Reichswehr

"...1934 is used entirely for the implementation of a program of extraordinary magnitude [...] thanks to the S.R., the Deuxième Bureau was able to identify (for the purpose of the High Command and the government) the principal aspects of the endeavor and penetrate the meaning and purpose of the new creations..."[83]

From February 1934, H.E.'s invisible ink letters provided a weekly report about the increasing motorization and mechanization of the German army, which progressed according to an apparently well-established program. That was, at least, Schlesser's belief. But his disposition didn't permit him to be satisfied with just piecemeal intelligence transmitted by H.E.—he wanted to understand the entire program.

On April 20, 1934, disregarding Rivet's prudent instructions, Schlesser arrived in Berlin, at 69 Kissingerstrasse, the home of Georges

Blun, correspondent of the French newspaper *Le Journal.* With the support of the editor, Gerar-Dubot, he and Lemoine had crafted identity papers in the name of St. George, journalist and reporter.

Summoned by a letter delivered to the *post restante*, Schmidt met with him the next day at noon at "La Taverne," a restaurant on Friedrichstrasse. His surprise was as intense as his joy. Their common complicity seemed to unite the two men. Schlesser explained his problem:

"Everything that you have sent us, especially about the motorization of the 3rd Cavalry Division, situated along the Rhine, proves that the Reichswehr has recently established a rearmament program based on certain principles, knowledge of which we believe will help us take the offensive. It is crucial that we know their operational doctrine and the program. Do you think, through your brother,[84] you could provide details of it?"

The request did not take H.E. by surprise; the spy had clearly taken into account the fact that the sporadic intelligence he had been collecting and transmitting was underpinned by fundamental decisions that had hitherto escaped him.

"Of course," he replied. "The Kriegsakademie should be able to address your concerns. Give me a couple of days to try to get something from Rudolf."

"Meanwhile," said Schlesser, "I would like to know more about the status of your move to Ketschendorf. Where are you at with it?"

"Here's the address—the property is called 'Bienenhaus'. It takes about a half hour by taxi. You can see for yourself where we are at with the work. I am expecting to move in sometime next month."

Before separating, a rendezvous was made for April 23, 1934 at 7 p.m. in the bar of the Hotel Adlon.

"It's Heydrich's favorite place," said H.E., laughing. "With a little luck you can catch a glimpse of all the pretty girls in his court."

Schlesser went to Ketschendorf. Not far from the Spree, just outside a beautiful villa surrounded by a small garden, workers were busy constructing an immense building, which opened onto a small yard where two vans were parked.

Ignorant of any and all soap-making techniques, he caught a glimpse of—without being able to identify its purpose—the construction of cement vats, while a plumber worked on a boiler. Large shelves line the back of the studio. No doubt, the work was well advanced. Reassured, the officer spent the evening of April 22 with Maurice Dejean and Georges Blun.

At no point was there any reference to Schmidt. Discretion was required. Blun's role was to step in only in case of extreme emergency. He ignored, and would always ignore, anything from H.E.

They did, however, discuss at length the political situation of the Third Reich. Goering's recent decision (of April 10, 1934) to hand over his powers of the Gestapo to Himmler, was also the subject of much conversation. A sharp journalist and attentive observer of Germany, Georges Blun offered his perspective on the event after which Dejean painted a striking picture of the situation:

"This is yet another victory for the S.S. It is also a sign of Goering's weakness—he is no longer able to control unrest of the S.A. in Prussia. This will all end in bloodshed!"

Schlesser again devoted the day of April 23 to Maurice Dejean. In addition to addressing various service issues, they made a careful study of H.E.'s situation. The system of remunerating the informant through the intermediary of *postes restantes* was complicated and becoming increasingly risky. The police state which the Third Reich was becoming would soon invade the privacy of the clients of the *postes restantes*; the Forschungsamt itself would certainly find a way to exercise its prying talents on the letters posted in them.

In a month, Schmidt would have moved his family to Ketschendorf and would be leading, at least on the surface, a bourgeois existence, as both a bureaucrat and a businessman. This would present an opportunity to modify the correspondence arrangements with him and above all to end his regular visits to the post office.

Schlesser decided to settle this issue with H.E. The two men met in the smoky bar of the Adlon. Schmidt pulled a large envelope out of his briefcase.

"Photographs of the radio service code for the month of May, and tables of daily keys for April and May. I hope Monsieur Barsac has not had any more difficulties with seizing and decoding its messages?"

Schlesser, who was fully aware of Bertrand's problems, nodded his head. He thanked H.E., who continued: "I had dinner with my brother last night—he had invited his adjutant from the Kriegsakademie, who is also a specialist in armored tanks. I was able to guide the conversation onto the topic of military training provided at the academy. I retained the essence of the discussion and you are right…

"In November 1933 the Reichswehrministerium clearly established a general armament plan for 1934. Rudolf has received mandatory directives to incorporate into his schedule an entire program of instruction based on the new doctrine being used during the process of creating large units."

The bar suddenly got louder as a large blond man accompanied by a very beautiful young woman entered. "It's Heydrich," noted H.E., indicating the new arrival. Oblivious to the situation, Schlesser gestured eagerly for his companion to continue. H.E. obliged.

"My brother and his adjutant have discussed at length the orientation of this doctrine. It must meet the demands of a mobile war. They spoke of blitzes launched by surprise with highly mobile armored formations capable of raiding more than one hundred kilometers on the flanks and rear of the opponent. They remarked upon Heydrich's satisfaction with a request for the creation of motorized cycles in all major units. 'It is essential,' Rudolf stressed, 'that mechanized units are no longer hindered by physical barriers such as broken bridges, blocked roads, potholes, etc., during their front-line movements.'"

As the informant reported his findings, Schlesser began to piece together the technical information disclosed by Schmidt over the past three months. In his mind, he reconstructed the mechanized formations and tanks promptly reported by H.E., incorporating them into the modern conception of war in the same manner that Colonel Rudolf Schmidt was currently teaching at the Berlin War College. Mobility and speed must accompany the massive movement of motorized and armored units; such was the offensive and tactical direction of the German Army,[85] all stemming from the policy defined by Hitler.

The report he had to make was beginning to take shape in his mind. Upon his return to Paris, its importance would offer him the opportunity to present it directly to the Army General Staff.

Then, the burning question:

"And aviation?"

"My brother spoke about Goering's creation of a premier squadron. It will be presented to Hitler next month. I should be able to tell you more, perhaps even provide you with documents, at our next meeting in Switzerland. I have to be there in early July on behalf of the Chiffrierstelle and the Forschungsamt."

The conversation turned to Schmidt's move to Ketschendorf and the measures he must take to secure his safety. Schlesser was insistent on this point. He dispensed safety advice for Schmidt's travel and methods of correspondence.

"To be honest, I have little confidence in how we are delivering your remuneration to you," he said. "Since you are going to be selling soap, is it not possible to imagine that you have a customer in France?"

H.E. immediately understood. "No—I cannot expand my business and get into export. However, I have developed special processes for making cosmetic soaps and toiletries. I would like to patent them. If you have in France one or more firms that can implement my methods, I could sell a manufacturing license and periodically retrieve a percentage of the sales. By playing it properly, one could manage the transfer of funds this way."

"Excellent," exclaimed Schlesser, already certain that Rex would find a suitably competent and complacent Gallic soap maker. "The matter would need to be resolved in no more than two or three months. And thus we will only rarely make use of the *poste restante*, in cases of emergency and without compromising ourselves either. Don't forget the emergency phone number—it is still valid."

"Agreed," replied Schmidt. "Notify the person who will be on the receiving end of phone that my message will be brief. I will keep it to announcing the death of my uncle Kurt. That will mean that I will wait for two hours in the waiting room of the Charlottenburg station. I will have a white suitcase between my legs."

"Understood," nodded Schlesser. H.E. continued: "I'll bring with me to Switzerland an organizational chart and documentation that Schimpf and Schapper have drafted on the Forschungsamt. The work is at an advanced stage and is quite important."

A noisy mass of young girls and young S.S. officers had now gathered around. Schmidt identified each of them in turn: Walter Schellenber,[86] Helmut Knochen,[87] Otto Skorzeny…[88]

"I am not very comfortable here," said the French officer. "Let's go out for dinner."

On the evening of April 25, Schlesser returned to Paris, after informing Dejean of the decisions taken with Schmidt, and having given him the documents to be sent via diplomatic valise.

A few hours after his arrival at the Gare du Nord in Paris, Schlesser was in the boss's office along with Perruche and Rex. Rivet made only a brief allusion to the security measures that had been so blithely violated. He appreciated the results of the trip and approved the safety measures adopted in Schmidt's interest.

"I am going to insist," he concluded, "that the Chief of Staff hears you. The situation in Germany is taking a sharp turn, we know this for definite. It is reconstituting its military forces according to its foreign policy objectives—aggressively. Internally, the government is going to exceptional lengths to thwart any opposition. The higher ranks must understand the danger."

After a moment's reflection, Rivet added: "We must follow closely any industrial developments, especially those in aviation. H.E.'s work is remarkable, but we must leave him in his already overloaded areas: the Chiffrierstelle, the N.S.D.A.P., the Kriegsakademie, now the Forschungsamt—and the soap factory! That's more than enough."

Turning toward Schlesser, he said, "Don't waste any time figuring out this licensing issue with Rex. I expect it to be completed in less than a fortnight."

Once again, Lemoine had the solution. Around the middle of May 1934, while having lunch with Schlesser, he proposed the following: "My friend, commissioner of home intelligence services of Seine-et-Oise introduced me to a young industrialist,[89] a reserve officer, who opened a soap factory near Versailles. He hinted to him that I am part of the Deuxième Bureau. I explained to the young man, who seemed a good sort, that we knew a German chemist who was wishing to sell a manufacturing license of cosmetic soaps and toiletries."

"'This is excellent timing,' the industrialist immediately responded. 'I am looking to extend my product line.'

"I told him that we would take care of the licensing fees in thanks for his kindness. Case closed. Can I notify Schmidt and place him in contact with our man?"

And so it was done. It was agreed that the purchase of the license would include an initial disbursement of funds and then, based on monthly statements, percentages on more or less real sales of the products.

"One final word before we leave, sir. I understood that we have had only a small amount of intelligence in the field of aviation. If all goes well before you leave for your command duties,[90] I'd like to propose a new recruit who is well positioned."

Schlesser, though intrigued, would not have the pleasure of discovering this new recruit. The groundwork undertaken by Rex would not come to fruition until 1935. The recruit in question was the brother of General Erhard Milch, Secretary of State at the Ministry of Aviation, future Marshal and Inspector General of the Luftwaffe. An ambitious and crazy homosexual, he would deliver to us all the expansion plans of the German Air Force for more than three years.

The Forschungsamt

As he had previously suggested, H.E. had a desire to take advantage of a mission to Bern to have some fun in France. He had proposed a rendezvous in Evian for July 4, 1934, and announced that he would be delivering an important supply of intelligence.

Rex, always accommodating, had convinced Schlesser and Bertrand that a meeting in the summer in a busy spa town posed no risk. He himself usually spent three weeks at the Royal Hotel there around the same time.

"This resort will be like Mürren, nobody will pay attention to us," he assured them.

Since Mürren and Schlesser's trip to Berlin, a number of significant events had taken place in Germany. Himmler and Heydrich had both left Munich and were ruling from Berlin, 8 Prinz-Albertstrasse and 103 Wilhelmstrasse respectively. Their rivalry with Roehm, head of the S.A., had accelerated so much so that it was like watching a drama in the theater.

H.E.'s message from June 25, 1934 confirming the rendezvous at the Royal Hotel for July 4 at 11 a.m. declared an imminent, brutal action by Goering and Hitler against Roehm and his minions—"We need to clean house."[91] It took place on the night of June 30–July 1, 1934, and would later become known as the "Night of the Long Knives."

On July 4, on the terrace of the Royal Hotel, still reeling from the bloody purge, H.E. provided a detailed account of the events to Schlesser, Bertrand, and Rex. He comforted himself with a double whiskey.

"Hitler is now the absolute master, but the S.S. won't stop there. From Schapper I know that something is brewing in Austria."[92]

"A Nazi insurrection?" questioned Schlesser.

"A coup, indeed. They will never stop."

Abruptly changing the conversation, H.E. thanked Schlesser and Rex for the sale of the license. A deal had been reached in late June.

"I am finally at home with my family. Ketschendorf is nice and my factory has been in operation for two weeks. I spoke to an advertising agency who will publicize our products."

"Bravo," interrupted Rex. "All this is perfect. You told us about a huge piece of intelligence and you've arrived here with nothing but your hands in your pockets!"

"I do not want to run the risk of being checked by customs or the French police. My official papers cover me in Switzerland, but not in France. I will arrive in Montreux first. I invite you to find me there when you wish, in any case at least before July 7 as I have to return to Bern before returning to Berlin on July 8."

"I applaud your caution," said Schlesser. "Will we have to photograph the documents in Montreux?"

"Not at all, I will take care of everything that needs to be photographed. However, I have some additional comments on the organization and operation of the Forschungsamt that I need to add after you have read it."

Schmidt spent most of his day in Evian playing roulette at the casino. Whether he won or lost, he was still cheerful when he stopped gambling at 7 p.m. to join the three Frenchmen for cocktails, a large dinner, and to answer their numerous questions. At 1 a.m., he returned to Switzerland on the last of the shuttle boats that catered to the casinos.

The next day, around 11 a.m., they met in Montreux, albeit without Rex. The sun was warm, the skies perfectly clear, so they decided to spend the day at Caux, which could be reached within a few minutes by the funicular. One could still feel alone there even when there were huge crowds. The view of the Alps was impressive: Mont Blanc, Lake Geneva, the Rhône valley upstream. The restaurant was huge and the park equally so. It would be easy to dine there while remaining in hiding and working. Confident in their privacy, Schmidt distributed the sheaf of documentation he pulled from his enormous briefcase.

Bertrand delightedly examined the photographs of the Enigma rubrics for June and July 1934, along with a reproduction of a wiring panel of the machine, but Schlesser had the lion's share:

- photographs of the directives signed by Goering in June 1934 ordering the completion within two years of six bomber squadrons, two fighter squadrons, and twenty-one reconnaissance squadrons for a total of about 1,400 aircraft. An entire development and industrial implementation program, which we would follow closely, hopefully with the assistance of the miracle informant announced by Rex;[93]

- an authentic document from the Kriegsakademie providing a detailed order of battle for reconnaissance detachments and motorized anti-tank units;
- Finally, an important memorandum on the Forschungsamt with "*GEHEIME REICHSSACHE*" printed on the cover, followed by a text for which the translation below gives an idea of the strict secrecy surrounding this institution:

1. This is a state secret under the Penal Code of the Reich (High Treason) and within the framework of the Act of April 24, 1934.[94]
2. To be read only persons authorized by the F.A. and who have acknowledged receipt of the document.
3. To be delivered in an unsealed envelope and by a trusted courier.
4. Any sort of reproduction (text or extracts) shall be strictly prohibited.
5. The recipients are responsible for the protection of this document and its secrets. Any such infraction will carry with it the most severe penalties up to capital punishment.

A shiver ran up Schlesser's spine after reading the menacing list of requirements. He observed Schmidt for some time, admiring him, though clearly worried:

"Oh!" Schmidt exclaimed, laughing, "Rest assured, I know what risk is. Like all officials at the F.A. I had to take an oath of secrecy and silence. I fall under Articles 88 to 93 of the Penal Code which gives the Reich the power to confiscate all of my property and to punish me by death. I don't care. I am now at the very heart of the private lives of the Nazis. Even better than the inner workings of the Gestapo, even better than the external appearance of the Abwehr, the F.A. collects the most crucial secrets of all."

Schmidt lit up as he spoke. Something like enthusiasm but infinitely stronger was driving him. His reaction reflected his pride when responding so well to the expectations of his employers. He continued: "Without appearing to do so, the F.A. makes the important decisions on all fronts: diplomatic and political, economic and financial, military, judicial, police. All done inconspicuously, as Hitler and Goering, sole masters of the F.A., do not want to expose it to the enormous possibilities of investigation and inquisition. It is Goering, and Goering alone, who prescribes or authorizes any eavesdropping or interception activities. He alone decides the operation."

"He will be quickly overwhelmed!" Schlesser remarked.

"Undoubtedly," Schmidt replied, "But at present, as it is a young organization and without tradition, it is important to impose strict rules of operation and security. One cannot take too many precautions—in terms of physical location as well. The F.A. is leaving Behrenstrasse,[95] where it felt ill at ease and was at risk of being discovered. It has moved into a more private setting, an inner building on 116–126 Schillerstrasse. During the transfer of the archives, I took this copy of the memorandum.

"If someone notices its disappearance, I wouldn't want to be in the shoes of the movers!" H.E. observed, chuckling. "Keep it, read it tomorrow and we'll talk in Evian between sessions at the casino."

*

In 1937, three years later, Schlesser told me about that meeting with H.E. He had cracked open his safe as head of the S.C.R., a position he had taken in recent weeks after a brief command of the 11th Cuirassiers Regiment in Paris. Confidential and respectful, like an officiating priest, he extracted from the famous tabernacle the memorandum and offered it to me for my contemplation.

I turned through the forty pages of the precious document again and again: the first part contained the general mission of the Forschungsamt and its central organization, the second described the location of various posts (Forschungsstellen) based upon the internal and external objectives, the third part dealt with the exploitation and dissemination of intelligence collected, and another was devoted to ciphers, codes and decryption.

"It's this part that falls within H.E.'s jurisdiction as representative of the Chiffrierstelle at the F.A.," Schlesser told me. "There are four of us here[96] who know and are familiar with this document. With you, we will be five. Rex himself, who did not come to Montreux, has not been entrusted access. Schmidt's life is at stake."

I was impressed and proud of the trust they had in me. In a lower voice and a severe tone that was unusual for him, Schlesser added: "If any danger threatens our archives, and if I were absent or unable to handle the situation, here is the combination and key to the safe, it is for you to safeguard the contents and to destroy them if necessary. You would start with this document."

This decision to confide in me was provoked by a message from H.E. He had reported that the F.A. was intercepting telephone conversations between Paris and our embassy in Berlin (as we had suspected) and were deciphering the French diplomatic code, which was very serious and had to be reported at once to Quai d'Orsay. This was done that same evening without revealing our source.

While I was flipping through the memorandum, Schlesser was commenting on its contents.

"The Germans are quite verbose, but they have meticulous organizational skills. You will notice that the Forschungsamt, in order to have a monopoly over interceptions and wiretapping, has had to impose itself over administrations or services that were already conducting interceptions and wiretapping on their behalf: the Reichspost, the Ministry of the Interior, the Gestapo, the Abwehr, etc..."

"I would be surprised," I said to Schlesser, "if there were not unauthorized interceptions already taking place."

"That's my opinion as well. It took all of Goering's authority, and sometimes even that of the Führer, to address this jurisdictional issue. In Evian, I combed through the document for an entire night and asked H.E. what sort of progress had been made a year after the creation of the F.A. I was amazed to learn that already twelve posts (Forschungsstellen A)[97] specialized in wiretapping inside the Reich covered the whole of Germany through covert collaboration with the Reichspost. Since mid-1933, they had given Goering and Hitler a mass of intelligence on opposition against the regime and against the S.A. It was the results of such eavesdropping that populated the first concentration camps and drove the Führer to call for executions in late June and early July 1934. It was also this intelligence that provoked hostility toward figures such as General von Schleicher[98] and his wife, Gregor Strasser[99] and many others whom he had assassinated."

I had noticed in the H.E. file, also kept in the safe, which I was seeing for the first time, a sub-folder named E. Bericht. I enquired into its significance:

"This is the simplification of *Entzifferungsbericht*. These are the decoding records performed by the F.A. for the past two years. They are of interest for a variety of reasons and are for the most part of a diplomatic nature. You will find there the interceptions between Berlin, Paris, Rome, London, Warsaw, Prague, along with others. Certainly the Germans are controlling much of the diplomatic activity taking place in Europe.

"With the exception of Moscow, it seems," I observed.

"Exactly. H.E. has confirmed to us that the Soviets do not speak very much and that their radio transmissions have not yet been penetrated, which is not the case for us. Fourteen times in two years, the Foreign Ministry has been forced to modify its code. I see by the last message from H.E. that once again, the French Embassy has been trapped."

Before leaving me for lunch, he added, disillusioned: "I wonder if our Foreign Affairs are taking our warnings seriously?"

The timing was perfect for me to familiarize myself with the mysterious Forschungsamt, given that ever since I arrived at the Bureau in 1935 I'd heard mention of it from time to time, in confidence, from Rivet or Perruche. For the first time I had access to H.E.'s reports, at least those that were in the possession of our Counterespionage Service.

Whatever was within the S.R.'s jurisdiction was with Perruche, and, understandably, Bertrand jealously guarded the secrets of the Cipher Service, especially those concerning Enigma. I plunged head-first into the files.

Alongside the posts responsible for wiretapping (Forschungsstellen A), additional posts were added in 1934 specializing in the interception of radio messages (Forschungsstellen B for domestic and C for foreign messages), communications by teleprinter (Forschungsstellen D1), by telegram (Forschungsstellen D2) and letters (Forschungsstellen F).

Guiding and centralizing stations (*Forschungsleitstellen*) organized interceptions by region and when possible, analyzed them locally on the spot. This was the case in Stuttgart, which maintained surveillance over the south of Germany and Western Europe. I recall that in order to relieve this post of the high levels of incoming intelligence, H.E., opportunely, was responsible for organizing a supplemental interception post in Switzerland. This was a responsibility that required one to be on constant alert, and Schmidt was responsible from the very beginning, acting as liaison between Forschungsstellen B and C, the oldest ones, created in 1934 in Templin, near Berlin.

Schlesser's account, written on his return from Evian on July 8, 1934 noted that Goering's orders to Forschungsamt staff, who were gathered for the inauguration of the Templin station, were to capture and decode radio messages from all points of the globe. Templin was outfitted with the most advanced listening equipment, including adaptive antennae. There were about a hundred staff, mostly from the Nazi Party. The cipher technicians came from the Chiffrierstelle or were educated by the organization. Their decoding abilities were excellent, all spoke several languages and were able to capture messages with exceptional speed.

In addition to Templin, five other Forschungsstellen B and C were in operation by 1937 in Glienicke, Lübben, Lissa (near Breslau), Köln-Deutz (near Cologne) and Constance. The central office of the Forschungsamt, abandoned in April 1935, was the Ministry of Aviation headquarters on Behrenstrasse.

The move offered the potential for serious problems. It had to be quick, discreet, and could not interrupt their work. There were a mass of papers to be transferred, tons of equipment, furniture, safes... Overwhelmed by the magnitude of his task, accused of not having properly ensured the security of the transfer of archives ("certain" secret documents disappeared under suspicious circumstances), Schimpf, the unfortunate Forschungsamt boss, committed suicide on April 10, 1935. Schmidt didn't show the least bit of remorse when reporting this to us.

Goering replaced Schmipf with his friend, Prince Christoph von Hesse, Minister of State in Prussia. The new location was enormous and heavily guarded. Security devices were installed on every floor; the areas dedicated to deciphering and decryption services were subject to even stricter security measures. Dormitories, a mess hall and a bar were installed for the staff, of whom one thousand worked continuously, 24 hours a day. Tasks were divided into six offices: administration, personnel, research, cryptography, analysis, equipment. Bureau IV— cryptography—was the most important. The leaders were two friends of Schmidt: Schapper and Schröder, and reporting to them were 240 technicians and cipher specialists. For the month of December 1935, they deciphered, sometimes in less than an hour, 2,200 posts of various origins, mainly French, English and Italian—but nothing from the U.S.S.R.

The average for 1935 was impressive: 34,000 internal communications and 8,500 external (radio, telephone, and other forms of communication) were retained for analysis by the Abwehr, the Foreign Affairs Bureau, the Gestapo, High Command, the Finance Bureau and more. To achieve such a high level of performance, more than thirty million interceptions coming in from all directions were combed through in just twelve months. On a daily basis, Goering received between fifty and one hundred "brown files," which summarized the most important information. He then submitted a relevant selection of that data to the Führer.

"The interior of Germany is being scrutinized with a fine-toothed comb," said Schlesser, who had just joined me, and to whom I was revealing the amazement of my discoveries. "Not even the slightest diplomatic or military maneuvers escape the eyes and ears of the Reich. We will have a great deal of work to do in order to put the brakes on the bleeding…"

*

Supplier to the death camps, *eminence grise* for Hitler's criminal policy, will we ever know everything that the Third Reich owes to the Forschungsamt?

Poring over my documentation and my memories, I continue to be haunted by the Machiavellian power of the Nazis and our inability to account for all of their evils. It's barely enough that the Nuremberg trial made reference to the organization. Only the U.S. prosecutor Justice Robert, sensing the Forschungsamt's critical involvement, requested an explanation from Goering on March 14, 1946. The defendant's response was set out in the minutes of the hearing. Here are the basics:

"The expression [Forschungsamt] was a nothing more than a term used to conceal covert operations. At the time we took control, there was a great deal of confusion with regards to the technical research being conducted and who had control over crucial intelligence.

"This is why I created the Research Unit, in other words, a department meant to centralize the supervision of all technical processes, telephone, radio, telegraph, etc. As I was then the Reich Minister of Aviation, I could not integrate these services directly into my ministry and so I thus choose this designation as a façade."

Jackson's curiosity didn't stop there, raising another question on March 18, 1946: "In 1933, you oversaw a special espionage organization which aimed to monitor telephone conversations[100] inside and outside of Germany, no?"

Goering's response (see the minutes from the trial on March 18, 1946) was: "I explained that I had installed a special intelligence organization which monitored conversations with foreigners or calls that came in from abroad, but also from one foreign country to another. Likewise, this same organization was monitoring conversations from within Germany [...] Anything that was of interest to the Ministry of Foreign Affairs was transmitted to them. Those that were important to the Führer were submitted to him. Intelligence that was of value to the army was sent to the Ministry of War, the Air Force, or to the Finance Ministry. It was me, or my adjutant, who made the decisions. In every office, there was an employee whose only responsibility was only to deliver the reports to the chief himself [...] Later, the police tried to take control of the organization. I did not allow this to happen. It is quite possible that the police installed its own listening posts. But no official monitoring could have been accomplished without being connected to the Ministry of the Reichspost, and even then it was mandatory for it to pass through me."

And that was it. A heavy silence fell over the Forschungsamt.

THE FORSCHUNGSAMT*
(General organization in 1940)

Central Service—Berlin. 116 to 126 Schillerstrasse
Bureau 1
    Section 1—Organization, Security
    Section 2—Administration
Bureau 2
    Section 3 –Personnel
Bureau 3
    Section 4—Centralization and allocation of research
    Section 5—Centralization and allocation of reports
Bureau 4
Cryptography
    Section 6—Scientific issues—Codes
    Section 7—Anglo-Saxon, Spanish, Portuguese, Asian matters
    Section 8—Francophone, Italian, Dutch, Belgian, Swiss matters
    Section 9—Slavic, Nordic and miscellaneous matters

---

* Table based on intelligence and documentation furnished by H.E. and by historic German services.

Bureau 5
Analysis
   Section 10—Synthesis, reporting
   Section 11—Foreign policy
   Section 12—Economic policy
   Section 13—Domestic policy
Bureau 6
   Section 14—Technical research
   Section 15—Technical achievements

EXTERNAL SERVICES
Sept Forschungsleitstellen (FLS)
(same as the internal organization of the Central Service)

Regional Centralization (files-archives)
Management of specialized positions (FS)
Localized analysis:
   Berlin
   Hamburg
   Cologne
   Stuttgart
   Munich
   Breslau
   Vienna

Forschungesstellen (FS)
Specialized positions for wiretapping and surveillance

FS A—Telephone interception and surveillance (A1 and A2 foreign languages, A3 German). Berlin Königsberg, Danzig, Litzmannstadt, Kattowitz, Stuttgard, Breslau, Stettin, Dresden, Vienna, Cologne, Nuremberg, Nordhausen, Munich, Frankfurt, Hamburg. (Beginning in 1941 all major occupied cities.)
FS B—Domestic radio interception and surveillance
FS C—Foreign radio interception and monitoring. Templin, Glienicke, Lübben, Leha, Lissa, Eutin, Cologne, Deutz, Constance. (Beginning in 1941: Sofia, Amsterdam, Plodiv, Reval.)
FS D—telephone and telegraph surveillance. Postal services for the Reich and the army (including occupied countries)
FS F—Postal surveillance

Nota. In 1941 the wiretapping of telephones commenced in Paris, Bordeaux, Bayonne, Dijon, and Lille. Lyon and Marseille were added in 1943.

Goering left historians completely ignorant of his actual part in the consolidation of Nazi power and Hitler's and political decisions. Not until 1940 was H.E. able to reveal to us the effects of his activities.

This regrettable silence is perhaps explained by the secrets and history of the organization itself. If it was true—as Schmidt demonstrated to us—that Goering reigned supreme over the intelligence gathered from various interceptions—pushing the perversion so far that he had his own personal phone tapped in order to verify the quality of work of his services—it was also true that this was no longer likely after the creation of the R.S.H.A.[101] on September 27, 1939.

From that moment on, contrary to his statement at Nuremberg, the unofficial wiretapping conducted by the police and the S.D. increased in number with the complicity of the Reichspost. Gradually, the S.S. invested every bit of the state administrative machinery and took what they could to use to their own advantage.

The Wehrmacht itself always maintained wiretapping and decoding services for its own needs; as for the Ministry of Foreign Affairs, despite Goering's efforts, they never gave up their very modest means of diplomatic interceptions.

And thus the tentacular grip of the Forschungsamt gradually began to weaken from 1940 to 1944, just as the authority and role of its founder did. This decline was actually only relative until November 1943, when it was then precipitated by two tragic events: the death of Prince Christoph von Hesse, head of the F.A., who was killed in Italy during a mission, and the destruction in Berlin of the Schillerstrasse buildings following the aerial bombardment of November 22, 1943, resulting in the loss of a significant part of the equipment and archives of the service.

Whatever was left, placed under the supervision of Schapper, was transferred to Klettendorf near Breslau and stored—a precaution that was clearly too late—in the barracks of an air defense regiment. Torn to pieces, but still alive due to Goering's determination, the F.A. continued to operate its external radio interceptions though in an increasingly limited manner. On January 10, 1945, the threat of a Soviet offensive led by Marshal Konev on the outskirts of Breslau resulted in Schapper's decision to dissolve the Forschungsamt and to burn the entirety of its archives. Plagued by the effects of his drug use, Goering, hiding out in Berlin, could do nothing but witness the collapse of his super intelligence service and wait in disgrace for the collapse of the Third Reich.

Revealing the Third Reich's plans

After the Montreux–Evian rendezvous in July 1934, with the exception of a brief interlude in Copenhagen in August, the meetings with H.E. were held in Switzerland, where he continued his mission for the Forschungsamt.

In Zurich, from January 19 to 21, 1935, he announced the preparation of a law that would reintroduce compulsory military service. It would increase the strength of the Reichswehr from 100,000 to 500,000 men. Using his Nazi cover, Schmidt had managed since October 1, 1934 to be entrusted with the local cell of the N.S.D.A.P. and the responsibility of civil defense for his town, and in that position he learned that a major espionage case in Poland's favor was under investigation. Surveillance of telephone conversations and postal correspondence from a Captain Sosnowski of the Polish S.R. triggered the arrest of three young women from Berlin's "high society" who were in contact with two officers from the Kriegsministerium: "The repression will be terrible; the Führer wants to make an example of them,"[102] said H.E. without the slightest manifestation of anxiety.

H.E.'s artisanal soap factory in Ketschendorf had proved successful. He was able to open a retail store in Berlin-Charlottenburg, 11, Knesebeckstrasse. "Financial yields" from the sale of the patent license to the French firm arrived regularly. It was the perfect cover for his operations.

A meeting was scheduled between October 18 and 20 in Bern with Perruche and Bertrand. From January 24 to 26, 1936 there would be a meeting in Basel with Rex present. At each meeting Bertrand was provided with his ration of codes and keys, and Perruche with intelligence on any new developments in the Reichswehr. Both were presented with full reports on the evolution of the internal situation of the Reich, on the growing authority of the S.S. and Heydrich, and on the astounding output of the Forschungsamt, which continued to populate the concentration camps and loot the secrets of Western diplomacy.

The January 1936 rendezvous in Basel took place at the Hotel Euler near the station. It was a cozy establishment, frequented by financiers and businessmen from all over Europe. Rex was well known there; he no longer completed any of the usual forms during check-in. He had at his disposal a luxurious suite on the first floor, where the agents met inconspicuously in the evening, their talk muffled by the music provided by the indispensable radio.

After announcing Hitler's plan to overthrow the Rhineland,[103] Schmidt handed over a huge package of documents to the Frenchmen. He had received them from his brother by promising to destroy them in the furnace at his soap factory.

Colonel Rudolf Schmidt had left his command of the 13th Infantry Regiment on November 1, 1935. He now had a gratifying position at the Army General Staff in Berlin.[104] Like any new boss with a certain degree of ambition, he started by cleaning house: he collected a mass of notes, staffing tables, maneuver reports, conference proceedings, and papers of minimal importance and entrusted his brother to burn everything as per the rules.

Perruche would draw conclusions of rare importance from these papers destined for the furnace. On his return to Paris, he presented his findings in a ten-page report to High Command. It painted an alarming picture of the German army on the eve of the events of March 7, 1936.

For the first time the appearance of tank divisions (there were already three in number) was evident. Thanks to the intelligence provided by the Luftwaffe representative during a Kriegsspiel attended by Colonel

Schmidt, the head of the S.R. was able to identify sixty squadrons and assess the rate of production at 200 aircraft per month. It was estimated that their goal was 10,000.

The head of the Deuxième Bureau of the Army General Staff would rely heavily on this work in order to prepare his intelligence bulletin for March 1, 1936. The commander and the government would be the recipients of the bulletin, from which they would learn, in addition to the imminent threat to the Rhineland,[105] of the no less obvious evolution of the Reichswehr.

The conclusion was extremely serious: it heralded the probability of combined actions and massive mechanized units and air forces in the future. And whoever read this would clearly understand that it provided a glimpse of the German tactics of tomorrow.

On March 7, 1936 at 5 a.m., three battalions of the Reichswehr cautiously traversed the Rhine. Sixteen others would join them as soon as the watchful Forschungsamt had given assurance that the British and French diplomats at the highest level had determined not to respond with force. For Hitler, this was confirmation of the rampant laxity of democracies. The lesson would not be wasted.

*

"The era of political tension preceding mobilization has ended. That of sudden action has begun. German strength, still inferior, is in a state of continual mobilization. Other strikes will follow."

Such was the lesson that the Deuxième Bureau officially learned from the event intended for the High Command and the government, without either one or the other deigning to seek further explanation of these alarming statements.

"Whom do we serve?" raged Rivet at the weekly meeting following Sarraut's bombastic tirade against the Führer. "One would believe that they're only reading Gringoire,[106] only listening to gossip and keeping their heads in the clouds!"

"They" were of course not only our governments, or our allies, but also our chiefs. Having been abundantly forewarned, they still turned a deaf ear and shirked the evidence.

"Each time Gamelin summons me—and that's rare—it's to talk about a dog that's been run over," continued Rivet, disgusted. "As for the ministers, for the most part I never see them! They want to hear what pleases them and to hear only what they want to hear!"

*

On March 29, 1936, with 44.5 million votes of 45 million cast, the German people ratified Hitler's policy.

On April 24, 1936 in Lucerne, H.E. brought a variety of intelligence to Perruche and new documents to Bertrand: ciphers used between the military and civil authorities, internal ciphers for the Abwehr, monthly batches of Enigma keys for April and May 1936. Upon his return to Lucerne, the chief of the Intelligence Bureau came to chat with me. He did not hide his bitterness.

"Schmidt has told me about the Führer's triumph. He described the anguish that gripped the German General Staff during the first half of March. There was a palpable fear as a result of the March 7, 1936 military strike.

"'You have missed the last chance to stop Hitler without having to go to war,' he said, claiming that this was his brother's opinion."

"What is worrying," said Perruche, "is that this opinion is not from one of our commanders or even less of one who governs our country!"

On October 17, 1936, the head of the S.R. returned satisfied after another meeting in Basel. He then reported the result to us in Rivet's office.

H.E. had completed his mission in Bern. The surveillance post of the Forschungsamt had finally been installed and the results in Switzerland, Italy and France were good.

"I have advised our agent to henceforth limit his movements abroad," said Perruche. "He is very busy with his duties and his personal affairs.

The atmosphere in Germany demands one to be extra prudent. If personal contact is necessary, we will confer with Rex about the best way to achieve it. As for the monthly key supplies for Enigma, I feel that their request is not entirely urgent at the moment."

Bertrand didn't even flinch. He must have been tired of providing the Polish with intelligence while knowing that there was no hope of any return. Perruche, who kept his feelings to himself, announced the promotion of Rudolf Schmidt to the rank of general, as of October 1, 1936.

"His presence in the Army General Staff is a blessing. His brother gave me two additional documents of great value. The first, from June 23, 1936, concerns the organization of the mobilization of Reich forces. The other is an O.K.H. study from October 8, 1936[107] on the progress of the Reichswehr restructuring plan."

At that point the head of the S.R. pulled two documents marked "*GEHEIM*" out of his briefcase. It was in the second document that General Schmidt presented his findings.

Thanks to the establishment of the obligatory two years of military service placed into law on August 24, 1936, increasing the size of the major units is ahead of schedule. However, the insufficient recruitment of management and delays in procuring provisions is jeopardizing the progress of the mobilization program. The general was recommending measures to facilitate the rapid incorporation of young recruits (a reduction in the duration of university studies, a decrease from eighteen to seventeen years of age for volunteers). Above all he stressed the implementation of a four-year plan. He sees this as vital in order to achieve the rearmament program on time.

"The timing is good," said Rivet. "Maurice Dejean told us this morning that Goering has received full authorization to implement this plan."

The boss went on: "This intelligence and this document will arrive on the Chief of Staff's desk this afternoon. The high command will finally understand how serious the situation is. That the Third Reich is sinking into a war economy."

War! Would the situation finally strike a chord in those who bore responsibility in France?

The secret conference

November 6, 1937, 8 a.m. Georges Blun was woken by the phone ringing.

"Sorry to wake you. I have a sad announcement to make. Uncle Kurt died last night. His family is expecting you."

Taken aback, Blun wanted to reply, but the call was disconnected. He suddenly understood. He must be at the Charlottenburg station within two hours.

*

At 10 a.m. in the waiting room. Schmidt, seated with a white suitcase between his legs, was reading the *Völkischer Beobachter*.[108] Someone appeared beside him and without any introduction addressed him: "Is there a message for Uncle Kurt's family?"

H.E. observed his interlocutor, greeted him and got up to respond. "Of course, would you like to take a stroll outside?" The two men walked away from the station, taking Wilmersdorferstrasse toward Kurfürstendamm.

While walking, Schmidt slipped Blun a thick envelope: "Don't waste any time in sending this to our friends. This is very important, very serious." Then he disappeared.

*

At 11 a.m., Blun was received by Maurice Dejean at the French Embassy on Pariser Platz. He handed the message over with only a brief comment regarding H.E.'s recommendation.

Our Berlin correspondent opened the envelope alone, read the contents and rushed into the ambassador's office. Before sending the documents to Paris by diplomatic valise, Dejean considered it essential to communicate personally with André François-Poncet. The S.R. representatives had recently agreed upon this protocol.

What the French representative read, which I will summarize below, provoked exclamations. Dejean's words were representative: "My God, it's not possible! This is war!"

*

For nearly three hours on the afternoon of November 5, 1937, a secret conference gathered around the Führer at the Reich Chancellery, including Minister of War von Blomberg, the commanders of the Army,[109] Navy,[110] and Air Force,[111] and the foreign Minister, von Neurath.

Hitler presented an expansion program for Germany that would be phased in over ten years, from 1938 to 1948. Austria and Czechoslovakia were the first targets for absorption. To Blomberg and Fritsch, who expressed reservations and objections about the plan, the Führer curtly replied that the vital necessity of land for the German people justified his decisions. He considered them as final and binding whatever the consequences, including war. It was his will if he should disappear. Hitler provided extensive analysis of those countries concerned about its expansion policy, in particular Britain and France, whom he characterized as hateful enemies. As part of his bellicose stance, and having taken into account the rearmament plan and the resources of Germany, the distribution of steel production among the three branches came to a halt. Ignoring the urgent needs expressed by Goering on the part of the Luftwaffe and von Fritsch for the Army, the Führer gave priority to the Navy, allocating it 20,000 tons of steel. He justified his decision by pointing out the weakness of the German Navy in comparison to the British fleet and highlighting the need to build as many submarines as possible in the shortest time.

At the end of his typewritten report, Schmidt set a meeting in Basel for November 15, 1937. The pretext he would use to justify his trip to Switzerland would be a matter concerning the Forschungsstelle post in Basel. He would go on to provide further details.

Impressed, François-Poncet consulted Dejean on how much credit should be given to such sensational revelations. Our correspondent confirmed the outstanding quality of the informant without revealing his identity or his duties. By mutual agreement, the diplomats decided to send an urgent telegram to Quai d'Orsay.

The event was far too serious to postpone an announcement. A more comprehensive report from the ambassador would need to follow by diplomatic valise. A few hours later on the same day, November 6, 1937, the same diplomatic valise carried the letter from Schmidt to Paris. It would be delivered to 2bis, avenue de Tourville the next day at noon.

Its arrival hit the Bureau like a bombshell. In Schlesser's absence, I attended the impromptu meeting called by Rivet on the afternoon of November 7.

In the past year alone, Rex, during his "business" travels to Berlin, had had direct contact with Schmidt and collected intelligence from him, particularly the Enigma codes. Several times a month, the informant conveyed his intelligence to us in invisible ink. He was keeping us abreast of developments about the Reich's military policy. On a number of occasions, he had warned us against our coding methods.[112] This time, his revelations carried such importance and magnitude that the exceptional method of transmission appeared justified. A heavy silence followed the communication of the message.

"For H.E. to once again take the risk to leave Germany with such documents, the matter must be much more serious than we thought," observed Perruche, breaking the silence after what felt like hours. "I will personally go to Basel."

"From where could he have learned such intelligence?" wondered a concerned Rivet.

"His brother is now in Weimar!"

The boss was right. Since October 1, 1937, General Rudolf Schmidt had taken command of the 1st Armored Division and had left Berlin. Whatever its source, the warning was clear and carried serious implications. This had to be brought immediately to the attention of the Army General Staff and the government.

"In short, it's the Anschluss," continued Rivet who had reported on the growing unrest brought about by the Nazis following the politician Seyss-Inquart in Austria.

When the opportunity arose, I pointed out that our agents embedded within the Abwehr had been reporting the attention being paid to Austria and the propaganda efforts being made there for several months. For Perruche, though, the threat to Czechoslovakia seemed even more worrying.

"The Czechs will fight," he affirmed. "They have reinforced their border with Germany and have built powerful barricades based on models of the Maginot Line. If Hitler attempts to show his strength, as Schmidt claims he's going to do, it will be war! We must understand this from the outset and be prepared to confront him!"

While Rivet left to take these dramatic omens to Boulevard Saint-Germain,[113] Perruche and Bertrand agreed to the terms of their trip to Basel with Rex.

On November 12, 1937 at 11 a.m., Daladier, Minister of War, summoned Rivet. Finally he would be able to review our intelligence and underline the gravity of the situation:

"A disappointing meeting," noted the boss in his logbook. "The Minister barely alluded to H.E.'s intelligence. He is, however, interested in the activities of the German S.R. The situation resulting from the presence of Francoists and Republican Spanish in France continues to concern him. He reiterates the questions he posed to me on September 2 regarding the expulsion of Francoists that Monsieur Dormoy[114] had initiated. I answer: 'Look inside.'"

At Hotel Euler in Basel, on November 15, Perruche, Bertrand, and Rex encountered a strangely aggressive Schmidt.

"One would think that your diplomats in Berlin are completely unconscious. What's the use of me alerting you to the work being conducting by the Forschungsamt? Why did they open the envelope that had been specifically intended for you? Why did they utilize codes that had been breached for months to send a telegram to Paris, in which were included the main points of my report? It's over! I no longer want to have these people act as your intermediaries. I want to work alone: completely alone!"

This unusual burst of aggression puzzled his three interlocutors. Rex was the first to respond.

"Calm down. Can you tell us what has happened?"

"This is what happened: on November 6, 1937 at 4.20 p.m., the French Embassy sent a telegram to Paris in its hackneyed code. It communicates part of what I stated in my letter and announces the delivery of a detailed report. The telegram was intercepted by Glienicke's Forschungsstelle and decoded in Berlin in less than twenty-four hours. It has been on Goering's desk since November 8. You can imagine what will be next!"

Perruche and Bertrand looked surprised, dismayed. Once again, Rex broke the silence: "Nothing here would indicate that you are personally at risk."

"Monsieur Lemoine, you are too familiar with this line of work to think that the Abwehr, the Gestapo and the Forschungsamt will not closely collaborate to locate the source of this indiscretion."

Softening his tone, Schmidt added, "I will still have to monitor the progress of the investigation. You have to agree that the imprudence of your embassy is unforgivable! I'll say it again that I no longer want any dealings with them. My intention is to work alone. This is the best way to avoid being betrayed by anyone."

"Understood," punctuated Perruche, eager to learn more about the famous conference of November 5.

One might be forgiven for thinking that H.E.'s irritation stemmed from his fear of being discovered as a spy and the resulting consequences for him and his family. That assumption would be wrong. What most exasperated him was the flippancy with which his warnings seemed to have been received. With reason, he felt that the work he was engaged in deserved better consideration and a more convincing analysis. What would he have thought had he known that the intelligence he had been delivering regarding the Enigma secrets remained completely unexploited by France, as it had been since the beginning?

Before explaining to Perruche what he had learned about the rendezvous of November 5, he pulled out of his bag the November and December 1937 ciphers for the machine along with a few diplomatic messages intercepted by the Forschungsamt.

Bertrand left with Rex to photograph the documents. Alone with the head of the S.R., Schmidt launched into his long story:

"My brother was summoned to Berlin on November 2 to discuss with the Reichswehrministerium the necessary preparations of his armored division for war. Remember that this is a first, a kind of prototype, and that the Führer had his own ideas about its deployment. Rudolf returned home. He no longer has an apartment in the capital. On November 3 and 4 under the leadership of General von Fritsch, he participated in a Kriegsspiel, the theme of which, surprisingly, was an offensive against Czechoslovakia.

"To thank the generals who participated in the exercise, von Fritsch invited them to a reception at the Reich Chancellery on November 5, 1937 from 6 p.m. to 9 p.m. It was a brilliant event: the crème de la crème of the army and diplomatic figures, about fifty people overall. Champagne, sherry, port…

"At around 8.30 p.m. Hitler, Goering, Blomberg, Fritsch, Raeder and von Neurath came to join everyone in the lounge. This is where my brother encountered his comrade Colonel Hossbach, personal adjutant to the Führer. These two are long-time friends. They keep no secrets from each other. Hossbach had just come from attending a meeting with these great leaders in Hitler's private apartment. He had been responsible for taking the minutes. Still in shock from what he had heard, he confided in Rudolf much of what had been said during the conference."

"Is this what you have summarized here?" Perruche interrupted.

"That's it. A ball had been organized to follow the Führer's reception, which my brother and Hossbach had no intention of attending. Instead they had dinner together where they were able to continue their conversation and share their impressions about the afternoon meeting.

"Upon returning home, around 11 p.m., my brother, stunned, recounted to me what he had heard. He was going to see Hossbach the following day to help him clarify his account.

"I sensed the matter was too serious not to alert you right away."

"You did the right thing," Perruche said approvingly.

"It would have been perfect, without the stupidity of your embassy," continued H.E., decidedly resentful. "I came close to sending them another letter. Fortunately I kept it with me. It is the supplement to the November 5 conference. Rudolf gave it to me before he left for Weimar, a few hours after I had been informed by Schapper about the interception of François-Poncet's encrypted telegram. I still shudder from it!"

At that moment, Schmidt pulled from the inner pocket of his jacket a piece of paper on which a rough map of Europe had been sketched out. The different countries were designated by specific different colors. A line crossed through France, appearing to cut it in half and marking the spheres of influence.

"What I am giving you here," said H.E., "is what the Führer had asked Hossbach to recreate after the November 5 meeting. This schema has to be submitted to Goebbels. It will undoubtedly serve as propaganda for the Third Reich. My brother was so alarmed that he recreated it right before me in order to explain Hitler's insane projects…" The document, arriving after Schmidt's revelations about the November 5 conference, created quite a sensation in Paris. General Gauche, Chief of the Deuxième Bureau, the first recipient of the map on November 16, 1937, later reported the impact of this extraordinary piece of intelligence:[115]

> "A map attained in late 1937 shows the entirety of Europe condemned to be gradually overtaken between 1938 and 1948, all falling under the tutelage of Hitler, except a portion of coastline around the Mediterranean basin reserved for his Italian partner […]
>
> "The map, devoid of any text, drawing its modest elegance from simple boundary lines between two spheres of influence and a series of dates written in a bold and threatening style, caused an uproar […]"
>
> "This document, of an unquestionable authenticity […] offers an invaluable

glimpse at the hallucinatory rhythm of Hitler's successive undertakings and the expansion policy he intends to implement [...]"

"The map has been photographed and distributed.[116] Later, examination of the armistice clauses would allow one to make an interesting parallel [...] The boundaries of the 'free zone' established by the 1940 armistice correspond to those of the French Mediterranean area reserved for Italy as seen in this document. A disturbing coincidence that leads one to think that if the Germans did not occupy the whole of France in 1940, it was out of respect for their previous commitments with Italy."

*

The crucial nature of the intelligence revealed by H.E. would provoke a meeting of the Standing Committee of National Defense on December 8, 1937.[117]

And so the high assembly studied "the impact of the international situation on the general conduct of the war, its military leadership and its preparation."

Daladier stated that such a "development now conferred upon the Mediterranean a level of importance that it did not have prior to the formation of the Berlin–Rome Axis." He insisted that "Germany still remained the main enemy."

Gamelin reinforced the point. Focusing on recent S.R. intelligence he declared: "After dealing with the Czechoslovakian and Austrian issues, Germany might be tempted to attack us by way of Belgium or Switzerland while collaborating with Italy [...] The big danger is through Belgium [...] Until now I was skeptical (with regards to the idea of a sudden attack) though now I am well aware of the potential threat this could pose [...] such a danger will only be possible if we do not remain vigilant over our fortifications."

Strong words. An obvious foresight of the fate that was in store for us. In reading the minutes from this conference of the civilian and military officials leading our defense, I remain confused by the obstinate clinging to the theory that limits a sudden attack to the Maginot Line while "the big danger is through Belgium." I am saddened at the lack of resolve and lack of responsibility.

To close this chapter, during which we came to learn within forty-eight hours the Führer's historic decision of November 5, 1937, I would like to recall what could be considered its epilogue.

Representing one of the main charges against the major German war criminals, this secret conference would be one of the key elements identified in the judgment of the International Military Tribunal at Nuremberg:

"Colonel Hossbach's minutes of the November 5, 1937 meeting[118] represent a critically important document [...] Hitler understood that his statements would be considered, if he died, as his last will and testament.

"The motivating theme was the conquest of 'vital living space'— *Lebensraum*.

"The German problem can only be solved by force [...] Everyone present knew perfectly well that Austria and Czechoslovakia would be annexed at the first opportunity." (Translation of an excerpt from the official minutes of the hearing on October 1, 1945.)

On November 26, 1945, U.S. Attorney Aldeman, in his terrible indictment against Goering and the other defendants stated his belief that the meeting of November 5, 1937 "left no doubt about the intent of Nazi crimes against peace."

Canaris' search for the leak

At 2 p.m. on December 9, 1937, Admiral Canaris passed through the metal gate that secured the long hallway of the third floor of 72–76 Tirpitz-Ufer.

His gait was slow, his face anxious. Small and thin, his white hair added to the distinction of his face, which was framed by his dark eyebrows. An Iron Cross First Class shone brightly on his dark uniform.

The head of the Abwehr stopped briefly in the small office next to his own. He asked Wera Schwarte, his faithful secretary, if she had received any telephone calls for him. With her negative response, he asked her to invite Lieutenant Colonel Bamler[119] to join him in his office.

It was a large room, well lit by two windows through which could be seen falling snowflakes, and a few barges on the Landwehr canal.

On his desk sat a model of the Dresden cruiser, a reminder of the admiral's military record. A conference table, chairs, a leather sofa, and a huge safe comprise most of the furniture in the room.

As soon as he entered the office, two dachshunds with long white hair rushed over to him, "*Ruhig! Ruhig!*"[120] Gently, he stroked and caressed them. He sat down and the two dogs took their place at his feet.

While waiting for Bamler, he slowly read the message on the brown slip of paper—the characteristic form of secret documents released by the Forschungsamt. His shaking left hand reflected his nervousness. He set the paper down and began to play with a bronze paperweight, the gift of a Japanese naval attaché. Three little monkeys symbolize through their respective poses the Abwehr's line of conduct, which the admiral liked to call (and who knows for how much longer?) the "headquarters of the Reich Security": see, hear, and remain silent.

After knocking on the door, Bamler entered quietly.

"Anything new?" asked Canaris.

"Still nothing," replied the officer.

Goering, who had sent him the November 11 brown memorandum, was the subject of the admiral's preoccupation.

"Not a single day goes by without the Minister-President[121] summoning or phoning me. He wants our investigation to succeed at all costs. The indiscretion that followed the conference on November 5, and which was to France's advantage, has turned into an obsession for him."

Canaris paused for a moment before adding, sadly: "For me too. I called a meeting at 3 p.m. with Doctor Kurzbach, Regierungsrat (R.R.) at the Forschungsamt and Doctor Best, Director at the Ministry of the Interior. With where we're at, it is essential that we involve the Gestapo in our investigation. It will also be necessary for the Forschungsamt to extend the scope of its monitoring, to increase their efforts, and collaborate more closely with us.

"On Goering's instructions, only the Abwehr has been involved in this serious matter of intelligence leaks. It requires tact and discretion. At all costs we must avoid the Führer from learning about this incident."

Bamler had questioned the Chancellery staff himself, and Canaris had informed von Blomberg and Fristsch of the confidential mission that had been assigned to him. He gathered their opinions along with those of Raeder and von Neurath.

All those present at the Chancellery reception were scrutinized by Section III of the Abwehr. Everyone was known. No one had noticed anything unusual. Hossbach, one of Hitler's close collaborators interviewed by Canaris, was caught up in conjectures.

At the end of a month of disappointing work, Goering authorized the admiral to expand his investigative resources, all while maintaining the management and responsibility of the inquiry.

After reviewing the investigation with Bamler, the head of the Abwehr summarized what he intended to propose to the Gestapo and Forschungsamt:

- Increased monitoring of the French Embassy, its personnel and any foreigners in contact with them;
- Systematic investigation of all Germans in connection with any officials from the French Embassy. Monitoring of their meetings, and their phones;
- Introduction of an informant in the bar-restaurant "La Taverne," a popular meeting place for journalists and French personalities;
- Centralization of intelligence by the Abwehr collected by the Gestapo and Forschungsamt.

And so it was decided during the meeting that representatives from the three organizations would collaborate together on the origins of the leak.

An order was given to Doctor Kurzbach, the Forschungsamt representative, to compile the minutes of the secret tripartite meeting and to provide Goering a copy of them as soon as possible. It was appropriate that the Minister-President knew about the provisions and commented on the possibility of listening to the conversations of the Reich Chancellery, if the findings of the investigation deemed it necessary.

The Anschluss

H.E., triumphant and beaming, delivered photographs of Kurzbach's minutes to Schlesser in Bern on the evening of January 26, 1938. They were dated December 10, 1937.

Seven pages of state secrets!

Schmidt had reason to be jubilant. To intercept such intelligence represented quite a coup, but what satisfied him even more was the Abwehr's inability to discover the origin of the leak.

The situation was hilarious, because he could see the investigation descending into a quagmire where it would flounder about without coming away with any clues that could place him in jeopardy. Even more comical was the fact that the investigators were focusing their suspicions on an outspoken character, known as I.S.[122] The joke didn't stop there either, as Hossbach wasn't allowing anyone to focus their suspicions on any of the personnel surrounding Hitler.

Schlesser returned from Switzerland on January 29. His mood was confident and enthusiastic. He handed photographs of the daily Enigma keys for January and February 1938 to Bertrand, and to Rivet, he gave "a harvest of documents which will allow one to take stock of the Wehrmacht's level of military preparedness."[123] Included in this collection was a detailed order of battle for General Rudolf Schmidt's 1st Armored Division. On January 30, he spoke with me again about the investigation launched by Canaris.

"Schmidt is priceless. He managed to hold on to this document from the F.A. for several hours. He went home during lunch time to photograph it. The report is full of lessons. Without it we would never have suspected the full extent of the F.A.'s abilities and its formidable authority. Above all, it proves the exceptional importance the Germans have attributed to the secrets revealed during the November 5 meeting. Incidentally, this also reveals the level of the negligence of our foreign affairs and laxity of safety measures utilized by our embassies. The direction of research to find the cause of the leak is reassuring, but it nevertheless remains," concluded Schlesser, "that we must intensify the precautions. H.E. must be forced to be even more prudent."

We all agreed to a certain number of provisions. The two mail boxes in Paris reserved for Schmidt would be replaced by two new addresses, never before used. A correspondence relay would be based in Geneva through the kindness of a Swiss lawyer who was a personal friend of Schlesser.[124] This relay would be used in the case of rising tensions between France and Germany. A new invisible ink formula would be also proposed to Schmidt.

Any direct or indirect contact with the French Embassy in Berlin was banned. Funds paid to Schmidt would be transmitted exclusively through the commercial channels of his soap business or registered in his name in a Swiss bank in Basel. Neither Rex nor any other intelligence officers would be permitted to meet H.E. in Germany. Finally, during our next meeting, Schlesser would explore with him the opportunity of changing his assignment and limiting his functions. Absolute priority must be given to gathering intelligence of military and diplomatic nature.

"Which means," grumbled Bertrand, "you are going to encourage him to leave the Chiffrierstelle."

"Which means," replied Rivet, "that we have entered into a very acute phase of Hitler's expansion program."

"Exactly," confirmed Schlesser. "Schmidt gave me a copy of a telegram on January 26, 1938 which had been intercepted on November 23, 1937 and decoded in late December by the Forschungsamt. It was William Bullitt, the American ambassador in Paris who had sent a telegraph to Washington. During his meeting with Goering, on November 20, the latter confirmed to him that the annexation of Austria by Germany was inevitable and would be achieved in the coming months. And thus it would be happening soon. This is General Rudolf Schmidt's opinion as well. It's also what our informants embedded with the Abwehr are communicating to us."

The actual events—and H.E.—would confirm our fears.

Shock and awe on February 4, 1938: Von Blomberg and von Fritsch, supposedly both embroiled in sex scandals, were forced to "resign for health reasons." In truth, they were paying for their coldness towards the regime and their reservations about the Führer's expansion plan.

"From now on," he proclaimed, "I alone will assume the direct command of all the armed forces." As a result, he created the Oberkommando der Wehrmacht (O.K.W.)[125] which he entrusted to General Keitel. Goering, who was aiming for the Ministry of War, received as compensation the title of Air Marshal.

As absolute master of the army, and with all domestic opposition suppressed, Hitler had cleared the way for himself. He was now able to implement the program that he had proposed on November 5, 1937.

On February 12, 1938, he forced the Austrian Chancellor Schuschnigg to take the Nazi Seyss-Inquart into his government.

On February 25, a letter from Schmidt revealed to us the existence of Operation "Otto." This was the code name for military action planned against Austria. The document included within it the composition of units placed under alert: three infantry divisions and one armored division—that of his brother!

On March 10, the military was ordered to begin its movement.

*

The accumulation of threatening intelligence against Austria and Czechoslovakia made Rivet determined to send two officers to Prague and Warsaw to supplement the intelligence of our allies and to develop with them direct radio links with our Bureau at 2bis, avenue de Tourville. Colonel Arnaud, head of our technical service, and Bertrand were charged with the mission.

For security reasons, the recommendations of which were not entirely unknown to H.E., it was decided that they would avoid Germany altogether and go through Austria. Even though they were well aware of the threats hanging over the country, they began their journey on the evening of March 10. They wanted to take stock of the domestic situation in Vienna on the eve of the referendum initiated by the courageous Chancellor Schuschnigg, which was intended to oppose the demands of the Führer and to defend Austria's independence.

Having arrived in Vienna several hours late on the morning of March 11, they were quickly brought up to speed.

Hitler had demanded that Schuschnigg rescind his position to the Nazi Seyss-Inquart and defer the referendum to a later date.

The city was in turmoil, with loud-mouthed S.A. officers swarming everywhere: in cars and on bikes, flying banners as if they were masters of the street. Austrian armed troops occupied the station and the strategic points of the capital.

The taxi driver who drove my two companions from the Westbahnhof (West Station) to the Ostbahnhof (East Station) struggled to move through the excited crowd.

"We're expecting the Führer," he said indifferently.

A huge portrait of Hitler hid part of the façade of the opera that had already been decorated with red swastika flags.

At the Ostbahnhof, just as they were going to board the train to Prague, Commander Salland, our military attaché in Austria, arrived on the platform. Nervous. Worried.

"I have received orders to take you immediately to Paris!" Stunned, Arnaud and Bertrand demanded an explanation.

"The situation has suddenly grown tense. We are expecting a Nazi invasion with the participation of the Wehrmacht at any moment. In France, the Chautemps cabinet has resigned. Your boss fears that the borders will close and mobilization measures will be initiated. He wants you to return to your posts as soon as possible."

While they continued their conversation, a familiar pat on the shoulder caused Bertrand to look behind him. Surprise! It was Lieutenant Colonel Langer, smiling, calm: "I came to meet you. I suspect that the events are going to cause difficulties at the borders. I don't want you to have any trouble crossing ours!"

His attention was praiseworthy, but his motivation was perhaps not entirely selfless. The Poles knew that Arnaud and Bertrand had a stopover of a few hours in Prague. They would meet our representative there, Commander Gouyoux, as well as Colonel Moravec, head of the Czech S.R. No doubt Langer had been ordered by his Bureau to find out the Czech attitude with regards to the threats against Austria and Czechoslovakia. The presence of two Frenchmen could help facilitate contact and an exchange of views that the current state of diplomatic relations between the two countries would be unable to achieve. Need we recall that the Czechs and Poles were not on very good terms? An aggressive Poland was still laying claim over the territory of Teschen.

Disappointed, Arnaud and Bertrand, accompanied by Langer and Salland, went to the French Embassy. They placed a call to Rivet. The order to take the first available train was confirmed. This "first train" would in fact be the last train to Paris until Austria resumed normal relations with the outside world.

"Langer was appalled," Bertrand told us upon his return. "All the same, we were able to tell him everything that we needed to say. The Poles were gravely concerned for themselves. As for Austria, she is already one hundred percent German. Constant checks are conducted by the Hitler Youth, the Gestapo is everywhere, and everywhere they are starting to hunt for Jews. At the Westbahnhof, climbing onto the train for Paris, we saw people gesture with their fingers: '*Es sind zwei Juden…*' These are two Jews! Undoubtedly an allusion to our prominent noses and our apparent flight to France…"

*

On March 11, on the Führer's and Goering's orders,[126] Seyss-Inquart took power in Vienna. He "called in" the German troops. They crossed the border on March 12, and took less than forty-eight hours to cover three hundred kilometers.

On March 14, at 6 p.m., Hitler entered the Austrian capital to the cheers of Nazis. The Anschluss was complete.

Approximately 99 percent of the Austrians who participated in the referendum approved Germany's annexation of Austria. Within only a few days, the Gestapo had arrested sixty thousand people. Thousands of Jews and political opponents, including former Chancellor Schuschnigg, were deported to Dachau. In this coldblooded witch hunt Eichmann, Kaltenbrünner,[127] and of course Seyss-Inquart, the new master of Austria, all knew how to exert their power effectively.

No one reacted to the coup. Protests from the West were no more than lip service. They invoked the people's right to self-determination just so they could keep a clear conscience.

France was herself in a ministerial crisis—without a government.[128]

Italy, the nation most directly interested in the events, didn't make a move. It had been linked to Germany since October 24, 1936. The partition of the spheres of influence in Europe, as reflected in the map drawn by Hitler and reproduced by H.E., kept them happy enough. Britain observed the events from its safe little island. "Impossible! In no way are we able to risk a global war for Austria, which is indisputably a German country," the British military attaché would say to the head of the Deuxième Bureau on March 17, 1936.

In truth, our allies were not yet fully aware of the threat that the Third Reich posed to peace. It was not for lack of communicating what we knew. Rivet's journal was evidence enough.

Ever since Schmidt alerted us to the expansion plan approved by the Führer on November 5, 1937, communications between our boss and the future General Menzies, deputy chief of the S.I.S., had greatly increased. For his part, Dunderdale made regular visits to 2bis, following with us the developments of the Austrian crisis. Without revealing the source of our intelligence, we insisted on the reality of the threat and the danger of an armed conflict. For the S.I.S., the Anschluss was a clear indication of the danger and ruthless resolution of Hitler.

From March 1938 our allies expanded their investigative efforts in Europe and would work more closely with us in the struggle against the Third Reich's espionage and propaganda. They would also finally launch serious research into unraveling the mysteries of the Enigma machine and begin to petition Bertrand for H.E.'s precious intelligence.

A serious warning for Rex

On March 17, 1938, in a brief message Schmidt set a date for a rendezvous in Basel four days later, on March 21.

Bertrand and Schlesser went alone; Lemoine, not in Paris, could not be reached. His faithful assistant Drach told us he had been in Germany since March 9, but otherwise we had no news of or from him. Strange—it was not like Rex to be absent for more than three or four days at a time without notifying us.

At the rendezvous, held once more at Hotel Euler, H.E. was less nervous than he had been at recent meetings, apparently reassured by the developments in the Canaris investigation. "The Forschungsamt is constantly listening in on the French Embassy. Communications are recorded on discs then sent to Goering. I don't think anything suspicious has been intercepted; I no longer set foot in the Tavern. You may want to ask your diplomats to do the same."

"Of course," replied Schlesser, who had visited Maurice Dejean on January 30, 1938.

"I was determined to see you," said H.E., "as I have found some crucial intelligence in the reports of the F.A. You know that Goering has been monitoring and recording his personal telephone calls? This reassures him that his own Bureau is functioning properly. It also provides a record of his actions and the reactions of those with whom he was conversing.

"On March 15, after congratulating the Führer on his return from Vienna, Goering addressed the issue of Czechoslovakia. The recording of the conversation leaves no doubt about the intentions of the two men. They discussed the matter at length, its launch and the risks involved: 'We must find a plausible excuse,' worried Hitler, who wanted to be done with this as quickly as possible. Goering agreed. He placed great effort on what he has called an 'irrefutable diplomatic opportunity'. It could be, for example, the assassination of a diplomat to the German Embassy in Prague.

"Like bandits!" Schlesser remarked indignantly.

H.E. nodded seriously and continued: "Another piece of intelligence collected from the Chiffrierstelle confirms the preparation of the actions to be taken in the Sudetenland. We have been charged by the O.K.H. to create a special Enigma code for this operation. Experiments must be conducted with it during a Kriegsspiel scheduled for early April. The Wehrmacht must prepare the attack on Czechoslovakia and the occupation of the Sudetenland fortifications."

Schmidt gave Bertrand the special code created for the maneuvers, and a new code that had been in police service since March 1. He added a few details regarding the creation of units equipped with coding machines—but that wasn't all. Carefully sorting through his things, he gently pulled out of his briefcase a document marked "*GEHEIM*."

"This is a report from O.K.H. on the mobilization of military forces engaged in Austria. I was able to acquire it without any difficulty. One particular section concerns the Chiffrierstelle. We are requested to offer our comments and suggestions. You will read in the chapter on 'transmissions' the observations from command on the failures of the Enigma machine. Many users neglect to follow the operating instructions for it. The settings are poorly executed. Security measures are barely respected. There is much to do in terms of training qualified technicians."

Schlesser leafed through the report. It was invaluable. The findings underscored how quickly forces were being concentrated along the Austrian border (within 24 hours), but also highlighted the slow and nevertheless limited mobilization that involved only educated reservists.

"The Wehrmacht is not yet fully prepared," my boss would later tell me upon his return to Paris. "This is perhaps the last chance we have to stop them in their tracks!"

Before leaving Schmidt, he told him what had been decided to better ensure his safety. The measures were greatly appreciated, in particular the postal relay through Geneva and the depositing of funds in Basel.[129]

Tactfully, Schlesser also addressed the problem regarding the informant's multiple responsibilities, his limits and the potential dangers resulting from such burdens. "The discovery of the Chancellery leak from November 6, 1937 cut the leaders of the Reich security forces to the quick. The Canaris investigation will not be satisfied unless it reaches some conclusions. We must proceed with caution and limit our risks."

Sensitive to his arguments, H.E. promised to consider an arrangement requiring less movement on his part. He could focus on the Forschungsamt, where Schapper continued to assign him.

"We'll talk more about this," concluded Schlesser, sliding the usual well-furnished envelope into H.E.'s hand.

The day after Schlesser and Bertrand's return to Paris, I noticed that my boss had been closed up in his office with Rivet for a long time. The door connecting our offices, usually open, remained closed. Shortly after Rivet's departure, Schlesser called me in. "There's a problem. Rex has just returned from Germany. He was stopped by the Gestapo and detained for eight days in Berlin."

I jumped. "How did this happen? How was Lemoine released? Under what conditions? Can we still trust him? What about H.E.?"

"So many questions!" jested Schlesser. He answered me, laughing, pleased with my strong reaction: "Rivet is not too worried. Rex came right away to inform him. He wasn't forced to reveal anything. This is not the first time that our man has had an encounter with the German police, as indeed he's had with many other foreign police forces. He is very strong. He plays with his reputation and the sort of international prestige that surrounds him."

Taking a more serious tone, he added: "Obviously this could all go very wrong. I myself am seeing Lemoine tomorrow morning and will draw my own conclusions. Until then, keep this incident strictly secret."

I was puzzled and not at all reassured by Schlesser's vague explanation. I was even less confident the next day, as he told me the results of his long interview with Rex.

"He is too sure of himself," he said to me immediately. "One day he is going to learn the hard way. For years—and especially since 1938—he has placed adverts in the French and German press offering sales representative jobs or industrial correspondent jobs. The responses that seem most interesting to him, he follows up by requesting an appointment, usually in Paris at his old address, 27 rue de Madrid. During the first meetings, he and his assistant Drach question the candidate closely, seeking to understand the strengths and weaknesses of their interviewees. They name-drop their connections within economic circles. They emphasize the importance of the missions that have been entrusted to them by multinational companies. 'Cabinet Lemoine' is in charge of finding employees to represent French industrial firms in relation to foreign companies or governments. They speak loud and clear. They pay well. When they are convinced they can get something out of a rookie, they gradually clarify their concerns to finally reveal what they actually want in terms of intelligence."

"All this seems very risky," I replied. "Sooner or later, Rex or Drach are bound to fall on provocateurs or clever policemen who are able to sniff out their game of fraud."

As it turned out, that is exactly what had just happened. A letter from Paris had been intercepted by the Forschungsamt. In the letter with the letterhead of 27, rue de Madrid, Lemoine—under the name of Verdier—made an appointment for March 9, 1938 at the Hotel Dom in Cologne with a young engineer from Rheinmetall. He had sent his C.V. to Rex after reading an ad in the city newspaper offering representation in Germany for a large French industrial firm. In his personal note, the German revealed the burden of his family responsibilities and emphasized his extensive relationships with those in the industrial sector of the Ruhr. This was more than enough to entice Lemoine. Section H3 of the Berlin Gestapo[130] seized the photograph of the letter intercepted by the Forschungsstelle F in Cologne, made the connection between Verdier, 27, rue de Madrid, and the famous "Lemoine," officer of the French Deuxième Bureau of the same address, well known to the Abwehr and German police since 1920.

Courteously apprehended at the Hotel Dom, Lemoine was transferred to Alexanderplatz in Berlin. There, he was interrogated in turn by section head Doctor Lipik, a big blond man of about forty years, and by Kieffer, an astute Kriminalrat with piercing black eyes, thoroughly familiar with the Rex dossier. He even showed him his identity file, which had been established in 1920 under his original name of Stallman.

Unfazed, Lemoine, without denying his affiliation with the Deuxième Bureau, noted that this fact alone did not warrant prosecution. "Apparently," said Schlesser, "Lemoine told them: 'Admiral Canaris was in Paris a few months ago to visit the World's Fair. He wasn't embarrassed to take advantage of his presence in France and offer his insight to officials of the Abwehr.[131] He wasn't worried.'"

I opened my eyes wide and exclaimed: "It takes some nerve to compare oneself with the head of the Abwehr!"

"One has to admit that it's certainly possible," continued Schlesser. "As for the recruitment work he was being charged for, Rex's work, in fact, contrary to that of Canaris, was infinitely more dangerous for France. Finally, the beast had the audacity to offer assistance to the police in Austria, where the Wehrmacht had just entered. He dangled before them his exceptional access to intelligence on the communists and Soviet activities taking place there."

Incredulous, I struggled to stifle a snort.

"But it's true!" Schlesser said loudly. "For a long time he has been in contact with a Soviet agent Bertrand knows well, nicknamed Walter Scott. Most often they meet in Holland or Austria. Their primary focus is on the trading of diplomatic codes from any possible source. Bertrand is certainly benefiting from the relationship. As for Walter Scott, he is overly talkative and needy, but he has great respect for Rex. Recently, on his return from Moscow, he offered a beautiful mink coat to Mrs. Lemoine. He says that it has been delivered to Paris by Soviet diplomatic valise. In any case, Kieffer was highly interested by Lemoine's proposal. The latter was astute enough to verify his claims by gathering specific information about the organization—about the Austrian Communist Party and the methods of the Soviet S.R., such as he understood from his contacts with Walter Scott."

*

I'll stop Schlesser's story here for now and let the two Germans to finish—since 1945 my offices have had the opportunity to interrogate them.

Captain Richard Protze, head of section IIIF of the Abwehr in Berlin from 1933 to 1939 told the story thus: "The French intelligence agent, or rather, the official representative of the Deuxième Bureau, Lemoine, whose real name is Stallman, had been noticed in Germany by his recruitment letters posted to the advantage of the French S.R. We eventually came to understand the significance of these letters since most were signed either 'Lemoine' or 'Verdier'. The stationery was always the same, the address 27, rue de Madrid also, so it was not difficult for the Germans to set out in pursuit of Lemoine."

The S.S. Hauptsturmführer Gunther Sadzik of the Gestapo in Berlin continued the story: "… Lemoine had been arrested before the annexation of Austria to Germany and transferred to the Stapo on Alexanderplatz in Berlin, which had a file on him.

"Lipik, Chief of Abt H 3, and Kieffer Kriminalrat at Abt H 3, both specialists in espionage and French matters, proceeded with their interrogation.

"Lemoine was an invaluable French spy […] who has provided statements of unquestionable importance […] I assume that with the Abwehr's agreement, the unusual decision was taken to make Lemoine an agent for Germany. Released, Lemoine had been 'manipulated' by Kieffer.

"The Abt H3, under the direction of Lipik and Kieffer, achieved during that same period—1938—brilliant successes in Austria, in Vienna. It would appear that these successes are due to the revelations and the collaboration with Lemoine…"

*

For my part, I could not stop there. There were too many gray areas in the report concerning Lemoine's findings. I suggested to Schlesser that I meet Rex this time, taking the Divisional Commissioner of

Territorial Surveillance, Jean Osvald, with me. A high-class detective and a remarkable espionage specialist for more than a decade, he was a loyal collaborator in our Bureau, and a friend. Osvald had the additional advantage of knowing Rex, his team, and Drach in particular.

The next day the three of us had lunch together at the Rotisserie Perigourdine on Place Saint-Michel. I had not seen Lemoine for several months. I found him emaciated, aged, and tired in appearance. At sixty-seven, he looked like he was well into his seventies. Was it the emotional shock of his arrest? Was it already the illness that was to take him from us eight years later? Both, perhaps.

From the outset I made it clear that our meeting was about his German adventure. Without shying away from the subject, remaining at ease, and fully aware of the reasons for Osvald's presence, Lemoine recounted almost word-for-word the story he had told Schlesser. With Osvald's support, I asked the question that had been troubled me:

"What did you give them? That is, why were you released so quickly…?"

"Not much, except for a few promises, that with your agreement, I could keep or not keep. You are aware that I often meet with Walter Scott in Vienna. I was put in touch by him with Communist circles in the city. Some names I had in my address book, others simply in my head. I delivered them. I also offered to provide diplomatic codes that I had negotiated with Scott. They concern Hungary, Czechoslovakia and Italy. From memory I provided details about these documents: volumes, forms, dates, etc… I know from H.E. that the Forschungsamt is already decrypting messages from these countries. The reward would not be of great value. If the Bureau believes that it would be worthwhile to coax the Gestapo with such documents, I can play that game…"

I did not insist and kept my answer to myself. I was sure that it had been Rex's reputation, as much as his abilities, that had impressed the Nazi police. What a boon for the Gestapo to hand over the oldest and most famous recruiters of the Deuxième Bureau—and right under the nose of the Abwehr.

With lunch finished, and with Rex having left, Osvald stated categorically: "He has completely fooled them! No one would doubt the sincerity of his explanations."

This was my opinion as well. I shared this with Schlesser, and proposed that he should prohibit Lemoine from offering any further feedback regarding this matter.

"I strongly agree," concluded my boss. "We have a duty to remember this, but here in the Bureau, we must move past it." Rex will need to take certain measures: changing his address, not writing indiscriminately, refraining from leaving France, and, above all, severing any and all contact with H.E."

The end of Czechoslovakia

On April 8, 1938, a letter from Schmidt arrived (via Switzerland—the relay was excellent) at the Bureau, confirming the operational plan for Czechoslovakia. The action was due to unfold in September. Our relations with the Czech S.R. were far too important, and there existed such a sense of trust and honor therein, that we immediately informed Colonel Kalina, the Czechoslovakian military attaché in Paris, of our plans. And—what a surprise!—Kalina confirmed our intelligence. He even gave details on the Sudetenland's Führer, Conrad Henlein. There was no doubt about it: the Nazis were setting the stage for the decisive crisis.

New letters from H.E. informed us about interceptions and codes deciphered by the Forschungsamt for diplomatic communications between Prague, London and Paris. Most of them reflected Britain's commitment to refrain from any intervention in the case of conflict regarding the Sudeten. France had also agreed to abstain.

In a message intercepted and decrypted on April 18, 1938, our minister in Prague reported to the Quay d'Orsay a conversation from April 17, 1938 with Benès. In the conversation, the President of the Czechoslovakian Republic informed Monsieur de Lacroix that he feared France would not react if Germany attacked the Sudetenland.

Meanwhile, Goering had prepared for Hitler an analysis of all such interceptions—we were given the essential points of this analysis by H.E. on April 20. The evidence supplied confirmed France's passive attitude with certainty.

Rivet, disgusted, rushed to Daladier, who had been appointed as Council President in April 1938. His request for a meeting was so unusual and pressing that the Chief of Staff, Clapier, immediately admitted him.

In a spirited but eloquent presentation, the boss summarized the military threats hanging over Czechoslovakia, stressing the Czechs' justified concern that France was resolved, despite its commitments, not to intervene in a German-Czech conflict, and that discussion of this resolution was increasingly widespread, especially in Berlin.

Daladier appeared overwhelmed, irritated. "Who would ever make such an allegation?" His tone was ruthless.

Rivet assured Daladier of the quality of our sources, disclosing the German interceptions of encrypted messages exchanged between capitals.

"… The President, outraged, promises to reject these claims by way of diplomatic channels…" Such is the conclusion of the interview that I drew from our boss's journal.

A few days later, Commander Gouyoux, our representative in Prague, came to Paris in a panic. He exploded into Schlesser's office.

"What game are you playing? Monsieur de Lacroix just received orders from Georges Bonnet to engage the Czechoslovakian government to make concessions with the Sudeten Germans.[132] We have to do everything we can to avoid war; Moravec[133] wants to know what you think."

Rivet, to whom the outburst was directed, offered a weary gesture. "I can state that Daladier has not kept his word. Britain has no involvement in Central Europe. It is by no means decided to intervene in an armed conflict with regards to the Sudetenland. This is an alibi for France, which is determined to do nothing."

"This means," stated Gouyoux with irony and bitterness, "that the assistance treaty will have no impact. Basic honesty requires me to warn Moravec not to count on any support."

*

On May 23, 1938, Perruche and Bertrand met H.E. in Basel. The harvest was rich: Enigma keys for May and June 1938, radio service codes with an accompanying chart of secret codes, and various obsolete codes given to the Abwehr and intended for the pleasure of foreign intelligence services.

Bertrand hastened to deliver everything to our military attaché in Bern, to be sent on by diplomatic valise to Warsaw, where Bertrand himself would be the very next day. There, he would meet Colonel Arnaud, resulting in a communication to Colonels Mayer and Langer regarding the intelligence gathered by the French S.R. on the situation in Central Europe and the preparations being made by the Wehrmacht. This was serious. A permanent radio link between 2bis in Paris and the Polish Intelligence Bureau was installed.

Schmidt shared with Perruche the organization of the German army: it had fifty-six active divisions, including five armored, and about thirty more reserve divisions. Rudolf Schmidt had revealed to his brother an important initiative on the part of the Führer and Keitel. On April 21, 1938, they wrote a memorandum to the attention of the Army High Command, outlining the preparations for the Fall Grün (Green Plan), a surprise attack against the Sudetenland. The provocation could, apparently, be caused by a serious incident such as the assassination of a German diplomat. This was the second time that such a possibility had been mentioned by Hitler, and H.E. made it clear that he believed that it had been left to Heydrich's S.S. to organize the assassination of Eisenlohr, Reich Minister in Prague.

At the Abwehr's request, a surveillance post was set up at Mittel-Walde on the Czech border. It was plugged into an international cable, so it could capture conversations pertinent to the Sudetenland and to fortifications defending access to the region.

What worried us—Schlesser and myself—was the intelligence that Perruche was reporting on the Forschungsamt's relentless work and the amazing results it had been able to achieve. Since 13 May, priority had been given to monitoring the telephone and telegraph interceptions coming out of the embassies and capitals primarily concerned with the Sudetenland: Berlin, London, Paris, Prague. The wiretapping was constant: twenty-four hours a day, seven days a week. Every encrypted message that was intercepted (an average of 100 per day) was usually decoded in under a day, sometimes even in an hour. Only a rare few took longer to decode.

H.E.'s revelations, which would later be confirmed by material in archives discovered after the war, were again brought to Daladier's attention by our boss. No reaction. On May 23, 1938 he informed Colonel Moravec, who had come to Paris to plead the case of his country, of the situation. The poor soul was desperate. The hypocritical and complicit maneuvers of the French and British governments to force Czechoslovakia to allow itself to be mutilated would continue, without anyone showing the least amount of concern about the distressing spectacle that the Forschungsamt was presenting to Hitler.

But events were soon to take a turn for the worse...

May–June 1938:
Encrypted telephone and telegram communications from Daladier and Georges Bonnet are sent to François-Poncet, our ambassador in Berlin, ostensibly stating the desire for peace in France. Several coded telegrams from Daladier and Georges Bonnet to Monsieur de Lacroix in Prague advise him to do everything possible in order to avoid war. Telephone conversations[134] and encrypted telegrams from Osusky, the Czech ambassador to Paris, confirm to his Minister of Foreign Affairs in Prague France's pacifist position, which is aligned with that of Britain.

July 16, 1938:
A Paris cable to de Lacroix in Prague requests that he inform the Czech government that France would reconsider the treaty of mutual assistance if an armed conflict were to occur following an uprising of the German population in the Sudetenland.[135]

Late August 1938:
Several encrypted telegrams are sent to London by Lord Runciman, Chamberlain's envoy in Prague, stating the need to cede the Sudetenland to the Reich.

September 15, 1938:
A letter from H.E. received on September 15, 1938 confirms Hitler's decision to act on the Sudetenland on September 25.[136] An avalanche of interceptions reveal the Allies' panic when faced with the declining situation in Czechoslovakia and the Führer's

ominous preparations. He decides to show his force,[137] even though he knows he will not have to make use of it.

There is growing Anglo-French pressure on the Czech government, urging it to surrender the Sudetenland to the Reich. There is obstinate resistance from Benès, despite Lord Runciman's insistence. Runciman will return to London on September 16 to give an account of his mission and to reaffirm his opinion.

September 17, 1938:
An encrypted telegram arrives from de Lacroix in Paris:
"Benès confided in me that he had once expected to cede to Germany 8,000 sq km of land that was inhabited by Germans…" A similar telegram was sent to London by Newton, Great Britain's representative in Prague.

We are pleased to have some hope of resolution, but suspect it will not last. The crisis between the Allies and the Czechs reaches its maximum intensity on the night of Tuesday, September 20.

September 20–21, 1938:
At 10 p.m., in a burst of legitimate pride, Benès informs France and England that he is refusing their suggestions, he intends to put into play the clauses of the Czech-German Treaty of 1925 and seek the arbitration of the International Court at The Hague.

There is complete panic in Paris and London—Hitler will not fail to take notice of this and act by force. He had said as much to Chamberlain, who had traveled to Berchtesgaden on September 15 to beg for peace.

Not wanting war, the French and English make one approach after another, threats followed by pleas, telegram after telegram. Benès' willpower is weakening. His strength is exhausted. The Forschungsamt is just lying in wait for him.

At 10.45 p.m. he yields, and asks Paris and London to take responsibility before the people and before history. He calls on both governments to confirm by telegram their wish to see Czechoslovakia submit to German demands and their decision not to intervene in an armed conflict in case of refusal.

Agitation in Paris.

Closed-door meetings in Daladier's office.

Contact with London.

At 11.30 p.m., we wake the President of the Republic, Albert Lebrun, who was in Rambouillet. "Surrender."

At 12.30 a.m. on September 21, 1938, with Chamberlain's agreement, Georges Bonnet sends a telegram to Benès.

September 29, 1938:
Munich. Implored by Chamberlain, accepted by Daladier, imposed on Benès, organized

by Mussolini, red with pride in his fleeting role as conciliator. Soviet Russia was absent. Czechoslovakia was gone.

With a grotesque irony unique to the situation, Hitler congratulates Chamberlain and Daladier for their determination and their courtesy in the face of what he calls the insolence and rudeness of the Czechs. In his pocket are the brown papers from the Forschungsamt—recording all the bitter remarks, the criticisms, indeed insults that were uttered against our representatives by the Czech diplomats in London, Paris and Prague.

An imperious Führer dictates his law: on October 1, 1938, the Wehrmacht will occupy the Sudetenland.

On August 9, 1938, H.E. arrived in Paris for a short stay, centering on a meeting with his "employers" to discuss his future work in light of his next assignment with the Forschungsamt, but allowing some time for relaxation in this beautiful yet unfamiliar city. He stayed in a hotel near Madeleine, where Perruche and Bertrand joined him.

H.E. had been granted some time off from the Chiffrierstelle before taking on the management of the important post of the Templin Forschungsamt on October 1, 1938. His work would certainly require most of his attention during the initial months and he would not be able to move about too easily. "But nevertheless I will stay connected with my former service where I have excellent comrades. If major changes occur with regards to the creation of ciphers and the structure of the Enigma machine, I will be informed.[138] I am not sorry to leave this service where, in spite of all my work, I was still a subordinate. Now I'll be my own boss."

Schmidt was back on his feet. Proud of this flattering assignment, he no longer had much reason to envy his brother, who had nevertheless been promoted to lieutenant general on June 1, 1938.

At fifty-two, Rudolf Schmidt was in the middle of a brilliant military career. He was favored among the soldiers in Berlin, which was in fact quite rare; and the Führer was appreciative of his competence, reserve and strict discipline, though he was not lacking in deference.

While H.E. was praising his brother and noting the extent of his own responsibilities, he pulled out from a large package several documents from the O.K.W. reproducing the plans of German forces outlining the movements to be achieved by the large units and the successive steps that were intended to bring them to the Czechoslovakian border. Also included were the monthly Enigma keys for August and September 1938. And to Bertrand and Perruche, who were both preparing to blame his imprudence, he offered with a great laugh the selection of prepared meats that had been used to cover the precious documents.

"I had entrusted the package to Schaffner in the sleeper car of the train. He himself had explained that its contents would have suffered from the heat in my own compartment!"

These monthly keys would be the last set provided by Asché.

On August 22, 1938, Bertrand was carrying them to the Poles in Warsaw. He had entrusted a copy to Dunderdale, so they could be sent to London.

Schmidt did not linger in Paris. The restless situation in the Sudetenland demanded his presence in Berlin. The events of September had cut short his leave and required him to commence his role in Templin a few days earlier than expected. By September 28, 1938, on the eve of Munich, he had settled into his new position.

I wanted to take advantage of H.E.'s stay in Paris to witness this strange man, whose incredible and high-quality production had made him the subject of universal admiration in our Bureau.

On the evening of August 10, just after H.E. arrived in Paris, I, with Bertrand's consent and presence, settled into a table with our guest at the Moulin Rouge on Place Pigalle. Leisurely, I watched our man. Bertrand treated him with respect. Both men appeared to be very absorbed by the show. One cannot deny that the performance was sumptuous—an unlimited number of scantily clad women on stage never ceases to command attention.

During the interval, Schmidt ventured over to dance with some of the hostesses. This man in his fifties, though somewhat overweight, still looked elegant in his dark suit. Being a gentleman, he invited one of the ladies over to his table. At around 1 a.m., Bertrand discreetly disappeared. Moments later, I did likewise. A second blond-headed woman had replaced my comrade. The happy trio continued to drink into the night, their glasses overflowing with champagne.

*

The year 1938 ended without us having had any further direct contact with H.E., but his letters still arrived on a regular basis. In the first half of December, he confirmed the Führer's determination to continue with his annexation plans.

Through talks with his brother, H.E. had collected valuable intelligence about the development of armored weapons.[139] The creation of a sixth division was underway in the Sudetenland. Four light motorized divisions were newly equipped on the model of the armored division, albeit with fewer tanks.

The increased availability of Enigma encoding machines to large units, including the Air Force, was crucial in enabling motorized warfare on a large scale. About seventy signal battalions had been created or were in the process of being created. "These particular formations are aggressive in nature," commented Rivet. He informed us that our intelligence was the subject of a written communication to the High Command on December 19, 1938. It highlighted the newly achieved superiority of the Wehrmacht over our military.

To those who still question the value of having deferred by a year, on September 29, 1938, the commencement of an armed conflict, it must be observed that three months after Munich the balance of forces had already tipped in Germany's favor. This advantage would only continue to surge thanks to the increased productivity of the Reich's industry and the growth of its mobilized workforce (particularly with the incorporation of the populations of Austria and Sudetenland).

On January 15, 1939, Schmidt requested a meeting in Basel for January 29. This time, Squadron Leader Henri Navarre[140] would accompany Bertrand.

Here I must tell you about Navarre. He had joined the S.R. just over a year before the meeting in question. Though initially adjutant to Perruche,[141] he had by this point taken over responsibility of the German section whose staff had been considerably reinforced. This was a senior officer of rare intelligence: accurate, discreet, and cold. He had the elegance and distinction of a cavalier and also a sort of condescension tinged with a certain amount of flippancy regarding matters concerning the lives of soldiers beneath him. I would be lucky enough to win his trust and have the privilege of becoming friends with him. Indeed, it was he who encouraged me to write this book, so deep was his desire to bring justice to our Bureau. His disappointment was bitter when confronted with the lack of character and the shirking of responsibilities by our leaders. A few months before his death in June 1983, he recalled for me some of his memories and helped me clarify a few points of this story. He showed me his last communications with Schmidt, known only to himself, Rivet, Bertrand, Schlesser, Perruche and Rex—precious confidences that his reserved nature had until then buried deep in his memory.

The first contact Navarre had with H.E. was brief. Our informant, busy with his new duties in Templin, could not be away from his post for more than forty-eight hours. He pretended to have a necessary meeting with the Forschungsstelle in Bern in order to justify his absence. Navarre's temperament hardly lent itself to any useless fussing and time-wasting, and an extension of his stay in Basel was not in the interest of the Service.

On February 1, 1939 Navarre was back in Paris. He rushed into Schlesser's office. I too was present, as part of the intelligence that he returned fell under our jurisdiction. Before presenting it, he expressed Schmidt's surprise and regret at Rex's absence from the meeting.

"I did not know how to respond," he said to us in a reproachful tone. It was true. had not thought it necessary to inform our comrade, nor Bertrand, of Lemoine's incident during his stay in Germany in March 1938. Since the unfortunate affair in Cologne and Berlin, we had seen to it that Rex remained as inconspicuous as possible. We had kindly requested him to not be involved in the business of 2bis, especially in the H.E. affair. He had moved house and was now living on Boulevard Pershing. His "sales offices" were located on rue de Madrid and rue de Lisbon. His assistant, the unavoidable Drach, reigned supreme.

"Still, you should have warned me," Navarre concluded after hearing our explanations. He then reported the results of his mission. It was impressive: the Forschungsamt's activity was under heavy scrutiny, especially that of the Templin post.

"This Schmidt," Navarre confessed to us, "is a really great guy. He knows everything. His memory is so accurate. After a first meeting where he was quite reserved (as he did not know me), he opened up and was completely frank with me when he realized that with Bertrand we were a team, and especially when he came to understand that I knew the situation and its possibilities."

"His Forschungsstelle has at its disposal a number of foreign diplomatic codes, including French, English and American. Something like 15,000 pages had been photographed and delivered to him by the Austrians[142] and the Italians. His decoding task is simple."

"This is incredible," said Schlesser. "Despite the fact that we have recommended the Foreign Affairs Ministry to monitor their codes and to change them periodically, they remain the same…"

"Templin is not just decoding diplomatic messages," noted Navarre. "Our Navy is not much more advanced. The Germans are in possession of their codes too!"

Both Schlesser and I were stunned. Since July 1938 we had been convinced that the Abwehr's intelligence sources from our Navy had dried up. The arrest of Midshipman Aubert in Toulon had brought to an end his criminal trafficking of secret codes with the German Naval Intelligence Service in Hamburg.[143] There must be another source!

"I will be seeing Sanson soon,"[144] said Schlesser. "I would not be surprised if the leaks are coming from Italy this time, as H.E. seems to believe. Almost the entire staff is of Italian origin and in contact with the Italian S.R."

The very latest significant intelligence had been reported by Navarre: the preparation of the total invasion of Czechoslovakia. General

Rudolf Schmidt had been to Berlin on multiple occasions to discuss the logistics of the operation.

The action was scheduled for March 1939. H.E. was able to get from his brother the features of armored equipment that had recently been put into service or was currently in production.[145]

At the weekly meeting following Navarre and Bertrand's return in the early part of February 1939, Rivet provided us with the analysis of the intelligence he was proposing to give to the High Command. It highlighted increased industrial production, the intensive training of the reserves in camps, and the Abwehr's warning to its agents oriented on France to increase their vigilance. It concluded with a warning from H.E.: "… all of these measures corroborate the signs provided by a secure and well-placed agent according to which the Wehrmacht is preparing for the invasion of Czechoslovakia in mid-March 1939."

Kalina, the Czech military attaché, visited us daily. He was on the lookout, as was Dunderdale, whose concern reflected that of the S.I.S.

Once again I took a moment to open the logbook of our chief of service. I transcribed his notes, which reflected the intelligence and renewed warnings in the almost daily letters from H.E. for February and March 1939…

"*March 12, 1939*: The German intervention in Slovakia begins as scheduled and is announced by the S.R. in February and with specific details provided on March 6."

"*March 13, 1939*: Movements of German troops to the Czech borders."

On the same day Rivet noted the visit of Commander Glotin from the Deuxième Bureau of the Navy who had come on account of the famous case of naval codes. Our boss would make a decision to send Schlesser to Rome to investigate the scandal.

Again on that same day, General Gamelin called an emergency meeting of the War Cabinet. The secret minutes provide a report of his presentation:

... We have come to this fateful date of March 15 [...], the Czechs would be content to make an international appeal [...] the current situation may well end in a crisis, it could also end peacefully [...]. The surprise attack: up until now I was skeptical, though now I believe it could escalate into something dangerous [...]. If Germany wants to unleash the bulk of its efforts on us, it would still need to pass through Belgium [...] the French army should be able to pick up the pieces of the Belgian army and expand its watch. Later, with the British, it could be a matter of taking up the offensive once again [...]. As the British will only ever have forces arriving slowly, we ourselves must be prepared to take the offensive...

On July 18, 1939 four months later, under No. 03L24S./EMA, General Gamelin would draw conclusions for Daladier from the above and propose "measures to increase the size of the active army for the year 1940."

Going back to Rivet's journal:

"*March 14, 1939*: German intervention in Slovakia is becoming clearer. Decision expected by 15 as announced. Troop movements continue."

"*March 15, 1939*: German troops have entered into Czechoslovakia—Prague has been occupied. End of Czechoslovakia. Colonel Kalina just spoke to me about of the tragedy of his country..."

"*March 18, 1939*: France and Great Britain submit a formal protest in Berlin."

Hitler shrugged his shoulders and annexed Memel.[146] Case closed.

H.E. announces the Nazi plan for Poland

Since his appointment to head of the Templin Forschungsstelle, Schmidt had only been able to return to his Ketschendorf home occasionally. The journey took over an hour by road. On the other hand, he went almost every day to Schillerstrasse in Berlin to provide updates on his work.

The day after the seizure of Czechoslovakia, his boss, Prince Christoph von Hesse, came to visit him at his post to clarify his mission and to determine with him staffing and additional resources.

Thus we learned in early April 1939 that priority had been given to the interception of diplomatic telephone calls and radio messages from Poland, France, and England. H.E. also pointed out to us at the same time the unusual absence of the U.S.S.R. from this list.

As a result of von Hesse's visit, in May Templin was provided with new wiretapping equipment for both listening and recording, as well as decoding machines.[147] The machines, produced by the Siemens company, had been tested and developed at the Forschungsamt testing facility in Glienicke near Berlin. The commissioning of such sophisticated equipment delighted Schmidt. Since late April his post had been afflicted by the worst of difficulties while attempting to capture messages broadcast by the British via a multichannel system (*Mehrkanalsystem*: in other words, issuing multiple messages at the same frequency). He noted at the same time that the recent use of new diplomatic codes by the British and French had seriously complicated the task of his decoders.

"Well, well!" Schlesser exclaimed, delighted by this recent information. He had returned from Rome a few days ago, which reminded me of his interventions at the Palazzo Farnese:

"I had to put my foot down in order to get them to change their codes. I struggled to convince the diplomats and especially our naval attaché, that their safes had been broken into and looted."

With his usual mastery and determination, Schlesser had managed to demonstrate how the Italians were able to enter our embassy at night. Since 1928, the doorman Boccabella[148] had managed access for the S.I.M. agents (the Italian S.R.). He provided them with the means to reproduce the keys to the safes by skillfully taking imprints of the locks. The British and American embassies were in the same boat. Neglecting the most elementary prudence, Americans, British and French continued to hire staff, the majority of whom were foreign. The Italians were good allies, and provided the Forschungsamt with the stolen codes.

We were discussing this painful situation, which seemed to have been set straight, at least for the time being, when Perruche burst in. He had just received a letter from Schmidt. It was alarming, to say the least.

On April 3 and 11, Hitler's General Staff (the O.K.W.) had broadcast to the various commands of the Army, Air Force, and Navy secret guidelines directing them to examine the conditions for military action against Poland.[149] Responses were due back by May 1, 1939. On May 3 the Führer summoned several trusted generals, including our General Rudolf Schmidt, in order to specify his intentions based on the General Staff studies submitted on May 1. On May 12, the O.K.W. shared Hitler's observations with the army commanders and set forth the anticipated areas of operation.

"This is the plan from November 5, 1937—it is underway," concluded Perruche. "Are your agents embedded in the Abwehr providing you with intelligence that confirms any foreseeable action against Poland?"

I replied affirmatively and recalled the rush of Nazi propaganda put forth to convince the French public of the good intentions of the Third Reich: "Germany's only ambition is to recover from the East its nationals and territories. Its only enemy is communism."

On May 27, 1939, another letter from H.E. arrived. Rivet summarized the essential points at the weekly meeting of department heads: on May 23, Hitler met Goering, Raeder, Keitel, Brauchitsch, and Milch. Schmidt's brother heard echoes of the conference: Poland was to be attacked as soon as the opportunity arose, and sooner if necessity so dictated. Danzig would serve as a pretext. We had to isolate Poland. If Britain decided to intervene, it would mean war. It would be necessary to occupy the Netherlands... We all listened attentively, gravely. We knew the pledges granted to Poland by Britain after Munich. This despite its lack of preparation for an immediate conflict.

Each day we measured the narrowing gap between our military strength and Germany's.

"This time it will definitely be war," whispered the boss.

"Yes, but when?"

It would, of course, be H.E. who gave us the answer. Rivet's logbook drew the following conclusion; brutal in its conciseness.

"*June 9, 1939*: Letter from H.E. 'Pay attention to the end of August.'"

On the same day, the boss left for London, summoned by the deputy chief of the S.I.S., Menzies. He was accompanied by Navarre from the S.R. and Commander Brown from the C.E., so we could pool our resources in order to confront the impending tragedy together.

In Paris, the Polish military attaché was warned of the impending danger.

On June 14, 1939, General Gauché, head of the Deuxème Bureau of the Army General Staff, alerted the High Command and the government. His note, too conservative for my taste, communicated the essence of H.E.'s letter. Below I have reproduced the entirety of the text:

Army General Staff
Deuxième Bureau
No. 1153

Paris, June 14, 1939

TOP SECRET
INTELLIGENCE MEMORANDUM

The intelligence collected during the week of June 5 to 12, 1939 on the potential evolution of the situation confirms the eventuality of another crisis. An excellent intelligence source announces the possibility of new tensions for the month of August.

According to the informant, if by the end of August, a peaceful solution to the ongoing international problems has not been found, Germany, after having exhausted all possibilities of negotiation, will seek to resolve the Polish matter regardless of the attitude of the other powers. This would, for the Reich, concern the restitution of not only Danzig, but the former provinces of Posen and East Prussia.

To this effect, military action would be taken in the summer: two armored divisions and one light division will be strengthened and led on August 20 to the Neuhammer camp (Silesia, 55 kilometers southwest of Glogau).

This intelligence is of particular interest, for thanks to such information it has been possible to follow step by step the concentration of German forces from September 1938!

With regards to the questions of General Colson, Chief of Staff of the Army, who was particularly concerned by the extreme gravity of this memorandum and trying to find out to whom he should give credit, Gauché responded verbally with the highest praise that one could offer for the quality and effectiveness of an informant: "We find ourselves today, like last year concerning the Sudetenland, with the highest level of perfection the Deuxième Bureau could ever expect. It is not humanly possible to get any closer to the truth."[150]

I appreciate what he had to say, but still I deplore the overly conservative editorial tone of Gauché's memorandum. I must explain, if only because of the respectful esteem that the former head of the Deuxième Bureau has always inspired in me. His high conception of his mission and his intellectual honesty were in no way the reason. What was at stake was the actual principle of how such intelligence was exploited, as it still is, no doubt, today. The question deserves that one stops here and learns something.

In his outward expression of confidence in our informant, Gauché could not be clearer ("It is not humanly possible to get any closer to the truth"). The head of the Deuxième Bureau is more nuanced in his written account of the intelligence. He uses formulas that could only weaken his strength of conviction. H.E. writes: "… Poland will be attacked […] pay close attention to the end of August." Gauché carefully announces to High Command the "possibility of tension for the month of August." Gradually emptied of its effectiveness by a hierarchy that becomes more faint-hearted the closer one gets to the summit, the surest intelligence becomes nothing more than one piece of information among many. A good deal for a power that is expert in dodging, sparing with its decisions, and deaf to whatever it doesn't want to hear.

This intelligence from June 9, 1939, because it came from H.E., was considered "explosive" by us, and likely to cause immediate reactions. In fact, it would only be on August 23, 1939—two and a half months later, too late without a doubt—that those in power would come to realize the inevitability and imminence of the tragedy to which France had committed herself.

On this particular day, at 6 p.m. at the War Ministry, Daladier gathered Minister of Foreign Affairs Georges Bonnet, Navy Minister César Campinchi, Air Minister Guy La Chambre, Chief of Staff for National Defense General Gamelin, Chief of Navy General Staff Admiral Darlan, Chief of Staff for the Air Force General Vuillemin, Secretary General to the Ministry of Defense and War General Jacomet, Chief of Army General Staff Colson, etc…

Three questions were on the agenda:

1. Can France simply watch and not react as Poland is attacked?
2. Which resources does France have to put forth an opposition?
3. What measures should be taken?

The following answers were proposed:[151]

1. France has no choice. It must keep its commitments vis-à-vis Poland.[152]
2. Our resources:
   a. "The state of our aviation should no longer influence the decisions of the Government as it did in 1938" (statement by Guy La Chambre).
   b. The Army and Navy are ready (statements by Gamelin and Darlan). The mobilization itself will bring relief to Poland.
   c. President Daladier recalled the completion of our fortified system protecting and securing our borders.
3. In addition to the security arrangements in place in the northeast and the southeast, successive steps will be necessary to take in order to implement general coverage and mobilization.

The meeting lasted an hour and a half.

It is neither my intention nor within my jurisdiction to indulge in a historical exegesis. I am recalling the date and the results of this meeting in order to illustrate the depth of the abyss which, during these crucial hours, lay between the intelligence and the ability to exploit and take advantage of it.

Since November 1937, the S.R. had indicated that Poland was part of Hitler's program of invasion for 1939. This had been confirmed by Goebbels' propaganda throughout 1938.[153] But it was only on August 23, one week before the outbreak of hostilities, that French officials were asked to consider what stance to take when confronted with such a threat.

Since November 1937, still relying on the intelligence from H.E., the S.R. had denounced the Führer's intention to invade Belgium, as well as Holland, if Britain and France were to enter into war against him. On 23 August 1939, on the eve of war, the Head of Government, Minister of National Defense and War headed to the Maginot Line for reassurance and to reinforce security.

Since Munich, the ever-growing gap in the arms race to Germany's advantage had been underscored by yet further irrefutable intelligence. On August 23, 1939, the heads of the three armed forces declared that they were prepared for war.

These are the facts.

I am not seeking to release our Bureau from all responsibility regarding the High Command's poor assessment of its work and its warnings. When an intelligence bureau has the unique opportunity to take advantage of an intelligence network as valuable as this one, where it can rely on the absolute credibility of the intelligence from an agent introduced almost miraculously into the innermost secrets of the enemy, it is no doubt surprising that, eight years later, that bureau has not managed to shake up routines, overcome the barriers and bring the truth to those at the top. A tough law of discipline forced limits on its soldiers, even though there would be some who would rebel. Can one be sure, however, that the plain truth delivered to the very top ranks would have the power to change the behavior of such men?

From top to bottom, laxity anesthetized the nation. Our certitudes haunted our Bureau without crossing the walls other than timid forays into the corridors of power. Schlesser was the only one who dared speak loud and clear what we were all thinking: our fears, our indignation, our warnings. "We must see H.E. again before war breaks out," he had told me earlier that summer, around June 20.

Letters from our informant continued to arrive, one after another. The threat against Poland was taking shape. It would be necessary to clarify what would happen to him, his work, our connections, if a conflict were to occur.

With Rivet's and Perruche's approval, Schlesser proposed a meeting in Basel to Schmidt for the first days of July. His request was granted. As a precaution, we shipped to Bern by diplomatic valise a radio transceiver unit and instructions. It was the first portable set of its type; we had just captured it from an Abwehr agent. Restored and adapted for our use by the technicians of the establishment known as "Carrier Pigeon"[154] we hoped—without much enthusiasm—that it could be loaned to H.E. and returned for our benefit. Its size was important, its reliability uncertain, but H.E.'s resourcefulness was such that perhaps it could be useful to him one day.

This was not Schmidt's opinion.

"You have no idea of the effectiveness of the Forschungsamt's radio surveillance," he retorted to Schlesser, refusing outright the device being offered. To illustrate his claim, he listed the many international diplomatic and military interceptions made just by the Templin post.

"The results of our monitoring is placed on brown stationery."

He explained that the surveillance was mainly concentrated on telephone conversations and radio messages between British, American, French, and Polish diplomats stationed in Berlin by their countries.

A note from July 1, 1939 clarified for the Führer the main pieces of intelligence collected during the second half of June:

"The Foreign Office has repeatedly insisted that its ambassador acknowledge Britain's determination not to tolerate any military action against Poland…"

"If the Führer does not understand," the ambassador said over the phone, "it will end in a bloodbath…"

"I am sure," continued Schmidt, "that Sir Neville Henderson[155] knows that his conversations are being tapped. He intentionally stated such violent proposition knowing that they would be reported to Hitler."

"What was the reaction?" asked Schlesser.

"Nothing! Our Führer does not want to admit that the British are capable of reacting in such a way. He says they are bluffing. He says just as much when we produce remarks from Americans who assert their intentions to intervene in cases of serious conflict. As for the Poles, they have received instructions from Warsaw to stand firm when faced with any German demands.

"Goering is not as reassured as Hitler. You know that he has ordered that his own conversations be monitored as well. He is in almost daily contact with one of his good hunting friends, the Swedish engineer Birger Dahlerus, introduced to one another through official circles in London. Through his intermediary, he is attempting to gain a better understanding of the British and to avoid war. As for the French, their diplomatic stance is to highlight their absolute commitment to peace."

"Do you consider it completely impossible that peace might be maintained? Why are you so sure that the conflict will erupt near the end of August?"

H.E. provided pertinent answers to all these questions. "Everything I hear and read in the Forschungsamt proves that the Poles will yield nothing except by force. The British will respect their commitment, the French will follow their allies and the Russians will not move. Hitler will thus trigger a war. He is ready: the operation on Poland should start no later than the first day of September. All armored divisions have been alerted, including that of my brother. Movements to concentrate troops along the Polish border are underway and will be completed on August 20."

To conclude his presentation, H.E. handed over to Schlesser the order of battle of the armored divisions and various clarifications requested by the S.R. on the characteristics of tanks in service or under consideration, and their total number (about 3,500).

"I am afraid, Monsieur St. George, that this meeting will be the last before the outbreak of hostilities. I have to maintain the utmost caution. My country is under a police state increasingly subject to the S.S., Himmler and Heydrich are maneuvering to take possession of all the levers. They are researching the formation of a state over which they will be masters. They want to have their hand in every element that contributes to the security of Reich."[156]

My boss and his informant parted ways, not without emotion, both convinced that the outbreak of war was inevitable and fast approaching.

They had agreed that the only mail service they would maintain was the one via Switzerland. Schlesser had found a second address that could be used as a relay in Basel. Arrangements also had to be made for when royalty payments from the soap-making license were no longer possible. Funds would then be exclusively paid to H.E.'s bank account in Basel.

Throughout the entire month of August 1939, Schmidt's letters would continue to arrive with remarkable precision. Navarre, who received them in Paris, analyzed the evidence.[157]

> … From the end of July the S.R. will record all mobilization measures as well as the offensive deployment of German forces in the East and coverage facing the West […] On August 24, we knew that Hitler had met with his top generals and had explained to them that the offensive would be launched between August 26 and 28 […] The main source of this intelligence was from our great agent H.E. who during the month of August sent to us a very large number of letters in invisible ink, providing us all the deployment details of the German army. He stated that Hitler's intention was to reach, in a single movement, the old German-Russian border […] On the day the war will commence, we will be perfectly aware of the German stance facing both east and west.

General Gauché was responsible for interpreting the intelligence and transmitting it to High Command. They wouldn't be let down.

"… On August 23,[158] the head of the Deuxième Bureau was able to paint a vivid picture of the German concentration efforts and the threat it carries…"[159]

At dawn on September 1, 1939 the Wehrmacht invaded Poland under false pretenses: the corridor, Danzig. I was unable to stop myself that day from going back to the intelligence H.E. provided in 1932 regarding the Reichswehr's studies on the Polish military situation and the "threats" it posed to Germany.[160] Poland's fate had already been set back then.

In the afternoon of September 1, inspired by Rivet, Gauché went to Army Chief of Staff General Colson. France was not yet at war. It was important that the High Command was presented once again with the balance of forces, as the French alone would have to bear the initial shock.

"Once again I come back to the superiority of certain elements of the German army [...] I conclude that the French army could in no way, as weak as it is, make a claim of superiority [...]. Finally, I expressed my concern with these terms: never, at any period in her history, has France ever engaged in a war under such unfavorable conditions from the outset."[161]

Forced to abstain from any major offensive capable of relieving Poland, France, despite her commitments, would respond to the aggression by withdrawing into herself with the hope of escaping the worst.

*

At 3 p.m. on September 3, 1939, following Great Britain's example, France declared war on Germany.

CHAPTER III

France Defeated, England Saved

H.E.'s contribution to the Enigma case • The Allies work to decode Enigma • War • H.E.'s final warning • Enigma in the Battle of France • The Fall of France • The hundred days of Enigma

H.E.'s contribution to the Enigma case

Those authors—mainly Polish and English—who have examined the Enigma case in order to emphasize the technical characteristics, strategic importance and scientific and tactical consequences of the machine have never revealed the actual contributions of the French Intelligence Bureau. It is true that because they were not able to take advantage of H.E.'s substantial resources themselves, our compatriots have always cast a modest veil over the matter. This deficiency of foreign authors, with the exception of David Kahn,[162] relates to the "ignorance" of Winterbotham, who confesses in his book *Ultra*[163] to the "concession of contributions," which enabled the Polish and English scientists to achieve their goals and reduce the time required for their research by a period of time ranging from several years[164] to some seven months.[165]

Although such a final concession suggests that decoding the Enigma occurred too late to intervene effectively in France's campaign and the decisive Battle of Britain, it cannot satisfy an objective study of the documents and intelligence provided by H.E., as reflected in this book.

The intelligence supplied, as I recall, was of two varieties:

The first concerned the machine itself. The *Gebrauchsanweisung für die Chiffriermaschine Enigma*[166] is the secret instruction manual, fifteen pages in length, describing in detail, with photographs and diagrams, the actual machine; the *Schlüssel-anleitung für die Chiffriermaschine Enigma*[167] provides details of the operational procedures in fourteen pages. When the French S.R. handed these secret documents over to the Polish specialists at the end of 1931, the latter would discover what they had been in search of since 1928: the modifications made to the commercial machine which included the following: the addition of a wiring panel, movable plugs, various cables except for the internal wiring of the drums, the new return drum, the frequency and setting modes, and finally the mystery of the specific keys assigned to each message.

The second set of details concerned the daily settings of the machines. Despite such crucial intelligence from the French, the Polish researchers continued to struggle to understand the internal wiring of each moving drum. Originally these were just three in number and interchangeable.

In late 1932, the French S.R., thanks to H.E., provided the Polish mathematician Rejewski with the basis of a solution. These were the secret monthly installments of the settings used each day. Included was a plain-text sample along with its corresponding encrypted code.

Rejewski's written testimony is unequivocal: "These resources (from the French) provided the foundation for my calculations that led to, in part, the reconstruction of the machine itself and, secondly, the establishment of the first scientific method for deciphering the codes."

After a long and impartial technical study that he was quite willing to include me in, Gilbert Bloch, one of the best French experts of such problems with the Enigma, came to the following conclusion in February 1985: "Contrary to opinions expressed to date, the documents transmitted by Bertrand not only assisted in the success of the Polish, they indeed shaped it. This finding in no way diminishes the ability of the Poles."

That is not all. Until 1938, H.E. continued to supply intelligence and Enigma documents on a regular basis (including monthly installments of the settings, keys, modifications and improvements made to the machine). For an additional payment, he would even respond to seemingly intractable questions about encryption problems that our Polish friends were unsuccessful at solving.[168] Sometimes he would procure for us foreign codes that we could not reproduce... He provided the codes that the Abwehr was assigned to release into the Allied intelligence bureaus or on us.

I am even more perplexed when confronted by his inexhaustible resources.

The discretion of the Polish, like that of the British, both of whom were nevertheless always informed of our intelligence, prevented historians from identifying the exact role the French S.R. played in the fundamental discoveries that followed in 1933 regarding the reconstitution of the machine itself. The constant interest and considerable contributions provided by our allies regarding our collaboration and the cryptographic intelligence provided by H.E. until his transfer to the Forschungsamt (in September 1938) suggest that the French contribution played an important role regarding solutions to the scientific problems encountered during the research on the Enigma keys. I've observed, moreover, that the insurmountable difficulties that the Polish encountered while attempting to make the machine "speak" in December 1938, were overcome shortly after our informant left his post at the Chiffrierstelle.

One month before the outbreak of World War II, the Poles thus handed over to the French and English the fruits of their remarkable efforts, achieved over seven years with the continual support of our Intelligence Bureau.

Such an invaluable acquisition would allow British scientists to participate in the Battle of France and, moreover, to be ready in time to confront the terrible shock of the Battle of Britain, where the fate of the war would play out.

I witnessed first-hand this crucial and decisive phase of the Allied cooperation in the domain of ultra-secret decryption. Reporting on this period of collaboration allows me to bring to light the roles the French S.R. and H.E. played, and to highlight the recognition they both deserve.

The Allies work to decode Enigma

After the fruitless initiative with the British Code and Cipher School (G.C.&C.S.) by Bill Dunderdale, representative of the S.I.S. in Paris, and the delivery through his intermediary in late 1931 of instruction and decoding manuals for the Enigma machine, the British seemed to pay no particular attention to the matter, despite new resources and a few timid reminders from Bertrand.

Commander Denniston, head of the G.C.&C.S., accepted our documentation with obvious interest, but remained silent about any possible exploitation of the intelligence.

From initial contact in 1936 with my British correspondents in Paris and London, I had taken notice of the priority they were giving to their Empire and the relative weakness of their knowledge of European affairs, particularly that of the Germans. They seemed to rely on us in a good number of circumstances. Everything changed after the Anschluss on March 13, 1938. Their contact with us became much more frequent and detailed in nature. From my missions in England, I took away with me the impression of a service that was transforming and expanding in Europe. It was Bertrand's opinion that British researchers were eagerly soliciting his assistance and collaboration.

At Bletchley Park, an old impenetrable mansion situated some seventy kilometers northwest of London, the British cryptologists had vigorously resumed their secret research on the German military machine whose use during the Spanish war had served as a clear warning to them. Unaware, as we were, of the results of the research underway in Warsaw, and reluctant to strengthen their relations with the Polish S.R. for reasons that escaped me, I noted their satisfaction when in April 1938 Bertrand offered, through the intermediary of Bill

Dunderdale, to compare their cryptographic knowledge with ours and that of the Poles.

Before the rush of events, Rivet, our boss, was growing impatient with the lack of positive results. During 1938 Bertrand went to Warsaw three times (in March, May and August) determined to collect, in exchange for new intelligence from Asché, a certain amount of clarification on the status of the Enigma research. On May 27, 1938, eager to keep him happy, Lieutenant Colonel Langer took him to the Makotov forest, a few kilometers from Warsaw, to visit the covert station of the cryptographic services, which operated night and day, under heavy guard. Yet still nothing was revealed to him about the work of Rejewski's team and their results.

Lacking in confidence, he attempted to get Mayer and Langer to participate in a meeting with the British to discuss intelligence. Upon Bertrand's return to Paris, in view of the reluctance of our Polish friends to comply, our Counterintelligence Section fabricated a plan to force them to clarify their position. The deception was as follows: one of our agents embedded within the Abwehr was to convince our enemy, with supporting evidence, that the messages encrypted by Enigma had been read. We would have requested the Poles to provide this "evidence," which at the same time would allow us to get an idea of the state of their knowledge. In addition, we thought that such a maneuver would encourage the German cryptologists to modify their machines or their ciphers. (We knew that Asché always had the means to monitor the reaction of the Wehrmacht and to inform us of any changes.)

In late August 1938, confronted with this somewhat risky scenario, the Poles begged us not to do anything. As compensation, a formal promise was given to us that in the near future, they would pool their knowledge with ours and with that of the British.

December 15, 1938—a dramatic turn of events! The Germans put two additional drums into service on the Enigma machine without Schmidt being able to alert us.[169] Already faced with multiple problems posed by the increasing number of machines in operation (over 70,000) and the diversification of control systems employed by the different users (O.K.W., Navy, Army, Air Force, Abwehr, Gestapo, S.S., Administrations, Foreign Affairs, etc.) the Polish researchers found themselves, despite their "Bomba," incapable of reconstructing the settings and keys within a reasonable amount of time. This new situation would force them to hasten their decision to share their knowledge of the Enigma. At Christmas, they agreed to participate at a tripartite conference of experts in Paris.

The meeting took place at our Bureau, 2bis, avenue de Tourville, on January 9 and 10, 1939.[170] From a technical perspective, it was disappointing. Everyone maintained a level of reserve regarding the state of his own research. It was nevertheless positive in that it allowed the representatives of the three countries to get to know one another, to present their ideas on various methods of calculation, and to establish a network within which they could exchange information. All promised, with varying degrees of sincerity, to meet again, to share the fruits of their continued work, and to share intercepted Enigma messages.

Meanwhile, Hitler's audacious initiatives continued to escalate. In addition to Germany's rampant rearmament, and the increasing pressure from the Nazis, both domestically and abroad (of which H.E. provided an amazingly accurate image), a series of coups took place in Munich on September 29–30, 1938.[171] On March 15, 1939 the Führer entered Prague; the next day the Czech country became a "German Protectorate of Bohemia and Moravia." On March 22, the Reich marched into Memel, Lithuania. Faced with this cascade of crises, Great Britain, followed by France, offered its assurances to Poland on March 31, 1939. At the same time, Hitler signed a treaty of friendship with General Franco, the dictator of Spain.

The Enigma messages intercepted in France, as well as in England and Poland, were increasing in number, yet always deemed indecipherable by our cryptologists. The British, under the leadership of Denniston and his adjutant Knox, increased their efforts. Moving forward, they were intent on penetrating the mysteries of the Enigma. Based on documents from Asché, all of which were now in their possession, the G.C.&C.S. enlisted a team of specialists to commence intensive research at Bletchley.

In April and May 1939, Denniston suggested a meeting. Dunderdale, who represented him in Paris, was insistent upon it. The French, having been a supplier of foundational documentation and providing a network of cryptologists to collaborate, served as liaison. This did not meet with success on the Polish side.

However, the threat of conflict was becoming obvious. On April 7, Italy invaded Albania, on April 28 Hitler denounced the agreements with Britain and Poland. Stronger than ever, he made a claim for Danzig.

We continued to procrastinate, until suddenly, on June 30, 1939, a message from Lieutenant Colonel Langer invited the French and English to an emergency meeting in Warsaw. As a result of the military cooperation agreement signed on May 19, 1939 between General Gamelin and Minister of Military Affairs Kasprzycki, the Polish Cipher Bureau was finally allowed to collaborate with us—all cards on the table.

This time it was the British who kept everyone waiting. It was enough to make you cry! Impatient, Rivet himself intervened on July 16, 1939, appealing to the head of the S.I.S. to put pressure on Denniston. Finally, an agreement was reached for a three-way meeting in Warsaw, beginning on July 24, 1939.

I only learned about this historic meeting on August 9, 1939. I had had, for the past two years, the privilege of being the adjutant to the head of the S.C.R., Colonel Guy Schlesser. As my office was right next to his, the lines of communication were always open, so I was a full participant, willingly or not, in his professional and personal life. God knows it was full and rich!

H.E.'s existence fascinated Schlesser, not only because the C.E. was watching his every move, but because he continued to have personal contact with him. His boldness always amazed him. His effectiveness filled him with admiration. For quite some time he had been aware of his decisive role in the research being conducted on the Enigma. Both of us enthusiastically followed the evolution of the case, in which the S.R.'s—as well as the C.E.'s—interest had remained prodigious.

Bertrand, whom we hadn't seen since his return from Warsaw on July 30, 1939, tiptoed into Schlesser's office that day, busy and more mysterious than ever. With the windows and doors shut tight—other than mine, of course—we listened to his story:

"I've just returned from Bourget. I put Langer on a plane to London after having lunch with him and Rivet at Drouant. The drinks were flowing; we at least owed him that much. Over two days he helped me unpack some extraordinary parcels that he brought with him from Warsaw by Polish valise."

We were dumbfounded. Amused, Bertrand continued his tale. A broad smile spoke volumes about his satisfaction and pride.

"With the tools contained here, the Germans will be damned if they want to go to war!"

We implored him to go on.

"This time our venture has been successful! With our intelligence and their science, our friends have constructed several replicas of the Enigma machine. True to their commitment to us, I was offered the first! They have actually given me two reproductions: one is for us, the other is for the English. I will carry it to London in a few days."

Bertrand was beaming and eager to keep talking. He went on to tell us about the presentation in Poland of the reconstituted German machine and the "accessories" needed to get it to "speak": perforated cards and the Bomba.

Everything had been arranged for the surprise. The French and the English (i.e. Denniston and Knox) were led by Langer out of Warsaw to Piry to the famous "wooden station" that Bertrand had visited the year before. In the vast concrete shelter, under military surveillance night and day, the head of the Polish Cipher Bureau wasted no time revealing the work of its cryptologists and the A.V.A. firm. For the visitors it was an astonishing and emotional moment!

"So!" exclaimed Schlesser, impatient, "Can we start deciphering now?"

"Not so fast! To decode these messages, we need more than just the machine—we also need the keys to its settings. The Poles have spent seven months trying to reconstruct them and still haven't had any success. And the Germans have introduced yet another new modification,[172] making their messages all the more difficult to penetrate."

"If I understand correctly," observed my boss, in a cruel tone, "they've provided you with unusable material and left the effort of making the machine speak to the British and us."

Shocked, Bertrand vehemently defended the Poles. He underscored their merits and the vital importance of their achievements. "Without them, we would have no hope of tapping into the Enigma messages for years. You must understand, there would be no hope without the Polish!"

"It is Asché, really, who is saying this," Schlesser continued, unmoved by our friend's irritation. "Why is it that for seven years we have been in the dark about what has been going on in Warsaw?"

Tense yet undeterred, Bertrand persuaded us that we were unable to imagine the complexity of the problem and to admit to the legitimacy of the discretion taken by the Poles. I was sure that privately he deplored their intense reservations. But today, in possession of what he called the "miracle machine," he forgot his complaints and regained his pride.

*

On August 16, 1939, at approximately 7 p.m., Bertand arrived in London accompanied by Bill Dunderdale's adjutant,[173] who was carrying a large British diplomatic valise.

Colonel Sir Stewart Menzies,[174] dressed in a tuxedo with the Legion of Honor rosette in his buttonhole, was waiting at Victoria Station with Denniston. Triumphantly, and with a profound sense of achievement, our comrade handed him a copy of the Enigma machine. Lieutenant Colonel Langer, who had arrived in the British capital earlier, told the British the secrets of perforated cards and the Bomba which, up until December 1938, had provided his service with the ability to make the machine "speak." He had failed to inform Bertrand, judging, and probably rightly so, that the French Cipher Services lacked the necessary enthusiasm required to exploit such valuable documentation.

*

On September 1, 1939, the war began. In London and Warsaw, and of course in Paris, the replica Enigma machines remained silent.

On March 6, 1940, more than half a year later, the machine at P.C. Bruno finally spoke for the first time, providing an output that was worthy of analysis. The logbook kept by the head of the S.R. paid witness to the event. Seven months of silence while tens of thousands of enemy machines continued in service. Seven months during which significant events had shaken Europe, during which thousands of intercepted messages had remained impenetrable. What had happened?

France, August 10, 1939: our Bureau had covertly begun production[175] on forty Enigma machines. It would be a long process. In any case, without any competent cryptologists, Bertrand had no way to provide the daily settings necessary to make machines "speak." Declaring the Cipher Service of the Army General Staff a failure had forced him to seek once again the assistance of British and Polish scientists. Once again it was the latter who would come to his aid, this time under dramatic circumstances.

Despite its heroic resistance, Poland was crushed within a matter of days. Between September 17 and 20, 1939, the Biuro Szyfrow with Rejewski, Zygalski, and Rozicki managed to seek refuge in Romania. They were able to save two Enigma machines; the others were destroyed to prevent them from falling into the hands of the Wehrmacht.

Lieutenant Colonel Langer and his team of twelve soldiers were interned at the Kalimanesti camp near Bucharest. The three civilians— Rejewski, Zygalski, and Rozicki—had been left to their own devices, and were soon picked up by Colonel Neuhauser, our representative in Romania. Thanks to him, these codebreakers would arrive in France in late September. The strong relationship that our Bureau enjoyed with the Romanian Special Services—in particular with Commander

Chistea, adjutant to the military attaché—meant we avoided any diplomatic obstacles and were able to secure the early release of the soldiers of the Biuro Szyfrow, who arrived in Paris on October 1, 1939. A few days later, with the agreement of the Polish Embassy and General Sikorski, the Polish commander-in-chief, the soldiers were posted to our Bureau and moved, along with both of the rescued Polish Enigma machines, to the Château de Vignolles, some fifty kilometers northeast of Paris. This was P.C. Bruno, a large house dating back to the nineteenth century, set in a large park, surrounded by walls and rigorously guarded. Upon mobilization, Bertrand, who had since been promoted, settled there with his services, supported by reservists and a team of seven Spanish cryptographers rescued from a military refugee camp for the republican army.

At the beginning of October, a British officer, Captain MacFarlane, became the representative for the S.I.S. He had at his disposal a teletype machine, which allowed him to correspond with London night and day.

Life at P.C. Bruno was monastic. While waiting for our (now) three reconstructions of the Enigma machine to "speak," we worked on consolidating the results of surveillance gathered through wiretapping. We deciphered what we could from the unencrypted messages, and conveyed any intelligence worthy of further exploitation to the neighboring northeast force headquarters.[176] Despite his frustration with the Enigma machines, Bertrand always saw this as a very active period for us, at least from an operational point of view.

Everything changed when the Polish specialists arrived in France; the outlook became much more positive, especially in the light of the exceptional work coming out of Bletchley at the beginning of September 1939. The outbreak of hostilities, in addition to the contributions of the Polish in August 1939,[177] acted as a catalyst at Bletchley. High-level mathematicians, recruited for the most part from Cambridge, had bolstered Denniston's team of researchers, hitherto unsuccessful at decoding: it was an army of great minds, including Gordon Welchmann and Alan Turing. Using the valuable intelligence acquired by the Polish as a starting point, Turing, a veritable genius by any standards, quickly developed perforated cards and Bombas adapted to the new configurations of enemy's Enigma machines in service. Their obscured messages would be made clear once again.

War

Absorbed by his work in Templin, and separated from his brother, who was engaged in operations with Army Group Rundstedt in Poland, H.E. decided to take a more cautious approach to his work, and reduced his level of output.

A brief letter, received in Paris on September 8, alerted us that the Forschungsamt had captured messages indicating the French High Command's intention to launch an attack in Saarland. Rivet noted this on the same day in his journal: "General Gamelin, alerted, has decided not to take any action…"

Schlesser's reaction to Gamelin's inaction was scornful. "Why not?" he commented, bitterly, "Are we really so impotent?"

A long silence then followed until the end of September, when a letter announced the upcoming transfer of General Rudolf Schmidt's panzer division to the Western Front. This short communication was followed by another period of silence, nearly a month in length, but by late October, H.E. became more talkative. His brother's division had shifted to a location between the Rhine and the Lahn, north of Koblenz. General Schmidt had understood from Hitler that he was to lead an attack in the west, but not before the end of winter in 1940.

Schmidt complained about the intrusion of the new security organization of the Third Reich—the R.S.H.A—into the activities of Forschungsamt and the increasing influence of the police apparatus dominated by the S.S.

On November 2, 1939, Rivet noted in his journal: "Summoned by Gamelin, who wants to know the value of intelligence reporting that a German attack on the Western Front is unlikely before the end of winter."

Of course, this related to Schmidt. Just like General Gauché regarding General Colson, Army Chief of Staff, the boss never failed to recognize the exceptional credit due for the intelligence provided by this informant.

Let us stop here for a moment and consider the question posed on November 2, 1939 by the commander-in-chief of the Allied armies, which deserves some attention due to its importance.

Schmidt, reflecting the thoughts of his brother (whom we all know was well positioned in the O.K.W.), had just notified the S.R. about the Führer's irrevocable decision to lead an attack in the west—"Not," he added, "before the end of the winter in 1940." However, in November 1939, an imminent offensive by the German army in the west would be announced eleven times, keeping Allied Command in a state of alert and distress.

If these alerts were not provoked by falsified evidence planted to reveal the reactions of the enemy, they may have been Hitler's real decisions to attack, which were then challenged by his generals under various pretexts: insufficient preparation, poor weather conditions, and so on. The S.R. had been unable to confirm the reality of threats with regards to any of these circumstances. Having been alerted eleven times, eleven times it had researched in vain the enemy's plans for any indisputable evidence of an attack, confirming to a certain extent, through observations made in the field, the value of H.E.'s intelligence: "Not before the end of winter in 1940."

Rivet's testimony, as reflected in his journal, illustrates the above, notably for the two principal alerts that forced Allied Command to react sharply, and in vain, despite the reassuring intelligence from our Bureau.

From November 7 to 12, 1939, both the Belgians and the Dutch expressed their concerns. Intelligence from various sources confirmed their fears of an imminent attack. On those same dates, the head of the S.R. noted: "The positioning of German forces and their size has changed very little in the west. There has been no further indication about attack plans with an introduction of sizable armored divisions.

"German threats are trumpeted to reinforce a peace offensive and to influence the neutral powers."

On November 13, Rivet concluded: "None of the intelligence coming from the delegations and military attachés (the Belgians, the Dutch, and other non-disclosed nations) and dates being offered regarding the forthcoming German offensive appear to be confirmed. The S.R. has nothing to announce."

After experiencing grave fears for their safety on Christmas night 1939, the Belgians and the Dutch faced new anguish between January 11 and 15, 1940.

On January 10, 1940 a Luftwaffe aircraft with a Wehrmacht liaison officer on board got lost over Belgian territory. Out of gas, he had to make an emergency landing at Mechelen-sur-Meuse, not far from the German border. The officer attempted to burn, unsuccessfully, the confidential files he was carrying. Partially burnt pieces were recovered by the Belgian Deuxième Bureau and reported to the king. What they revealed concerned the next German offensive across the Netherlands, Belgium, Luxembourg and the French Ardennes.

Some twenty-four hours later, having been informed of the events, General Gamelin appealed to the S.R.

Rivet reported the incident in his journal:

"*January 12, 1940*: Summoned by General Gamelin to a council of army generals to give the S.R.'s opinion on the document sent by the King of Belgium to the French commander-in-chief announcing a German attack on the Western Front in the very near future. [...] Opinion of the S.R.: 1) nothing has changed in terms of German operational plans; 2) there is no evidence to suggest that something is going to occur in the short term. Verification of this is underway."

"*January 13, 1940*: The S.R. has not collected any affirmative intelligence regarding troop movements. However, the Belgians are taking measures according to critical intelligence they claim to have received [...] Overnight, the head of S.R. is alerted by Gamelin's cabinet by way of a Belgian military attaché who repeated the gravity of the situation on the Belgian border. [...] Alerted by phone, our Dutch and Belgian posts reply that they have absolutely no intelligence of this nature."

"*January 14, 1940*: The Belgians have evacuated the regions of Eupen, Malmedy, and Verviers. They are calling in all available troops and dispatching them to the Ghent and Brussels sectors.

"The S.R. receives nothing positive, neither from the Belgian authorities nor from research organizations monitoring Germany, other than German movements or threats that could motivate such measures."

The evening of January 14 and the morning of January 15 seemed endless. The unrest that had taken hold of the staffs and ministerial cabinets overflowed onto us. The Bureau was in turmoil. We had to find justification for such alerts or demonstrate that such actions were being taken in vain.

In Brussels and The Hague, the German embassies were calm. Our agents embedded in the Abwehr revealed nothing concerning about the behavior of the German S.R. We heard nothing more from H.E., who was sticking to his warning: "Not until the end of winter in 1940."

In Luxembourg, as in Liège or in Metz, our comrades scrutinized the enemy's operational plans in vain. Each and every one of us spent two or three sleepless nights waiting for decisions that would never come. As for the urgent solicitations from High Command and the government, Rivet, imperturbable, merely answered with "R.A.S." (*rien à signaler*)—nothing to report.

January 15 ended with the boss writing: "The alert has fizzled out. There is a sense of calm tonight in Belgium. No further details of the famous Belgian document." I went into Rivet's office just as he was writing this sentence. It was 11 p.m. Perruche was with him, satisfied with the recognition shown regarding the significance of the S.R.'s intelligence, especially Schmidt's contribution. His caustic wit was on great form. Referring to commotion caused by emergency calls from the Belgian government and the preparations of the Allies to imagined threats, Perruche noted: "Hitler always manages to cause problems at the weekend. I must admit that this time it has caused panic. In this game of 'let's go'—'let's not go', Belgium will one day be invaded and we'll arrive too late."

During the days that followed, I would participate in a meeting of the heads of service. Schlesser had gone out of his way to assume command since January 1, 1940. He hardly ever left the war zone any more. His successor had not yet been assigned,[178] so I was responsible for sending out updates on current affairs.

"These false alarms must not alter our vigilance," Rivet advised us. "We have an idea from H.E. of Hitler's determination and O.K.W.'s opinion on the impossibility of a serious offensive before the end of March or April. The fact of the matter remains that the Wehrmacht has amassed 170 divisions for use in the west, of which ten are panzer units, and at any time the Führer may, despite the advice of his generals, give orders to attack."

"I imagine that Schmidt will know how to warn us," said Perruche, somewhat subdued. Like Bertrand, Navarre and myself, he was surprised by the agent's silence, which had now lasted three months.

H.E.'s silence would continue until February 27, 1940, so we were left guessing. Anxiety began to take hold of us when a short message read by Navarre informed us that H.E. would be spending some time in Italy. In fact, he had requested a rendezvous for Sunday, March 10, 1940, at the Hotel Eden on Lake Lugano in Switzerland.

Navarre did not entrust us with the information directly; the news spread quietly to those of us who were aware of Schmidt's existence (Bertrand, Rex, and myself in particular) along with the news that, as a precaution, all contact had been temporarily discontinued with our informant. It was plausible. It was not customary in the Bureau to seek out information about something deemed unnecessary to us.

H.E.'s final warning

Navarre returned from his mission in Italy on March 17, 1940. Starting from Paris, he had passed through Switzerland and arrived at Lugano on March 10, where he met with H.E.

For a long time—a very long time—I was unaware of this final rendezvous with our amazing agent. Indeed, it wasn't until 1974 that I learned about it for the first time, and then it was by chance, and very brief. Navarre, along with a few comrades and myself, was preparing a book on the intelligence services.[179] He was returning from Théoule where he had collected the memoirs of General Gustave Bertrand,[180] and had taken me aside to confide in me his impressions:

"I found him tired and bitter. He rejects any of the revelations on the Enigma machine that did not come from him. He disputes the accuracy of the intelligence. He is furious at what he calls the guilty indiscretions committed against H.E. He still considers himself the sole custodian of the secrets of this case. He fears that the family of our informant are still victims of public opinion."

Navarre stopped talking. Rarely did he show any outward expression of emotion, but at this time he seemed upset. After a pause, he resumed his story:

"His attachment to our traditions and his respect for Schmidt himself are quite moving. I kept myself from adding to Bertrand's suffering and exposing any further his vulnerability. I obviously did not speak to him about Schmidt's final meeting. It would have been too cruel!"

"Why so, General?"

"Oh, it's true? You were also unaware of the Lugano rendezvous?"

I didn't say anything. At that time, I had no reason to know more about the situation than Bertrand or any of my comrades. Nine years later, however, the circumstances were different. I was in the process of preparing this book, and the conditions under which the Bureau had lost contact with H.E. in 1940 seemed unclear to me. I had also noticed something intriguing in Rivet's journal entry for March 19, 1940: "… summoned by the General regarding important intelligence to communicate to him…" The day before this entry, Navarre had returned from Italy. This meeting with the commander-in-chief must surely have been related to his meeting with H.E.

I decided to ask Navarre. His friendly interest in my work had never wavered. Quite to the contrary. Gustave Bertrand had died, and we no longer had to fear the wrath of his sensitivity.

One day in May 1983 I was showing Navarre Rivet's journal, and making comments on what I'd found therein:

"I guess that the 'important intelligence' that was necessary to communicate to Gamelin was more of a military nature rather than diplomatic. Do you think this was the intelligence you collected in Lugano in March 1940?"

"Probably—Rivet did want me to go with him to see Gamelin then."

Finally, then, I would learn about that fateful meeting...

*

"We agreed—Rivet, Perruche and myself—that the Lugano rendezvous had to remain secret. There were several reasons for this, the primary one being Schmidt's safety. His long silence led us to believe that he too was worried about this. As you will see later, we were not wrong. Paradoxically, what made us take this decision without hesitation had to do with Bertrand's personality.

"He considered H.E. as his personal possession. Right from the beginning in 1931, he had never missed a meeting with him. This was the case even when the meetings were only remotely related to coding issues. In July 1939, he learned about Schmidt's meeting with Schlesser. No doubt you remember? It was such a drama!"

I nodded, remembering that for several days afterwards, Bertrand had given us the cold shoulder.

"In March 1940," Navarre continued, "it was impossible to distract our comrade from his work at P.C. Bruno. Every day, every hour, messages were coming in. We had to analyze them and attempt to read them. Under a heavy cloak of secrecy, we began to decipher the Enigma codes to benefit the High Command. The liaison with London and Bletchley Park was non-stop. At any one moment, there were decisions to make, confidential intelligence to exploit... Bertrand's presence was really quite essential."

At this point of his story, I allowed myself to interrupt Navarre:

"You don't believe that if he had been informed of the proposed rendezvous in Lugano, he would have taken it on himself to go?"

"Maybe, but it wasn't clear. Moreover, the Bureau had become accustomed—dare I say it—to Schmidt's silence. We rationalized it as a measure taken for his own safety, the remoteness of Templin from sources of intelligence other than the Forschungsamt, a lack of contact with his brother who was engaged with his large armored unit on the Western Front..."

"Whatever the reason, Rivet, Perruche, and myself have always respected the decision, even after the war. It was the slightest of adjustments vis-à-vis Bertrand. I myself had valid reasons for not being there. The government and the High Command were receiving contradictory intelligence on Italy's stance. Was it going to join arms with Germany or not? Indications of its hostility were multiplying. Six months prior, the Italian spies, driven by the Italian Embassy in Paris and its consulates in France were replaced with spies from the Abwehr.

"In Italy, a veritable razzia had befallen not only our staff but also that of the French, simply for being suspected of interacting with our intelligence services. Rivet had thus decided to send me to Italy. I had to try to unravel the real intentions of Il Duce and his entourage. You and Schlesser asked me to see if it was possible to convince the Italians to attenuate their conduct and whether a tentative agreement on an even exchange of prisoners arrested for espionage in France and Italy could be reached.[181]

"On March 10, 1940 at around noon, I found Schmidt at the bar of the Hotel Eden in Lugano. He had checked in the day before. The staff were particularly attentive to his needs given the extent of his spending and his generous tips. It was sunny; the view of the lake and the snow-covered Alps was impressive. While taking a stroll in the sun, we went to lunch on the Riva Paradiso. He had reserved a table set a little apart from the others on the terrace of a luxury restaurant. We were able to chat without any fear of being overheard.

"He had to leave the next morning for Basel, go to his bank (I understood the hint) and go to Templin on Tuesday, March 12.

"Asché was on his way back from Rome. He had exchanged the foreign codes with the specialized service of the S.I.M.,[182] provided an update on the possibility of a collaborative decoding effort, and collected various pieces of intelligence.

"This is how I learned that the relationship between the Abwehr, the Forschungsamt, and the Italians was closer than ever. I was also not completely surprised to learn that the Italians were intercepting encrypted messages from the French Embassy.

"But most of what Schmidt had to say was not to do with that. His brother had been appointed on February 1, 1940 to the head of the 39th Panzer Corps. Newly formed with two divisions, the 5th and 7th, headed by Rommel,[183] the corps was part of a group of seven armored divisions available to General von Rundstedt, commander of Army Group A, which was in the process of concentrating its forces on both sides of the Moselle in Luxembourg and on the Belgian border.

"On February 17, 1940 General Rudolf Schmidt was invited to lunch by Hitler. The Führer was on inspection and his aide-de-camp, Colonel Schmundt, former student of the Kriegsakademie and a friend of General Schmidt, had suggested that he gather for dinner a few commanders from some of the larger units whom he held in esteem and in whom he had confidence. Among them, Schmidt met von Manstein, Rundstedt's brilliant former Chief of Staff. He had just been assigned to the head of an army corps positioned next to Schmidt's 39th Panzer Corps.

"During the meal, Manstein, supported by Rundstedt, made a compelling presentation of his concept of Fall Gelb (Case Yellow, the operational plan in the west). Instead of concentrating the Wehrmacht forces in Belgium and Holland, Manstein, with Hitler's approval, suggested positioning them further south in the Ardennes along the Luxembourg and French borders. With a successful breach, the offensive would continue in a westerly direction toward the lower

Somme, so the northern Allied forces[184] would be caught in a veritable noose along with, of course, the Belgian and Dutch armies."

I interrupted Navarre once again:

"This is exactly what our agents embedded in the Abwehr fore-shadowed in March and April 1940 by informing us about the German S.R. surveys. The Wehrmacht Command wanted to know the nature of the obstacles it could possibly meet up against along the Sedan–Abbeville–Saint-Quentin line. I myself informed General Georges[185] of such intelligence while on my way to La Ferté-sous-Jouarre with General Rivet on April 13, 1940."

"Yes, that is precisely what happened! Today it is easy to see and regret that our intelligence did not have the impact it deserved. On March 19, 1940, both Rivet and I reported and commented on this crucial intelligence from H.E. to Gamelin. The commander-in-chief ordered a study on the hypothesis of such an attack. The Troisième Bureau of the Army General Staff and that of General Georges joined forces to conduct the study. They concluded their work in April 1940, and demonstrated that, due to the terrain of the Ardennes and the inadequacy of the road network, it would take weeks for the Wehrmacht to organize enough forces, tanks and artillery, in particular, to breach our lines of defense. The hypothesis was not definitively ruled out; it was simply considered less likely than an offensive through the Belgian plain, north of the Meuse. An overly cautious interpretation of intelligence all too often prevents one from recognizing the facts.

"Let's come back to H.E. I observed that he seemed worried. His precautionary measures were on the rise. I asked him if something was distressing him.

"'No, not really,' he replied. 'I knew that the S.D. had acquired evidence that the Poles had successfully reconstructed the Enigma machine. They scrutinized the staff of the Chiffrierstelle with a fine-toothed comb. I hope Monsieur Barsac and Monsieur Lemoine have given nothing to the Poles that could implicate me.' I reassured him as best I could, but I was surprised and worried.

"I asked him if he had any news of the investigation into the 'leaks' from November 1937 by the Reich Chancellery. The case clearly bothered him. He knew from Schapper that the investigation was ongoing. The small Chancellery staff, along with a few people who had at one time or another been in contact with the French Embassy, were always being tapped by the Forschungsamt and under surveillance by the Gestapo. Any sort of communication with anyone abroad was strictly controlled.

"All of this weighed heavily on Schmidt and explained his prolonged silence. I urged him not to make any appearances until further notice. If an important event needed to be communicated to us, for example the date that the German offensive would begin, it was agreed that he would arrange to go to Italy or Switzerland and alert us. I advised him that if he really felt in danger that he should flee to France. He jumped up and violently rejected such an offer:

"'I'd rather die! It would jeopardize my family and especially my brother. I will never do that.'

"Thereupon H.E. explained that he had to halt the operation of his soap factory. His partner had been drafted, and with the additional workload imposed on him since the beginning of the war, he was unable to manage his business alone. He was trying to liquidate his stock and sell the equipment. It was a big worry for him, and something he was unable to share with anyone.

"Despite constantly telling me that he was in no danger, he insisted on how necessary it was to be careful. I agreed, and handed him his envelope full of Swiss bills. We were about to part when he was overcome with emotion. I myself had a heavy heart. We both felt that we would not see each other again… He shook my hand for a long time asking me to send his best wishes to St. George, Barsac, Alison and Lemoine.

"'I so wanted to avoid war and to save my country from the disaster that is at its door!'

"These were his last words to me. I believe he was sincere.

"I was expected in Rome by March 11, 1940 by our military attaché, General Parisot. He had arranged meetings for me with our ambassador, André François-Poncet, who was on his way from Berlin to Rome, with Monseigneur Weaver at the Vatican, and various political and military figures. Out of all of these contacts, I came away with the impression that Italy's participation in the war alongside Germany was inevitable. Only the embassy had the slightest trace of optimism.

"The day before my return to Paris, I was invited to lunch with François-Poncet—nothing more than light conversation. At coffee time, the ambassador took me aside. Ciano[186] had confided in him that Mussolini was resisting the pressure of the Third Reich, but for how long? 'I notified Quai d'Orsay. They ordered me to do anything I could to preserve a neutral stance, and yet I had nothing serious to offer in return.'

"'I hope,' I said venomously to François-Poncet, remembering H.E.'s revelations, 'that all these exchanges of messages are confidential and have been carefully encrypted.'

"'Of course! From time to time, to deceive the Italians, we use the old codes they already know. Important messages are encrypted with new techniques. They are impenetrable.'

"I did not dare question the ambassador. I simply recommended to him that he use only the valise for the most serious and secret matters.

"On March 17 I was back and provided an account of my missions to Rivet and Perruche. You know, as I do, what came of their work. We had neither the influence nor the audience to be able to force anyone to take H.E.'s final pieces of intelligence into account…"

*

I never saw Navarre again. The day before his hospitalization at Val-de-Grâce, where he died a few days later, on June 23, 1983, he rang to tell me of the seriousness of his condition. He had the sincere thoughtfulness to wish me luck in writing this book.

Enigma in the Battle of France

While Navarre was abroad, the deciphering of the Enigma messages had advanced enough to become an effective tool for our High Command.

Using data provided by the Poles (perforated cards and the Bomba) British scientists had created a new perforated card better suited to the new configuration of the machine. Polish technicians were sequestered and on January 17 they had managed to break the key from October 28, 1939. It was the one in use in the twenty military regions of the Reich for their domestic contacts. A few days later, Bletchley had in turn broken the key from October 25, 1939.

The lag of nearly three months between intercepting and deciphering the message meant the effort did not produce anything useful but after a year of silence this advance was encouraging. The two "factories" then increased their efforts tenfold. The English, under the leadership of the remarkable Alan Turing, were performing wonders. Besides the development of perforated cards, Bletchley had embarked on the implementation of a Bombe derived from the Polish Bomba. Upon its commissioning, the time needed to decipher messages decreased considerably and messages intercepted about the Luftwaffe formations became decipherable. Their connections with the Army made it possible to identify and locate some of the large formations on the Western Front.

On March 6, 1940, Rivet considered it possible to make tactical use of the intelligence gathered in this way and he summoned Colonel Gauché, head of the Deuxième Bureau for General Gamelin, the commander-in-chief of the Allied armies, and Colonel Baril, head of the Deuxième Bureau for General Georges, commander-in-chief of the northeastern armies.[187]

Both were aware of the possibilities now available at our Bureau. Together, the three officers defined the conditions under which one could disseminate the Enigma intelligence, whether from the P.C. Bruno or from Bletchley. In no case should its origin be revealed. For the British the source was to be called "Ultra" and for the French it was "Source Z." The latter had exclusive responsibility of analyzing these two sources in the war zone according to the agreements on January 3, 1940 between General Menzies, chief of the S.I.S., and our boss.

On March 12, Commander Ferrand, head of the Deuxième Bureau

of the Air Force, was informed of the situation. The increasing number of deciphered messages mostly concerned the Luftwaffe. On that day, the captured interceptions from February 20, 1940 were delivered to Ferrand. Three weeks had been sufficient to break the key for this day, and revealed an important component of the order of battle of the German Air Force.

The rate would dramatically increase during the second half of March 1940. Every day, the Deuxième Bureau was supplied with intelligence through intercepted messages that had been deciphered in under a week, sometimes in less than twenty-four hours.

On April 6, 1940 Rivet's journal notes the satisfaction of General Georges' Deuxième Bureau. On the 20th of the same month, he said: "Source Z is starting to provide intelligence relative to the operations…"

*

March 6 and March 18, 1940: first results from deciphered Enigma messages. This document was particularly interesting because it revealed:

1. *sabotage preparations on the Danube;*
2. *intelligence gathered by S.R. on the preparations of the German offensive in the West (Holland); and*
3. *the good relations between French and Romanian intelligence services.*

*

On April 21, Rivet and I rushed over to see Gamelin. An Enigma message from April 20, decoded that very night and delivered to our counterespionage services, revealed that the Germans were reading the instructions that the commander-in-chief had transmitted by radio. Our traditional ciphers were truly outdated. I have come to lament the fact that the French army had never had at its disposal an encryption machine nearly as good as the German machine.[188]

On April 28, 1940, General Staff Headquarters were able to establish a model of the order of battle of the German Army on the Western Front, from the Dutch border to the Swiss border: 116 infantry divisions and ten panzer divisions.[189]

It was the eve of the Wehrmacht's decisive offensive on the Western Front.[190] Numerous indications from our intelligence and counterespionage services confirmed this. H.E. himself had warned us. More than ever, the assistance of Enigma proved invaluable.

Suddenly, on May 2, 1940, silence.

Bruno, like Bletchley, was confronted with messages that had suddenly become impenetrable. On May 1, 1940 the Wehrmacht, having become suspicious, secretly modified the procedures of creating the keys specific to each message. The decryption methods developed through so much hard work suddenly became useless.

On May 22, 1940, Bletchley regained control by deciphering the new codes. From this point until the end of the war, they remained the masters of the codes. A tireless researcher, Alan Turing had successfully developed his Bombe and adapted it to the new encryption procedures. In 1943, British scientists would put into operation what would be considered the first computer in the world: the "Colossus." It was an impressive apparatus due to its complexity and its size, but also because of its ability to solve in record time any combination of ciphers, including encrypted messages transmitted by teletype.

I observed in Rivet's journal:

May 23, 1940: "Meeting with Gauché and Baril, Source Z just thwarted a German attack on the Beaumont–Le Chêne front. We're almost able to read in its entirety the German operational plan."

May 25, 1940: "The key to the German code from the 25th was cracked at 9 p.m."

May 26, 1940: "Source Z indicates defensive measures being taken by certain aircrews of the Luftwaffe."

May 27, 1940: "A message from May 26 from the Luftwaffe mentions preparations for a massive air attack, code-named 'Paula'. Specifics are unclear."

May 28, 1940: "Z continues to charge forth at a rapid pace."

May 29, 1940: "Z indicates the 20th Bomber Wing's participation in Operation 'Paula'."

May 30, 1940: "Source Z: Paula, Ferrand-Paris[191] has been alerted."

May 31, 1940: "Z reveals the route to be taken by the Paula mission. South of Reims, Corbeil, Melun, Nangis, return by Sedan."

June 1, 1940: "Z confirms the concentration of bomber formations 1,500 meters over Sainte-Marie at 1 p.m. on June 3 with three escort fighter groups. General Vuillemin, who has been personally informed by Bertrand, does not seem able to oppose the operation, not having at his disposal a sufficient number of fighter planes due to a commitment on the front taking priority."

June 3, 1940:[192] "Bombing of Paris announced by Z: 906 victims, including 254 deaths at Renault and Citroën and surrounding areas."

The end of the Battle of France was near. On June 6, preparations for the closure of Bruno were underway. On June 9, everyone set off blindly for the south. Bletchley had already taken complete control of deciphering our interceptions. In the tragic disorder of defeat, the messages it decoded were the only pieces of intelligence that reached us for the next few days and—completely in vain—High Command and the French government were stricken with panic.

Rivet wrote his final account while in La Ferté-Saint-Aubin:

June 14, 1940: "… Command is utterly distraught. The service is still operational thanks to decoded messages… no one, however, is here to analyze them…"

This was the end.

The fall of France

On Thursday, May 9, 1940 at 8 a.m., General Rudolf Schmidt was summoned to the General Staff of General von Brauchitsch,[193] a few kilometers from his own command post south of the Bonn–Euskirchen line. He was received by Chief of Staff General Halder, along with General von Kleist, leader of the panzer group of Army Group A (von Rundstedt) and his colleagues—panzer corps commanders like him—Reinhardt and Guderian.

There was a huge map of the western theatre showing the locations of major German units, as well as those of the Dutch, Belgian and the Allies. For several hours, Halder developed the plan of attack through Luxembourg and the French Ardennes toward Sedan. The von Kleist panzer group was to be the spearhead. It was the arduous implementation of the offensive plan presented to Hitler on February 17, 1940 by von Manstein. Rudolf Schmidt was very familiar with the goals to be achieved. Since February 17, he had been thinking about this operation, the secret of which he had confided to his brother. His 39th Panzer Corps had to be in position at the Belgian border at the northern tip of Luxembourg by 6 p.m.

On May 10, preceded by shock troops from the Abwehr and specialist engineering teams, Schmidt's corps had to protect from the north—along the right flank—the actions of Reinhardt's and Guderian's panzer corps, which had embarked across Luxembourg and the Ardennes, in the direction of the Meuse valley on both sides of Sedan.

Two of Rudolf Schmidt's panzer divisions roared out at 5.30 a.m. In complete silence, they had moved into their launch positions under the cloak of darkness. The weather was nice: a light fog was still enveloping the valley. That day, they breached the first line of defenses of the Belgian fighters in the Ardennes. Under the cover of German air superiority, they rushed to the west, crossing the Ourthe (a tributary of the Meuse) on May 11. The next day, around noon, they lined up on the Meuse north of Dinant. The Belgian troops received orders to withdraw, destroying everything in their path. The major French cavalry units launched in Belgium had barely moved in along the right bank of the Meuse. Despite the difficulties of the terrain, despite the bottleneck of troops and equipment, despite sabotage on the narrow secondary roads running from east to west going from the German border to the Meuse valley, the 39th Panzer Corps had successfully crossed 150 kilometers in forty-eight hours. At the same time, still covered by Schmidt's tanks to the north, Guderian's 19th Panzer Corps and its 1,500 tanks crossed the French border. They had already crossed Luxembourg and Belgium without much opposition. Such a concentration of troops channeled into the base of the valley could have made them easy targets for Allied aircraft… but Guderian's troops would arrive on the banks of the Meuse on May 13 at 11 a.m.

At 4 p.m., under the protection of a deluge of fire and preceded by terrifying dive-bombing Stukas, Guderian's front-line units crossed the river on both sides of Sedan. From the right bank, Rundstedt, reigning supreme, opened a deadly breach in the French defenses. The sky was empty of Allied aircraft. Our troops comprised mostly of poorly educated and inadequately armed reservists, more or less anesthetized by the foul pacifist propaganda and the "humdrum" about the "phony war." Without the sufficient support of fortifications and artillery, they were in no position to resist. By the evening of the 13th, the breach was already five kilometers wide and six deep.

On the night of May 12/13, it was time for the light units of Rudolf Schmidt's panzer corps to cross the Meuse north of Dinant. Rommel's 7th Panzer Division rushed westwards toward Cambrai.

Rivet's journal mentions the date of May 24:

"… To the south of the Sambre and Meuse, there is a violent German push through Dinant and Sedan. Mezières, Charleville have fallen into the hands of the Germans. A few losses in certain French divisions at Sedan…"

On May 15, he noted:

"… Met with General Gamelin, to whom I explained our situation. Very concerned by the alarming news of the lightning advance of the Germans and the weak state of our troops who were under fire from aerial bombardment and armored ground forces…"

Guderian arrived at the mouth of the Somme on May 20; on the same day, Rommel reached the region of Arras. Rudolf Schmidt modified the direction of his march northward, charging through Belgium to finish the race in Rotterdam. The Netherlands had already surrendered on May 14. According to von Manstein's prediction, the noose would be closed around the Belgian army, the British Expeditionary Force, and the 7th and 1st French Armies within ten days. The only ones who would escape the hell of the entrenched camp at Dunkirk would be 220,000 British and 100,000 French.

A million prisoners, every piece of equipment from these large units, 100,000 killed or wounded—such was the sad result of the German maneuver that the French government and High Command had refused to consider.

*

"… Once again, our leaders have refused to accept the facts. They have let themselves be driven by their preconceived ideas," commented Rivet, bitter and pessimistic. "Expect the worst and prepare to retreat to the Loire…"

It was now June 1, 1940.

On this day, Rundstedt appointed Rudolf Schmidt to "General of Panzer Troops" (General der Panzertruppe). On June 6, Hitler awarded him the *Ritterkreuz*—the Knight's Cross. It was a flattering recognition of the lightning-fast deployment of his 39th Panzer Corps through Belgium, the Netherlands and France ending on the Swiss border in late May 1940 and testimony to the confidence his leaders and the Führer had in his mastery of armored tactics. It was he who now inspired Rundstedt (promoted to field marshal) in the use of tanks until the end of the campaign in France.

*

During this depressing campaign, Schlesser managed to take command of the 31st Dragoon Regiment. It was my responsibility to pass on his instructions to his successor, the excellent Colonel Guy d'Alès. Together, we had to prepare for the withdrawal of the S.C.R. to ensure the security of our archives and the safety of our employees. There was no news from H.E. in spite of a few cautious messages posted in Germany by our correspondents from Basel.

My first thought was to go to Lemoine. I met him on June 9 at his home on Boulevard Pershing. Suitcases cluttered the living room. A mass of papers were burning in the fireplace.

The news was not good.

The Germans were in Rouen and our Bureau's senior officers were en route to the Loire. Rivet predicted that the total evacuation of the service would be complete by the morning of June 11.

Rex was aware of the gravity of the situation. His sons, from whom he had had little news, were both on the front line and bravely performing their duties. He was justifiably proud.

"I am both surprised and worried," Rex told me, "that I have had no news from Schmidt for so long. It is not normal that he has not found a way of showing signs of life through Switzerland. What will happen if the Germans occupy Paris?"

Lemoine didn't know about the Lugano rendezvous. I assured him that communication with H.E. would eventually be reestablished. The night before, we had alerted our Geneva and Basel connections to suspend the delivery of any letters from our informant to Paris until further notice. At a later date we would provide them with the means to handle any messages should Schmidt attempt to contact us.

We then addressed Rex's personal situation:

"I expect Paris to be occupied in the coming days. The government is retreating to Bordeaux. We will certainly be in continual contact with it, even though I am unable to tell you today exactly when that will commence. No matter what happens, you will be able to find us at the headquarters of the National Defense Ministry."

And so this is how it was. Like all the other state agencies, we would flee south. One way or another, we would try to maintain our connections with High Command, our agents and metropolitan posts who were themselves moving toward the interior of the country.[194]

After my commentary, which my friend listened to in dismay, I asked him his plans.

"My wife and I intend to travel to La Rochelle, where my daughter lives. It's not far from Bordeaux. I will be waiting there for the arrival of a representative from the Bureau as soon as I know the address of the National Defense Ministry."

We parted, though not before I advised Lemoine once again not to leave behind anything that could be exploited by the enemy. I encourage him to be as careful as possible. I could not help feeling doubtful as to the effectiveness of the vacuum I had asked him to create. His colleagues—Drach in particular—handled so many matters and dealt with such a wide variety of issues that it seemed very difficult to understand the full consequences and to erase all traces.

*

On June 11, 1940, it was my turn to leave Paris. I did so with a heavy heart. Who would ever be able to understand the intensity of the tragedy that we had lived through? Everything was falling apart. Nothing was planned. There was no order—it was every man for himself.

While Italian aviation targeted the endless miserable convoys of refugees, we strove to save our staff and our archives, and to maintain contact with each other.

After many tribulations, which for my part I have recounted in my other book,[195] our exodus ended pitifully on June 23 at the Seminary of Bon Encontre, near Agen, the night before the armistice was signed with Germany.

I found Bertrand at the head of a strange procession of a dozen cars and a Parisian bus.[196]

"It's a miracle," he said. "I have been able to save my whole world—my archives and my Enigma. Tomorrow I will take MacFarlane to Cazaux[197] so we can fly him home to England. I will then try to evacuate my Spanish and Polish colleagues to North Africa."

Bertrand, of course, achieved his goal. A few days later, Bertrand began looking for a quiet refuge in which to pursue his mission in connection with London.

On June 19 Navarre went in search of some news in Bordeaux. There he found only evasions, contradictions, agitation, crowds, and panic… The next day, between two doors of the Prefecture, he stumbled upon Lemoine:

"You must leave France. The enemy is looking for you. You're too vulnerable…"

Navarre succeeded, after much difficulty, in obtaining Navy orders directing Lemoine, accompanied by his wife and Drach, to go to England. The port of Bordeaux was full to bursting, so we advised him to try to embark from Saint-Jean-de-Luz on a British warship. He had to present himself with his mission orders to the British consul in the city.

"I hope," Navarre told me at the Bon Encontre on June 24, "that our team was able to clear out before the Germans arrived on the Basque coast. Just in case, I gave everyone a way to find us."

No sooner had he finished his remarks than Rex's car entered the courtyard of the seminary. His wife and his assistant Drach, buried in luggage, seemed lifeless. Staggering, Rex got out of his car and told us about his odyssey.

"The British consul whom I saw on the night of June 20 in Saint-Jean-de-Luz told us to arrive at 5 a.m. the next day at the harbor pier, where there was a type of British minesweeper. Thousands of Polish soldiers were there to board the same boat. I managed to meet with the commander. The departure was scheduled for that evening. Due to the number of passengers, he asked me to bring for each of us a blanket, and a small suitcase with four days' worth of provisions. On the evening of the 21st, we returned to the dock. The Poles boarded. When it was our turn, around 10 p.m., we were directed to a location on the bridge in the middle of a crowd. I asked an officer if we could find somewhere that was a bit more sheltered—for my wife. I showed him our mission orders. His response was nothing more than a curse, as he hurled unpleasant insults against France in English.

"My blood was boiling. I told him in English that we would rather die in France than live and be insulted in England.

"It was nearly midnight. We left the boat and spent the night in the car. For the entire day of the 22nd I sought in vain a way for us to board a French boat headed to Morocco. In desperation, on the 23rd I decided to meet up with you. We edged our way through the crowd of refugees and retreating troops. It was difficult to make any progress. Finally, in Mont-de-Marsan, presenting our mission orders, which I had kept, we were able to sleep in a barracks and got hold of some petrol. Finally, here we are… exhausted!"

I found a corner in the seminary where the three of them were able to get some rest. On June 25, better informed of the overall situation created by the armistice,[198] we invited Lemoine, his wife, and Drach to take refuge on the French Riviera.

"No problem," Rex responded, having perked up after a good night's sleep. "I have money and friends in Saint-Raphael. I'll head to the gendarmerie where I will await your instructions."

Just before leaving, he opened his trunk and pulled out a box that he handed over. It contained confidential documents, codes of various nationalities, unsigned passports of Dutch, Swedish, Danish nationalities, blank ID cards, stamps of all kinds… a trove of counterfeiting paraphernalia!

I was amazed—even now I still shudder at the thought of his mad recklessness.

"I hope you have not left anything in Paris," I said again, noticing that among the codes there were two from the Chiffrierstelle.

"Both of those are outdated codes," observed Bertrand, "H.E. delivered them to us in August 1938 shortly before joining the Forschungsamt. He suggested that we try to sell them to the Italians to verify the nature of their relations with the Germans…"

A little embarrassed, Lemoine claimed that he and Drach had only kept the box because they believed the contents could still be useful. Anything that could have compromised us had been destroyed.

I was skeptical. I feared for H.E., and my premonition of trouble would prove to be well founded.

The hundred days of Enigma

"*The Battle of France is over. I expect that the Battle of Britain is about to begin.*

Upon this battle depends the survival of Christian civilization.

Upon it depends our own British life and the long continuity of our institutions and our Empire. The whole fury and might of the enemy must very soon be turned on us now.

Hitler knows that he will have to break us in this island or lose the war."[199]

The devastating occupation of Holland, Belgium and France was a dark cloud hanging over Europe. The Wehrmacht was in full, menacing control, at the peak of its material and moral power.

"*… we shall prove ourselves once more able to defend our island home, to ride out the storm of war, and to outlive the menace of tyranny, if necessary for years, if necessary alone…*"[200]

Our S.I.S. comrades would be alone for these hundred days, during which Europe's fate would be decided. Unaided from late June to late September 1940, they would meet the urgent intelligence needs of Britain.

Suspended since June 24, relations with our services would only be restored gradually and clandestinely from mid-July 1940. The intelligence network of General de Gaulle's Deuxième Bureau (the future B.C.R.A.[201]) wouldn't be effective for several months yet.

The S.I.S. itself, with the help of the Polish Intelligence Bureau and from what was left of the Allied S.R.s who had retreated to London, would not be working at full intelligence-gathering capacity from inside the occupied countries until September 1940.

The S.I.S. had no better way to penetrate into the gray areas and delve into the intentions of the enemy than intercepting and decoding radio messages from enemy. Miraculously, we had seen for a month (May 22, 1940) that the Polish contributions from July 1939 regarding the Enigma machine and its technical aspects were again operating flawlessly.

Miraculously, just when Hitler was planning the invasion of Britain and about to launch the Luftwaffe to attack the defenses and vital centers of Britain—starting with the destruction of the R.A.F.,[202] it was precisely the Enigma messages intended for the German Air Force, or from its large units, which were captured in greater numbers and deciphered with the greatest ease. The prodigious effort that Bletchley sustained during these one hundred days, for the sake of Britain, deserves that one stops here for a moment to remember that this would all probably have been in vain had the French S.R. not revealed the mysteries of the enemy's mechanical encryption in time.

I have stated that the German Enigma network in 1940 included tens of thousands of machines. Under the control and principal coordination of the Chiffrierstelle, each user (armed forces,[203] administrations, R.S.H.A., etc.) had its own cipher department. Each one created and broadcast its unique keys. Within large field units, there sometimes existed multiple different keys. It's clear to see from this the complexity of the cryptographers' task.

Following the Fall of France, the English were the only ones intercepting radio messages from the Axis. Four listening stations were developed in haste.[204] Subsequently, beginning in 1941, the number was increased to cover all regions from which enemy broadcasts could come.

On August 1 and 8, 1940, two Enigma messages from Goering ordered the Luftwaffe to prepare to crush the R.A.F. This was the indispensable prelude necessary to the success of Operation "Sea Lion" (the landing in England).

On 12 August, a message declared August 13 as the day the attack would commence. Every day, every night, powerful bomber formations and Luftwaffe fighters would try to render routes impassable and to destroy as many British aircraft as possible.

Assisted and occasionally guided by Ultra,[205] the R.A.F. Command succeeded—though at the cost of heavy losses—in overcoming the attacks, in which enemy losses reached upwards of 15–20 percent of its aircraft. Intercepted messages indicated that in late August the difficulties encountered by the Luftwaffe required it to stop and lick its wounds, and repair the lost or damaged equipment. It was a critical phase in this gigantic battle, when each party painfully regained its breath.

On September 5, an Enigma message deciphered in just thirty minutes informed the British of Goering's decision to launch a raid of 300 bombers on the London docks. It was terrible, despite the extensive defensive measures taken by the British Command.

On September 15, the heart of the capital came under attack. R.A.F. fighters launched their elite forces to oppose the most powerful waves of the raid. Thanks to Enigma, they intercepted the German fighters as soon as they crossed the English coastline. The British inflicted such heavy losses on their opponents that the Germans were forced to withdraw.

Two days later, on September 17, an Enigma message from Hitler ordered the dismantling of bases that had been equipped for the invasion of the British Isles.

The Battle of Britain was won.

The war, however, was certainly not over. Victory remained uncertain. At least now there existed a chance, safeguarded by the coolness and courage of a nation. In this great and decisive battle, the role of Enigma was real if not decisive. It would remain just as important during the course of fighting on land, at sea and in the air, until the Third Reich was crushed.

Bletchley, under the leadership of its scientists and in the wake of its successes, continued to strengthen its abilities and improve its performance.

Its work, buried deep in secrets which time has not completely brought to light, will go down in history if not as the decisive factor in the victory, then at least as a factor reducing the length of the conflict[206] and leading to scientific advances.

Bletchley's Bombe and the Colossus were descendants of the mathematical principles and Bomba developed by Polish scientists based on documents delivered by H.E.

"Colossus" would supply the Allied Enigma machines with essential data for their instantaneous settings in alignment with those being transmitted from the German machines.

Day after day, Ultra broadcast intelligence seized right from the very heart of the enemy. The origin would remain secret; the enemy never imagined the existence of the scientific resources of Bletchley, nor did it doubt the reliability of its own mechanical encryption.

*

"... I had hoped to be able to pay a visit to Bletchley Park in order to thank you and the members of the staff personally for the magnificent service which has been rendered to the Allied cause," wrote General Dwight Eisenhower to General Menzies, chief of the S.I.S. in July 1945.

"The intelligence which has emanated from you before and during this campaign has been of priceless value to me. It has simplified my task as a commander enormously. It has saved thousands of British and American lives and, in no small way, contributed to the speed with which the enemy was routed and eventually forced to surrender."

*

Letter addressed to Colonel Paul Paillole on the occasion of his appointment into the order of the british empire by General Menzies, head of the intelligence service during World War II

My dear friend,

Please excuse the time it has taken me to respond to your letter, but I assure you that I was truly touched by your feelings. I am naturally very pleased that you were wearing a badge that shows the good work we have done together. The association between the two Special Services was truly perfect and accordingly, the results were very, very rewarding.

I assure you that my hope will always be to see you again. Our bond is so tight that it cannot be broken by matters of service.

I hope that you are in good health, I must admit that I am a little tired, but one of these days I expect to take a real holiday!

With congratulations on your award, I send you my best wishes for your future.

Very truly yours,

Menzies

28-9-1946

*

In August 1945, through an affectionate communication from his friend Menzies, General Rivet, who had been unjustly dismissed from his Command,[207] learned about this letter.

The chief of the S.I.S. had likewise heard about it and shared the glowing testimony from the commander-in-chief of the Allied armies with our former servicemen. No one knew better than he the tortuous and tenacious path we had followed since 1931 in order to break the most sophisticated and most reliable code in the world. And no one could better appreciate the decisive contribution made by the French S.R. and its providential agent.

CHAPTER IV

The Pursuit

Confrontation • On the trail of H.E. • In pursuit of Rex • Rex in the hands of the Abwehr • The downfall of H.E. • The tragic fate of General Rudolf Schmidt • Ultra-Enigma safe and sound in the storm • From the Abwehr to the Gestapo: Rex's tribulations • The end for Rex

Confrontation

While Britain was entrenched on its island giving the world an example of courage and tenacity, we were preparing to combat the invaders and offer the S.I.S. the support of the Intelligence and Counterespionage Bureaus' staff.

On July 1, 1940 three resistance networks were created[208] with the help of our reservists and our honorable correspondents. It operated from that date under the leadership of Colonel Louis Rivet: an intelligence network originating from the Research Section (S.R.) with Perruche (the "Kléber" network); a counterespionage network (C.E.) over which I assumed leadership (S.S.M./F./T.R. network); and the aviation network (A.V.), with the Colonel Ronin at the head. This transfer of our methods of researching the enemy did not present any problems; most of our agents had resumed contact with their "employers" by the end of June. By contrast, H.E. remained silent. We prudently resisted reaching out to him.

The delivery of our "product" to our allies in England would be achieved progressively by radio and by mail. Radio contact with London recommenced on July 13, 1940 (see Rivet's journal)—the result of the "Olga connection" that united our two services until June 1940. A transmitter of 40W connected with an H.R.O. receiver was installed in Sayat, near Royat. It would ensure the continual success of our radio transmissions with our own Central European S.R. in Bucharest, Romania.

The Air Force Intelligence Bureau, which had been established in Cusset (near Vichy) created its own radio connection with the S.I.S. in August 1940. Finally, Bertrand himself, having clandestinely reconstituted his Cipher Service in the area of Uzès (in the Gard region)—it would have four Enigma machines—resumed regular contact with the S.I.S. from October 1, 1940. At that time, he would be able to recover his Polish technicians, who would continue to act under the direction of Lieutenant Colonel Langer.

Transmissions to London via our couriers were handled completely from Vichy by staff from the Canadian and U.S. embassies (Monsieur Dupuis; and Monsieurs Schow, Cassidy, and Sabalot, respectively). The Foreign Affairs valise occasionally provided opportunities to make contact with the British through our military attaché in Lisbon, Colonel de Brantes. It was the future wife of Georges Bidault, Suzy Borel, a diplomat assigned to the Ministry of Foreign Affairs in Vichy, who would discreetly place our mail inside the bag to be transported to Portugal with a safe agent.

During these one hundred days, during which the fate of the war would be played out, our contribution to the S.I.S.'s research effort would earn an expression of appreciation from its chief, General Menzies, that I have the pleasure of reproducing here:

"… In the weeks and months that followed the armistice, the intelligence from the French S.R. was for us of paramount importance. Our most valuable sources came to us from France."

For my part, I had moved the management of our clandestine service of the C.E. to Marseilles.[209] This choice was guided by several considerations: to conceal our archives and our resistance activity in the largest city of the so-called "free zone", where we could be ready to get down to work improving our relations with North Africa; to prepare for a probable fall; and to take advantage of the exceptional relationships that complemented and facilitated our work. Among the latter were those with Divisional Commissioner John Osvald, who was transferred from the Territorial Surveillance Bureau in Paris in July 1940 to take over as the Director of the Marseilles police; commissioners Robert Blémant and Simon Cottoni from the Territorial Surveillance Bureau in Marseilles and Nice; the Recordier brothers;[210] and General Granier, chief of staff of the military region. Finally, we moved to Marseilles to take advantage of the support of one of the best-equipped offices of our intelligence services in terms of personnel and technology.[211]

One of our initial concerns was to ensure the safety of those among our comrades who were sought by the enemy. Some were evacuated to North Africa, where they oversaw the organization of our Counterintelligence Service there; this was the case, for example, for Colonel Doudot, one of our agents embedded in the Abwehr who was among the most exposed. Others received missions to be conducted from the free zone, including Colonels Mangès and Johannès, who, having retreated from Metz, took over management of the Counterespionage Bureau in the S.S.M./F./T.R. network in Clermont-Ferrand. Others, in the end, simply had to comply with the security measures that we imposed in the so-called free zone while continuing the investigations of the Abwehr through the intermediary of armistice commissions.

The first person of concern should have been Lemoine, a.k.a. Rex. He was entirely elusive. Impatient for action and concerned about H.E.'s continued silence, he went to Vichy in September 1940 to locate any remaining traces of our services. His investigation ended when he discovered Rivet and Bertrand in their refuge at the *l'Office national du Retour à la Terre* ("National Office of the Return to the Land"), in the Hotel Saint-Mart in Chamalières (Puy-de-Dôme).

Rex wanted to resume his activities and travel to Spain and Portugal to try to get hold of Spanish codes. The interception and deciphering of radio messages between Madrid and Berlin was one of Rivet's concerns at a time when the Führer was seriously considering taking action against Gibraltar. Bertrand jumped at Lemoine's suggestion. A week later, Rex—with a diplomatic passport and a false identity—crossed the border.

For several months, Madame Lemoine was left alone at Saint-Raphaël. Once or twice, she went with her daughter to La Rochelle.

I was worried about Rex. In March 1941, our embedded agents alerted us to the Abwehr's growing interest in him. I hadn't heard anything about the results of his mission in Spain, but one fine day I learned that he was back in Saint-Raphaël and, far from being discreet, was resuming his barely legal financial activities with Drach: currency smuggling, illegal border crossings, black market trading…

I confided all of this to Perruche and Bertrand. With their agreement, I notified Rex through the gendarmerie of Saint-Raphaël that he and Drach were to appear on April 15, 1941 at 2.00 p.m. before the Director of the Marseilles police.

Unaware that the director was John Osvald, the two men were highly worried by this unusual summons, and were surprised and relieved to be welcomed by me in the office of the police chief. I went right into the thick of it:

"You must leave Saint-Raphaël and henceforth play dead. Two rooms have been reserved for you in Marseilles, at the Hotel Splendid, on Cours Lieutaud, starting on May 1. You can get in contact with the hotel manager of the hotel to make arrangements for your move."

Rex expressed his satisfaction with the situation, promising to go to Marseilles with his wife under these conditions. A wily old fox, he suspected that the residence that had been arranged for him, which being in Marseilles was not far from Osvald's presence, was our way of keeping an eye on him. It was a security measure for his own sake, of course, but the continual surveillance of his behavior and that of Drach was a bonus for us.

Both men were of German origin. Despite evidence of their loyalty and service to our Bureau, it was our duty to control any reactions provoked by Germany's brilliant victory and the upheaval it had caused.

"This man Drach," Osvald confided in me, "has never inspired much confidence in me. He is always in search of shady deals to earn money. Here at least, I'll be able to keep an eye on him."

The doorman of the Splendid, just like the hotel manager, had for some years been one of several trustworthy police informants. I left Osvald's office after warning Lemoine and Drach not to engage in any business related to their previous work for our Bureau. Until further notice, they were not to leave Marseilles without my permission. I emphasized to them the Abwehr's desire to establish themselves in the southern zone in order to monitor and neutralize any resistance efforts, and to track down all our former servicemen, who they believed remained in contact with the S.I.S.

Terser and more to-the-point than me, Osvald added in a non-nonsense tone: "No more false papers, no more trafficking, no more tall tales. If you have, see or do anything that seems out of the ordinary or unusual to you, come see me."

I had no concerns about Lemoine's and Drach's comfort. Rex had a few kilograms of gold and hundreds of louis in his luggage, as well as transferable securities of which I never knew the amount. As for Drach, paid monthly by Lemoine, he certainly had reserves and resources to enable him to face the future with confidence.

*

Let's return to Paris. On Friday, June 14, 1940 the Wehrmacht entered the capital. At 6 p.m. on the same day, Colonel Friedrich Rudolph, at the head of an Abwehr regiment, with a requisition order from General von Briesen (commander of Paris), was to present himself at the Hotel Lutetia, 46 boulevard Raspail. He gave the management twenty-four hours to clear the hotel of the few guests who were still lodging there.

On that same evening, he and about fifty of his subordinates moved into the hotel. Tall, blond, blue-eyed, burly, polite but distant, the officer spoke in good French with ease and authority.

It was Colonel Rudolph who would reign supreme over the Abwehr in France during the occupation—certainly one of the most experienced intelligence experts upon whom Canaris could count. Born in 1892, he was a cavalry officer in the Great War, and when assigned to the Abwehrstelle in Munster in 1930, he had been promoted to captain of the Cologne annex to work on the east of France, Luxembourg and Belgium. His exuberant activity immediately caught the attention of our counterintelligence post in Metz. Captain Doudot, our outstanding specialist, was in charge there and would not leave the post until the declaration of war.

Rudolph, despite opposition from our services and clear cuts in his network of informants, had obtained results that influenced Canaris to entrust to him the command of this important post in Munster. From there he would lead the majority of the Abwehr's research on France. He got to know our country well. While, in 1937, with our embedded agents—including among others, Doudot—we had learned about the majority of Rudolph's activities and frequently neutralized them, he had nevertheless been able to achieve notable successes, including intelligence about the fortifications of the Maginot Line.[212] His competence and dynamism had earned him not only Canaris' trust but also frequent and flattering promotions. Made colonel in 1940, no one was better qualified to be the first to enter Paris and jump on the objectives set by the Abwehr: military archives, police, diplomatic personalities of the French Special Services, and so on.

On the morning of that dark Friday, after an exhausting march through the night, Rudolph quickly and covertly spread out his police sections (Geheimfeldpolizei) into buildings where there might still be useful documentation for German intelligence: the Ministries of War, of the Interior, of Justice, of Foreign Affairs, Police Headquarters, etc. The directives were clear: let nothing disappear or become altered before the appropriate personnel could arrive to review and sort records; capture what deserved immediate analysis either on site or in Berlin; and finally find and if possible apprehend hundreds of individuals suspected of spying against the Reich. The list of suspects, provided by Berlin, was in Rudolph's hands. Figuring prominently on the list was Stallman, Rudolf, a.k.a. Lemoine, Rodolphe, and the addresses of his various Parisian homes: rue de Madrid, rue de Lisbon, boulevard Pershing.

This was an enormous task, which, in spite of the quality staff that surrounded him, the colonel would be unable to bring it to fruition without substantial reinforcements. This was especially true for the Abwehr's Counterintelligence Research group (III.F), which was in the urgent need of additional support.

On June 15, 1940, through personal communication with Canaris, Rudolph learned that he would be responsible for the entirety of France.[213] He was, some may say justifiably, happy and proud. The admiral informed him that he had appointed his own nephew, Major Alexander Waag, to assist Rudolph in the search of military intelligence, and that he was also assigning Major Oskar Reile to his C.E. group, whose staff would be significantly increased.

Reile's assignment pleased Rudolph greatly. He had learned of him in 1935 when Reile was leading a counterespionage group in Trèves for the Cassel Abwehrstelle. He was a confirmed counterespionage specialist who spoke French and knew France well. Until his posting in Paris, he led a regiment of the 16th Army, which had invaded Luxembourg on May 10 and continued its victorious route through Sedan, Abbeville, all the way to Metz and Verdun.

On June 20 at 4 p.m., Reile came to Rudolph and took possession of his apartment and offices on the third floor of the Hotel Lutetia. The next day, he met his senior staff, who were already at work: Major Adolf von Feldmann, Captains Leyerer Wilhelm, Georg Wiegand and Blang, and Lieutenant Hermann Niebuhr.

On June 22, Reile described his trip:[214]

"In the company of Captain Leyerer, I decided to take a moment in Paris and take stock of the situation and the secret documents that had been seized. The city still seemed dead. Many of its inhabitants had evacuated before it was declared an open city on June 13, 1940[215] [...] here and there soldiers, either alone or in groups, were slowly moving around the streets of the beautiful French capital and were admiring her beauties. I, alas, had no time to do so…"

The two officers thus made their way to the Ministry of Foreign Affairs on Quai d'Orsay, to the Ministry of War on boulevard Saint-Germain and the Ministry of the Interior on Place Beauvau. They finished their inspection at Police Headquarters.

Reile's impressions[216] indicate the violent cyclone of panic that swept through France and of the culpable negligence of its leaders: "There was no one in the buildings I visited. With a few exceptions, all of the ministry offices and the police were open. The archives had remained in place […] On the same day I also learned some sensational news: in the sealed cars of a train stationed at La Charité-sur-Loire were the secret archives of the French High Command. […] A few days later we made another important discovery. Captain Wiegand had found among the belongings at 11, rue des Saussaies in Paris, archives and files on national security that were in perfect order…"

I do not recall whether those responsible for these criminal activities were ever held accountable for their actions.

On the trail of H.E.

At around 7 p.m. on June 16, 1940, a brief telephone call from the Reich Chancellery informed Canaris that the Führer wanted to see him immediately.

In all the euphoria of victory, proud of the successes achieved by the Abwehr regiments, the admiral was convinced that Hitler was calling on him in order to express his satisfaction, examine the situation and discuss with him operations that were to follow. In his car, he had briefly noted the various issues he wanted to discuss as a result of his increased responsibilities.

To his amazement, he found Heydrich in the waiting room of the Chancellery; he had also been summoned urgently. A few minutes went by before a uniformed Goering opened the door of Hitler's office and silently signaled to them to enter.

The Führer was standing; his welcome was cold, barely polite. He held in his hand several brown papers from the Forschungsamt, which he handed to Canaris:

"Read it! This is very serious. There's a traitor in the Bureau. His deceit could derail everything. We must discover the culprit fast—I intend for him to be punished regardless of his seniority. Both of you must dedicate all of your resources to locating him. Admiral, you will send me an account of your findings."

The meeting ended almost as soon as it had begun. Goering was silent. He accompanied the two men into the waiting room. They were aghast. In almost a whisper, Goering related to them the essentials of the case:

"The Forschungsamt has intercepted and deciphered several telegrams from the Dutch ambassador to his government, and recorded telephone conversations between Belgian and Dutch military attachés with their capitals. It is clear there is a traitor, very well positioned, who has informed the diplomats of our offensive plans and the date of the attack in the West."

Goering took Canaris by the shoulder. The admiral's face betrayed his fatigue and dismay:

"It is fortunate that our organization allows us to read nearly all the telegrams exchanged in Europe and that the diplomats and foreign defense ministers don't want to believe it. Let's not forget that despite this, we still have not discovered the traitor who delivered the secrets of the meeting on November 5, 1937 to François-Poncet. The Führer, he too has not forgotten. Like me, he wonders if this is the same character running rampant among us."

Moments later, Canaris and Heydrich met in the office of the head of the Abwehr. They examined the brown papers carefully:

- On May 2, a message to Brussels from the Belgian Ambassador Adrien Nieuwenhuys: "… an attack against Belgium and Holland will take place next week…"
- On May 3, messages from the Vatican to the nuncios of the

Netherlands and Brussels: "Next invasion of Holland and Belgium."

• From May 5 to 9, a series of brown papers from Forschungsstelle A (wiretapping) in Berlin, reproducing the telephone calls from the Belgian and Dutch defense attachés.

The communication on 9 May at 9.45 p.m. between Colonel Sas (Dutch military attaché) and the Dutch Ministry of War dumbfounded Canaris and Heydrich:

"Post, do you recognize my voice? [217] This is Sas in Berlin. I have only one thing to say: tomorrow at dawn! Do you understand me? Copy!"

Post replied: "I understand, received letter 210." [218]

They were utterly shocked at these revelations, amazed at the level of recklessness on the part of the military attachés and diplomats in Berlin.

At length, they discussed every possible hypothesis. They compared the elements in the brown papers with the case of November 5, 1937. They were completely bewildered, and agreed to continue the investigation tirelessly together. Then the astute leader of R.S.H.A. took the opportunity to ask the head of the Abwehr for authorization to continue with him the necessary investigations in Belgium, Holland and France.

The proposal was clever. Up until now the Wehrmacht and the Abwehr had been stubbornly opposed to any intrusion from the R.S.H.A. in the Western European theaters of operation. The only police department authorized to act under the orders of the Abwehr in the newly occupied areas was the Geheimfeldpolizei (G.F.P.). No special dispensations had yet been granted. Canaris hesitated. Would he allow them to get involved? Would he allow others in on his assignment and, with the R.S.H.A., would they take advantage of the opportunity and overpower him?

Heydrich was insistent, tenacious, and persuasive:

"Believe me, admiral, it is in Brussels, at The Hague, and especially in Paris where, through a thorough and intense examination of the captured archives, we will have much better opportunities to identify the perpetrator—or perpetrators—of the November 1937 and May 1940 leaks. The enormous mass of documents in foreign languages to comb through, the multiple investigations to be made—these will require a considerable number of specialists, especially if we want to succeed quickly in order to satisfy the Führer. I would feel guilty if I did not offer my help."

Canaris was particularly sensitive to such arguments, as he was receiving exorbitant demands from Rudolph for reinforcements.

It was now after midnight. The admiral, subjected to these relentless requests since 10 May, was exhausted. He finally gave in to the perfidious insistence of his younger opponent. He would later recall this moment of weakness. Canaris gave his agreement in principle, reserving the right to cancel it if the O.K.W. leader, Keitel, was not of the same opinion.

"Be that as it may," he said, taking leave of Heydrich, "the missions you could send abroad, particularly in France, will have to be approved by my office. They will have to be in constant contact with my staff leaders responsible for their posts and will have to refrain from any initiatives outside of any assistance they must bring to the Wehrmacht in the interest of security."

"If you wish, tomorrow we will sign a memorandum agreeing to the protocol," concluded Heydrich, fully satisfied with the outcome of the meeting.

A few days later, small detachments from the R.S.H.A. arrived quietly in Paris. A regiment from the S.D., under the orders of S.S. Doctor Knochen, settled into 72, avenue Foch; another took possession, on Place Beauvau, of the premises of the National Security Bureau, despite the presence of a detachment from the Abwehr, which was already at work there. It was the Gestapo, along with the Sturmbannführer[219] Bömelburg and especially Hauptsturmführer[220] Kieffer, specialist in the fight against espionage, the very man who, not too long ago in Berlin, had called Lemoine in for questioning and released him. The case had hardly been forgotten…

Such S.S. detachments were precursors of a gradual and serious expansion. Their skills, as much as the services they offered to the German Army overseeing the occupation would permit them to gain the confidence of the Wehrmacht and the Abwehr while waiting to replace the latter institution in 1942. In February 1944, it would finally absorb it and Canaris would be discharged.

*

Since 1939, Admiral Canaris had dramatically restructured the Abwehr. Colonel Egbert von Bentivegni took over from Lieutenant Colonel Bamler as the head of Abwehr III (military security, counterespionage and misinformation). Perhaps one could blame Bamler for his failure in the search for the 1937 leaks? Whatever the case may be, it was to Lieutenant Colonel Joachim Rohleder, head of the special section of Counterintelligence, that Canaris and von Bentivegni assigned this old case, and to whom the Forschungsamt brown papers were disclosed. It was a good choice: Rohleder was a strapping forty-two-year-old trained in the harsh military discipline of the 8th Grenadiers Guard Regiment. He had learned the techniques of the Special Services in Spain as part of the Condor Legion. Canaris had taken notice of his qualities and brought him to Berlin in 1939:

"No consideration of the person or his rank should prohibit you in the search for traitors. The Führer will not accept failure."

Rohleder needed no additional motivation to launch himself, body and soul, into this treason case. It revolted his strong moral and patriotic convictions.

He had three leads: the French, into which investigations began in 1937, the Italians, and above all the Dutch.

Very soon this last lead would take him to General Hans Oster, a most intimate associate of Canaris. He was known within the Abwehr for his anti-Nazi sentiments. A personal friend of Colonel Sas,[221] a Dutch military attaché with whom he met on a daily basis since May 1, there was no doubt in Rohleder's mind that he must have indulged himself in the telling of a few guilty secrets. Was it a deliberate betrayal? An indiscretion? Recklessness?

In late June, Rohleder revealed his initial findings to the admiral.

"It's not possible!" the latter spontaneously retorted.

He was nevertheless open to the arguments of his subordinate, and ordered him to meet Oster and tell him frankly about his suspicions. Indignant, Oster violently refuted the accusation. Meanwhile, Rohleder continued his investigations into the Vatican lead. Delving into the archives of the Forschungsamt, he came upon disturbing telephone contacts between Oster and various Roman personalities, or those authorized to have access to the Pope.

Again he turned to his boss. This time the admiral was shaken, disturbed. He considered the scandal that could reverberate throughout his bureau. In the end it was his friendship with Oster that determined his attitude:

"We have no evidence, Rohleder. You must investigate elsewhere—in Paris, in the archives of the police, intelligence services, foreign affairs, in the documents that have been found in La Charité-sur-Loire.[222] Searching in all directions, we must be able to find a clue concerning the origin of these indiscretions—which, remember, date back well before 1940."

*

On July 28, 1940, Colonel Rohleder arrived at the Hotel Lutetia. In the presence of Colonel Rudolph, he summoned Reile and revealed the state of his research after having informed the two officers of the details of Canaris' audience with the Führer on June 16, 1940.

Captain Wiegand had made some sensational discoveries on rue des Saussaies.[223] The activity of the French Intelligence Bureau was prolific. Intact files were sent to Berlin in order to allow for closer inspection. Two or three particularly serious cases would fall under high treason, without Reile being able to identify the culprits. They were certainly very close to the Nazi leadership circles and the O.K.W.

Other less complicated cases were under investigation in Reile's offices.

Thanks to these files and folders relating to national security, an organizational chart of the French intelligence services could be drafted. Searches were conducted at the premises or apartments of Colonel Rivet's officers and employees;[224] thorough examinations of the homes of the suspects, Lemoine at the fore, led to the seizing of extensive documentation, which was analyzed at the Hotel Lutetia.

A few arrests were made in the Paris region by the Geheimfeldpolizei. Sixty-one suspected spies imprisoned in Paris were released. Many made excellent V.M.s,[225] that Reile and his assistants would use for their investigations in France and to aid in the penetration of activist circles.

Rohleder listened to the long report without interruption.

Reile, who seemed to have no particular sympathy for Canaris' envoy, noted the events in his memoirs with some bitterness, never paying him a single compliment. While noting the magnitude of the task, he was critical of the fact that the samples had been taken from the archive. He ordered that they not be moved from their original location,[226] and for photographic reproductions to be created of those documents that required additional analysis in Berlin. He also elaborated at length on his priorities during his visit:

"The day before our offensive in the West the Forschungsamt intercepted a telephone conversation between the Dutch military attaché and his government, announcing from a reliable source that the offensive would begin the next day. This intelligence could have had fatal consequences. We must find the traitor. In the French secret archives, there are certainly documents that report on Sas' intelligence and its origin. We must study the archives from 1937—we know that Ambassador François-Poncet was informed about what was happening in the Reich Chancellery, and that the French Command was receiving intelligence coming from the O.K.W."

Rudolph, very attentive, offered some advice on how he believed the work should be organized. He recommended not neglecting further investigations of those known by the Abwehr as agents of the French

S.R. He mentioned Lemoine in particular, whom he considered the most important. He had been familiar with his activities for years:

"It is essential to know where he is and to get our hands on him if he is in the occupied zone. If he is in the free zone, it will be necessary to set one or two V.M.s on his trail and follow his every step."

Rohleder's final recommendation was as follows:

"Forschungsamt posts are being installed in Lille, Bordeaux, Bayonne, Dijon and especially Paris. Work with them. Start wiretapping the homes of officers and employees of the French Deuxième Bureau right away."

*

On 15 August, Canaris came to Paris. He confirmed Rohleder's directives and stressed the importance of examining the French archives: "We must discover the origin of the Berlin betrayals and find Lemoine by any means necessary."

The results of the Abwehr's offensive would not take long to arrive.

The surveillance of Rex's home on boulevard Pershing enabled the Forschungsamt in Paris to intercept a card posted by Lemoine in Saint-Raphaël on 30 August 1940. The note authorized the building superintendent to hand the keys to his apartment over to his daughter. He didn't give his address. A few days later Rudolph sent a V.M. (agent) with a photograph of Lemoine to look for him in Saint-Raphaël. The search was in vain. Suspicious, Lemoine had moved to the Hotel Beau-Rivage under a false identity. Since the beginning of the month, he had been in Vichy, then Chamalières, and then finally Spain.

In October, Abwehr investigators discovered in the archives of the French G.Q.G., seized at La Charité-sur-Loire, a series of documents that made reference—in disturbing detail—to intelligence from the Deuxième Bureau concerning the crises of the Anschluss, Czechoslovakia, and Poland. Diplomatic conversations or messages between capital cities were clearly reported: Berlin, Vienna, Prague, London, Paris… Other documents related the measures reiterated to the French government from Belgian and Dutch military attachés about the threats to their country. They reported the information from their colleagues stationed in Berlin. One document from the "Vatican source" dated May 7, 1940 confirmed the imminence of the German offensive in the West.

Photographs of all these documents were sent to Berlin, along with a message suggesting to the Central Abwehr office to consider them in relation to the intelligence collected on the same dates by the Forschungsamt. "It seems," Rudolf wrote in his confidential transmission to Rohleder, "that leaks have been occurring in this organization for many years."

In December 1940, S.S. Sturmbannführer Kieffer who, with the Abwehr's agreement, was combing through the archives of the police headquarters, fell upon a voluminous dossier about Lemoine:

"We would need a wheelbarrow to transport it!" he exclaimed when reporting what he had found.

After several weeks of work, he extracted from the mass of papers the minutes from a hearing on December 3, 1938, that occurred at the Police Department regarding an Italian man who had arrived illegally in Paris. He was in possession of a note describing a German code from 1938 coming from the Chiffrierstelle. The Italian was clear in his testimony: it was Lemoine who had asked him, for a large reward, to offer the acquisition of this code to the government in Rome.

In the transmission of this report to the Langeron Police Department, Commissioner Gianvitti[227] noted that he had informed the Deuxième Bureau (S.R.–S.C.R.) of the case. "Lemoine," the police officer had written, "is known as an agent of the Deuxième Bureau and is in the business of trafficking codes." In my absence from Paris, Schlesser had received Gianvitti and confirmed that Rex's initiative was covered by our authorities. It resulted from an agreement with Bertrand, who was eager to test the nature of the relationship between the Italians and the Germans regarding encryption.

You will recall that on June 25, 1940 in Bon Encontre, near Agen, I had been shocked to discover the trafficking that Bertrand was involved in which he had assumed would be without consequence.

Kieffer's discovery was communicated to Berlin in late January 1941. "There is no doubt. In addition to leaks from the Forschungsamt, there have also been leaks from the Chiffrierstelle..."

Rohleder lost no time connecting it to the intelligence from the S.D. in Warsaw, which revealed that the Poles had succeeded in reproducing the Enigma machine.

A conference on February 4, 1941[228] brought together in Canaris' office General Erich Fellgiebel, boss of the transmissions bureau and the Chiffrierstelle, the head of R.S.H.A. Heydrich, Prince Christoph von Hesse, director of the Forschungsamt, and of course Rohleder.

The latter offered a complete assessment of the initial scouring of the French archives. He highlighted the various hypotheses regarding the origins of the leak in November 1937 and May 1940. At Canaris' request, he was careful not to mention Oster's name. It was just as well, given that responsibility could not be placed on him for leaks from the Chiffrierstelle and the Forschungsamt.

It was decided that each department head, with the help of S.S. police officers from the Gestapo, would examine in secret each of their employees who had worked for them since January 1, 1937: their origins, their lifestyle, the company they held, their state of mind... Particular attention would be given to personnel, military or civilian, who had had successive assignments in both departments involved in the leaks.

Rohleder coordinated the work. Unless something new arose, a meeting wouldn't be scheduled until May 1, 1941, during which they would take stock of progress. It seems that on May 1 the investigation had not progressed, for in June Canaris decided to go to Paris to confer with Rudolph and to provide a boost to the research being conducted in France. Yet Rohleder had gathered a dozen names of staff members of the Forschungsamt who had moved from the Chiffrierstelle since 1937. Among them: a certain Hans-Thilo Schmidt, brother of Rudolf Schmidt, general of armored troops.

As soon as his name was announced, the admiral threw his arms in the air:

"Really now, Rohleder, you're just looking for a scandal! After Oster, you'd dare throw aspersions on one of the largest families of the Reich and one of the most valued leaders of our army? Trust me, abandon that lead. It is in France that we will find the key to this mystery."

Not satisfied with the reaction of his leader, Rohleder nevertheless ordered the Forschungsamt and Gestapo to discreetly monitor the ten suspicious characters, including Hans-Thilo Schmidt.

In pursuit of Rex

On his return to the Hotel Lutetia on June 10, 1941, Canaris found a fevered atmosphere. The Abwehr's post in Paris had expanded greatly; it now had authority over the entirety of France. The growing number and significance of its current missions stifled the initial interest in the research of older cases.

Marshal Rundstedt, commander-in-chief of the Western operational area, flooded Rudolph with questions about the British forces. Meanwhile, General Otto von Stüpnagel, military commander in France in charge of security and law enforcement, was overwhelming Reile with orders and requests. Espionage and sabotage cases were multiplying as the free zone proved to be a breeding ground for resistance groups over whom the G.F.P. had no rights to exercise its authority. Arrests in the occupied zone revealed the resurgence of activities from the former Deuxième Bureau and its links with the S.I.S. Every day, the Reich ambassador in Paris, Otto Abetz, and his authorities were requesting assistance from the Abwehr for intelligence or investigations.

The admiral himself, after a series of missions in Spain at the Führer's request, harassed his Parisian authorities to infiltrate the Mediterranean region. This was both to prepare for a possible attack on Gibraltar, perhaps even on Morocco and North Africa, and to monitor British and pro-British activities.

This somewhat disorderly agitation did not go unnoticed by our agents embedded in the Abwehr. To the indignation of the occupying authorities, the repression of acts committed by the German intelligence services in the free zone and Africa was progressing well.[229] It slowed down Rudolph's efforts when they were not neutralized.

Canaris was well aware of the state of affairs in France. He remained obsessed by his inability to discover the traitor, or traitors, and Hitler's growing irritation was causing heads to roll. Only the interrogation of officers or colleagues closely related to the French Intelligence Service might be able to direct the research in a decisive manner. Unfortunately, this staff was inaccessible—in the southern zone, where the admiral refused to take brutal action such as a kidnapping or burglary.

There remained one solution: Lemoine.

His strong personality haunted the minds of all those in the intelligence services of the Third Reich who had had to deal with his multiple activities for many years on behalf of the French S.R. They had an admiration and a kind of respect for his daring and skill, which none of their employees could ever match. His arrest in Cologne at the time of the Anschluss, his hearing and his offer of service to Berlin persuaded Canaris and his Parisian colleagues that it should be possible to approach him and utilize his services.

Those officers of the Abwehr and S.S., such as Kieffer, who had studied his records in Berlin and the captured archives in France, knew that he had knowledge of much if not all of the leaked material. His trading of codes had certainly placed him in indirect if not direct contact with the Chiffrierstelle. Playing tactfully upon his German origins, upon the new situation in France, he could probably be "turned around" and provide the key to the mystery. He was now old, and of frail health. He liked the high life, and might respond to arguments that boosted both his pride, his susceptibility and his personal interests.

"I have your man," said Rudolph. "Captain George Wiegand. He has just come from working on National Security cases and those of the police headquarters. He speaks French well. He's clever. I can, with him, personally take care of this matter. I have old scores to settle with Lemoine."

The next day, Rudolph introduced Wiegand to Canaris. Wiegand was in his fifties and of medium height, slender and stylish. A slight bald patch near the front of his head and his remaining (albeit graying) brown hair gave his face a distinguished and serious look.

Briefly the admiral presented to the officer what he was expecting from him: someone who would take complete charge of the Lemoine case. "We must get the maximum benefit from this extraordinary character and know the contacts he had in Germany, notably those at the Chiffrierstelle." He recommended caution and absolute discretion.

"You are only to provide an account of your mission to Colonels Rudolph and Rohleder."

Flattered by the task and more than happy to leave the dusty offices of the rue des Saussaies, Wiegand, after having given his instructions to his adjutant Captain Bulang, set to work.

He recounted the approach he took for his mission during his hearing in 1946, which was conducted by our counterintelligence services.

Wiegand began by taking the diverse and voluminous files on Stallman, a.k.a. Lemoine, a.k.a. von Koenig, a.k.a. Verdier, back to Berlin and Paris. The traces of his various activities, and in particular his espionage work over the past thirty years, were numerous and enlightening.

With Kieffer who, for now and for some time to come, was playing the collaboration game properly with the Abwehr, he handed over the results of searches conducted on Lemoine's various homes, as well as those on Drach's and of their acolytes. Two address books from 1938 and 1939 were discovered in Rex's home. They were valuable: Wiegand found there a multitude of names and notes of his movements— amounts for anonymous payments were modest with the exception of two payments in 1938 in Basel, to the amount of 200,000 Swiss francs, which seemed incredible.

After months of work, Wiegand was thoroughly familiar with his case. He now also shared the conviction that Lemoine was the key figure who could lead them to the traitor. What they still had to discover was where Lemoine and his assistant Drach had fled. Ever since the fruitless search in Saint-Raphaël, nothing serious had been done to find the pair. Now, in the month of February 1942, an Italian agent of the Abwehr, back from a mission in Tunisia, told Wiegand that he had come across Lemoine and his wife on the Canebière in Marseilles. He had known them since before the war, but he refrained from approaching them. Wiegand decided to send a German colleague who spoke French and knew Marseilles well in search of the couple. Within a few weeks, she had located Lemoine at the Hotel Splendid and triumphantly returned to Paris.

Among the many villainous V.M.s recruited by the Abwehr since the occupation, Wiegand had discovered two individuals who had approached our authorities before the war. Their names, Marang and Marette, appeared in Lemoine's address book. What a piece of luck. Both seemed to be qualified to reconnect with him, to probe his feelings and to persuade him of the Germans' good intentions toward him. As incredible as it seems, everyone at both the Abwehr and the R.S.H.A. was full of respect for this man whom some might call the spy of the century, and who everyone imagined had been the éminence grise of the Deuxième Bureau since World War I.

Rudolph and Wiegand's achievement would be to "bring back" this genius of espionage to their advantage. Their ambition was to outpace Kieffer's S.S. Kommando. Driven by Heydrich, the latter was now participating more and more frequently in the functions of the Abwehr, and the glory would go to the first to get their hands on Lemoine.

For this operation of seduction, the first V.M. used by Wiegand would be Charles Marang, a Dutchman of about sixty years of age. Marang operated a business with his son in the Paris region. In 1939, Lemoine had introduced him to our Bureau. Captain Simoneau of the Parisian S.R. post, my classmate from St. Cyr, had taken care of him. He had offered him a few economic and military missions in the Netherlands, which Marang fulfilled voluntarily and correctly, enlisting his son Karel into his research. Wiegand was able to locate the two men from the information he found in Lemoine's address book. He had Karel arrested. With the intervention of Roechling,[230] a personal friend of Charles, he was released immediately. Summoned to the

Hotel Lutetia, Charles Marang was quick to affirm his identity. He was prepared to provide proof.

In July 1941, Simoneau, who was looking to recruit informants in Paris for our clandestine networks had thought of calling Marang back. He met them, formed his opinion and returned to the free zone with a bad overall impression. He wrote upon his return: "… I learned from Charles Marang that his son had been arrested and released by the Germans. He seemed aged and timorous. Assuming that he could be under surveillance, I did not try to pursue any further contact, which could perhaps be dangerous, and in any case without any benefit."

Simoneau's intuition would be beneficial.

*

A year later in June 1942, in Chamalières,[231] the head of the Marseilles police, my friend Osvald, informed me that Lemoine had told him about Charles Marang's visit at the Hotel Splendid. It had been proposed that he return to Paris, in full freedom, where the Germans would be happy to welcome him. Ready to brave new adventures and to play the game of double agent, Rex requested my instructions. After hearing Simoneau's opinion, my response was categorical: a refusal, accompanied by a demand for the immediate arrest of Marang, an agent of the Abwehr. It would be ineffective; Wiegand's envoy had already disappeared from the free zone. The warning was serious. We had to learn from this lesson.

In agreement with Rivet and Perruche, I met Lemoine in Marseilles in the last days of June 1942. He recounted in detail his meeting with Marang, but his story wasn't very satisfying. Rex was crafty enough to maneuver in such a way that we would be able to apprehend Marang, but it was clear that he did not want to burn bridges with the interlocutors who were representing our enemies. Was he arranging his place in a future he anticipated being favorable to Germany?

From the expression on my face, he understood that I was hardly convinced of his sincerity.

"What should I do now, my commander?"

"You must immediately leave France. We're asking you to go to North Africa."

Lemoine jumped. He objected vehemently for reasons of his business, his children, his age, his health… It's true, I found him increasingly aged, without energy, marked by illness. He had long and painful fits of coughing. I insisted. I put forth the possibility of a total occupation of France by the Wehrmacht, the dangers that would result for him and his family.

"I will alert one of our safe passage networks in Spain. You and Madame Lemoine will be able to reach Gibraltar safely, from where we will transport you to Morocco.

"For now go and get some fresh air and unwind in the Pyrenees. You will enjoy preparing your escape. I know of a lovely village at 1,300 meters above sea level, close to the Spanish border. There is an excellent inn and the brigade leader of the gendarmerie is a friend of ours…"

Rex in the hands of the Abwehr

Saillagouse was an old village in the Pyrenees a few hundred meters from the Spanish enclave of Llivia, close to the sanatoriums of Osséja and the Spanish village of Puigcerda. From there you could reach easily Ripoll and Barcelona. From Perpignan, you could access Saillagouse by either the RN116 from Perpignan to Bourg-Madame, or by rail.

Since 1941, this had been the hub of our covert crossings into Spain. The sergeant chief of the Bottet gendarmerie was the linchpin—it will surprise nobody that the customs officers and smugglers in the area were our best auxiliaries.

Within days, Lemoine and his wife had settled comfortably into an old inn typical of the Cerdanya region, and were already familiar with the villagers. Lemoine quietly gauged the advantages of the region and the opportunities for trafficking of all sorts across the border.

In Err, the neighboring village, he encountered an old acquaintance: the mayor, Bartholomew Lledos. He was a reserve captain, officer of the Legion of Honor; Rex had met him in Paris before the war through his business activities with foreign countries, particularly Denmark. He had convinced him to work for our Bureau. Lledos was able to complete a few assignments for us, notably through his intelligence on the economy of the Reich and on German-Soviet relations. Thanks to Lledos, Rex was able to rent a small furnished house close to the Saillagouse school. In the evening, by the fireside (evenings in the mountains can be rather chilly), they discussed their experiences. Lledos, who often went to Paris, didn't hesitate to flaunt his relationship with the Germans and his favor for Germany. This certainly did not fall on deaf ears.

In the quiet and fresh air of the high Cerdanya, Lemoine's heath gradually began to improve. He played "belote" (a card game) with the local peasants on rainy days, organized a few remunerative crossings toward the Llivia enclave, made black-market purchases for himself and his friends, played *bocce* with the gendarmes and took walks with his wife and his little dog, being greeted along the way as a well-known local. It was far from the tumultuous and captivating life of a spy in Marseilles. The doorman at the Hotel Splendid (where he had kept a room) forwarded his mail to him. This doorman was the only one, apart from Lemoine's children, Osvald, and me, to know about his retreat. It was under these conditions of secrecy and his sojourn close to the border that, at his insistence, we delayed the evacuation of the Lemoine couple to North Africa.

This was a mistake. I share this responsibility with Rivet, Perruche, and Bertrand.

*

At the end of September 1942, Rex received an urgent call from the doorman of the Splendid at the local phone booth in Saillagouse. One of his Swiss friends, de Ry, absolutely wanted to meet him. The demon of adventure took hold of our man once more: The next day, without our knowledge, he was in Marseilles. In the corner of the lobby at the

Splendid he found de Ry, a code trafficker like him. In the past, they had negotiated, with Bertrand's agreement, the sale of expired German codes provided by H.E.

This time de Ry was on the trail of the Italian Code "Imperio." The Roman official from the Ministry of War who was making the offer was serious, though demanding, with regards to financial guarantees. For proof of the reality of the offer, de Ry showed Lemoine photographs of the cover page as well as two pages of text on the code.

What was going through Lemoine's head at this moment for him to deliberately consider negotiating, undercover or not, any business with the Abwehr?

He rushed back to Saillagouse to see Lledos, and suggested that he make an offer to purchase the code for the Germans during his next trip to Paris. They would share the profits. Lledos accepted, happy to demonstrate his potential to the Germans.

On October 15, Lledos went to Paris. He asked his usual contacts to place him in contact with the Abwehr. On October 20 at 4 p.m. he had an appointment at the Hotel Lutetia with an officer from Section I (Intelligence Service). He presented him with the photographs of the Imperio documents, responded somehow or another to questions about the origin of the documents, and—horrifyingly—mentioned Lemoine's name. The officer asked him to wait for a moment, and an hour later he was being questioned by Rudolph and Wiegand.

On October 30, 1942, Lledos returned to Saillagouse and was at Lemoine's home:

"Everything is fine! The Germans are discussing the price, but they will take the Italian code.

"There is clearly no trust between the two Axis partners," sneered Rex.

"Certainly not," said Lledos. "The Germans want to meet with you to settle the deal. They are proposing that you and your wife come to Paris. You will be reimbursed for your costs, so you have nothing to fear. Quite to the contrary."

Lemoine thought about it. For the second time, he had been invited to visit the capital. It was very tempting. Yet he hesitated: if he were to ask for advice from the French, he would reveal his serious violation of their instructions. In the end, he yielded to his thirst for intrigue and adventure.

Two days later, he went to Err to inform Lledos that he would accept the offer. In 1945 he explained his behavior in writing:[232] "In the end, I decided to go to Paris. I gave our two passports to Lledos to affix to them the necessary visas for our journey [...] Lledos left at the beginning of November 1942. I didn't see him again. Later, I received a message from Marseilles announcing that I was going to be placed under arrest." It was December 10, 1942. On November 8, the Allies had landed in North Africa and the Wehrmacht occupied the so-called "free zone." To better understand what follows, we need to take into account two previous events:

On May 5, 1942 the head of R.S.H.A. himself, Heydrich, had come to Paris to induct S.S. General Karl-Albrecht Oberg as Höherer S.S. und Polizeiführer in France. It was Hitler who desired this, at Himmler's request. The Abwehr, the G.F.P., the Feldgendarmerie—in other words all of the military authorities—seemed incapable of exploiting the intelligence retrieved from the French archives, curtailing any resistance and suppressing espionage efforts in favor of the Allies. The Nazi police apparatus must gradually replace the organization of the Wehrmacht Special Services.

Canaris was not fooled by the maneuver. He felt that the effectiveness of his work and his duty were being contested. On several occasions the Führer protested the results of investigations entrusted to the Abwehr on the leaks that had fuelled the French intelligence bureau. All the admiral could do was stall.

In early June 1942, he reacted. He came to Paris. Gave Rudolph a sharp shaking. Dealt with the Lemoine case. It was he who decided that the cautious Wiegand should send Marang to Marseilles, where he returned empty-handed. In agreement with Ambassador Otto Abetz (who was not exactly excited to hear about Oberg's arrival), he organized a meeting in Paris at the Hotel Lutetia with the representatives[233] of Admiral Darlan, Army Chief of Staff, and of General Bridoux, War Minister for the Vichy government, in order to try and obtain the assistance of the French Special Services in the free zone.[234] It was a wasted effort. The S.S. and the Gestapo used it to their advantage, with each organization positioning itself in the southern zone in September 1942, with the complicity of certain leaders of the Vichy police.

*

Sought after like most of my classmates, I was hiding in the Royat region. I developed the new covert organization of our C.E. before heading to London (Christmas 1942) and then Algiers (January 1943).[235] Rivet had been in North Africa since November 10. I had lost contact with Perruche and Bertrand on November 8. I was convinced that, with the news of the occupation of the free zone, Lemoine had escaped to Spain. I knew from Bottet that everything had been prepared for such an escape. In 1946 his wife, Madame Lemoine, in a letter (of which I have the original), stated the reasons that prompted the couple to stay in France at the last moment: "A message from Marseilles on December 10, 1942 alerted us about a visit from the Germans to the Hotel Splendid where they had come to get us. We were planning to escape to Spain with the help of the local police. A few days later, we learned from a call from Marseilles, from one of our sons, Rolf Guy Lemoine, that he had been arrested by the Germans. He was speaking in such a way that I could tell a Gestapo agent was standing right next to him.[236] We decided not to flee..."

What Madame Lemoine did not know was that her son was in the hands of Kieffer, disappointed in his expedition to the Hotel Splendid where he had hoped to get hold of Rex before the Abwehr did. What she also did not know was that the Abwehr, since Lledos' visit to Paris, had taken measures to ensure her husband did not get away. On November 15, 1942, Wiegand assigned the mission to a second V.M. who was to take hold of Lemoine in Saillagouse. If he attempted to cross the border, the V.M., along with the local Feldgendarmerie post, had to take all steps to prevent it.

This second V.M. had been registered with the Abwehr since late 1940 under the number 7180. His alias was Hubertus; his actual name was Marette. He also had the advantage of having known Lemoine from long before the war. Together they had conducted "business" in Guyana, where Lemoine had the concession of a gold mine. Marette had offered his services to our Bureau, but whoever had received him in 1937 was not convinced of his potential or of his loyalty. Rex, knowing him, was tasked with evaluating him. Unenthusiastic himself, he had kept in touch with him, thinking he could be useful for operations on the borders of legality. The Abwehr now had plans for him. Wiegand and Rudolf would rely on him to shape their perspective concerning Rex. Arrest him or collaborate with him? It would ultimately be, as we will see, a mixed solution recommended by Berlin.

On February 21 and 22, 1943 Hubertus sent two lengthy reports to the Hotel Lutetia. Below are the essential points, which would be crucial to the attitude adopted by the Abwehr towards Lemoine:

> As soon as I was certain during the first meeting that I had with him in Saillagouse,[237] that this supposed retired banker was the man of the French S.R., I suddenly threw in his face that he belonged to the "Bureau." At first puzzled and reluctant, I allowed myself to confide in him, which then motivated him to do likewise. A few days later, we had become old friends talking openly about the situation and exchanging memories of our past […] He was living comfortably in this region which straddled the border and was a big spender in Saillagouse, as well as in Spain and Llivia. He was very friendly with all the civil and military authorities (police), and perfectly up to date with everything that was going on in the region […] Lemoine demonstrated a real and sincere love of Germany and truly wished for her victory[238] […] He told me verbatim: "I hate and despise the English as much as it is impossible to imagine, and if the marshal gave me orders to fight against the English and to rally on the side of the Germans, I would do so with all my heart and with great pleasure. The Germans have a courage that commands admiration and it is lamentable that the pernicious Anglo-Saxon propaganda blinds the world about the terrible danger which makes it run from the horrifying threat of communism that Germany alone is currently fighting. It is necessary that Germany wins the war, for if not, it is the end for all of Europe and its civilization. Under no

circumstances will I accept to live in a communist country…" I had Lemoine in my hands. He was aware of the searches conducted by the Germans in his offices and apartment, but he said: "They did not find anything because, before leaving, my wife and I spent two days destroying any incriminating documents in our possession concerning our French and foreign agents."

"You are entirely sure?" I retorted.

"Absolutely sure," he replied, "and none of our documents or those of the S.R. have fallen into German hands, although I know that many documents of the French Deuxième Bureau fell into the hands of the Germans in La Charité-sur-Loire in June 1940. These were not our documents."

To conclude, I can say that Lemoine is:

1. anti-English to the core, as is his wife; moreover,
2. thoroughly anti-Bolshevik; and
3. a real and sincere supporter of the German cause […].

Given his connections around the world and his potential, it would be most useful to rally his services which I believe he is entirely prepared to offer us.

Hubertus.

As an addendum, the agent specified the location of the Sainte-Lucie villa inhabited by Lemoine in Saillagouse. He attached a sketch of the locale. Rex's U-turn, which we should have foreseen and avoided by evacuating him from France, was explained as much by his circumstantial political beliefs as by his family situation, age and the skillful maneuvers of the Abwehr. It would lead to terrible consequences.

On February 25, 1943 at 3 p.m., Rudolf, Reile and Wiegand had the Hubertus reports in hand. They studied and analyzed them at length. At 6 p.m., Rudolf managed to get Canaris on the phone via the famous underground cable connecting Paris to Metz to Berlin, which was reserved for the exclusive use of the occupying authorities.[239] The admiral's instructions were clear: "Sequester Lemoine and his wife immediately. Treat them with respect, and keep the matter in absolute secrecy, including vis-à-vis the R.S.H.A. Do not consider anything else for the time being, only making him speak about his work with the French S.R."

On February 27, at 4.30 p.m. Wiegand, with Hubertus' sketch in front of him, set off for Saillagouse.

He described his mission in these terms:

"I was ordered to arrest the couple and transfer them to Paris. I arrived in Saillagouse with my driver Master Corporal Barth. Our V.M. (Hubertus) was visiting Lemoine at his house. I surprised him in the middle of his conversation with the couple. Lemoine was astonished. He told me word for word: 'I was expecting you tomorrow. You are obviously in possession of my picture, and you have come from Marseilles.'

"I replied that I indeed had one of his photos but I had not come from Marseilles, and that I did not belong to the Gestapo. He then let me know that someone had phoned him and that two men had inquired about him in Marseilles.

"The husband and wife were taken into a room at the Customs House since it was impossible to monitor them in their home.

"Apart from personal papers, nothing was found during the search of their home. A day before our departure, we found some money in a box. I gave him enough money to pay off his bills. The rest of the amount, around 30,000 francs, was left at the couple's disposal for their expenses in Paris.

"Lemoine spoke to me about his activities with the Deuxième Bureau. He told me that he would be willing to tell me everything and to be of assistance."[240]

The downfall of H.E.

Oh, what irony of fate! In the same Parisian palace, the Hotel Continental,[241] where not too long before he treated friends and on occasion his recruits like royalty, Lemoine, with one downfall after another, would shamelessly surrender himself to the Abwehr.

Rudolf, Reile, Rohleder, von Bentivegni, and even Canaris, all curious and triumphant, each took turns at taking delight in the haughtiness of a man in failing health and rubbing the old man's nose in the most hypocritical collaboration he had found himself in.

Captain Richard Protze, Rohleder's predecessor at the head of Section

III.F in Berlin would go to Holland where he would direct the German C.E. and refresh Rex's memory about his pre-war activities. It was he himself who set the Abwehr's conduct:[242] "Lemoine has been brought back to Paris not as a prisoner but as guest of honor. There can be no question of arrest…"

As for Rex, he would try to justify his felony. He wrote and signed the following:[243]

"I am French by naturalization and I worked for the French S.R. against Germany. I think I can say that I have done my duty to my country, France. […] Pétain and Laval honestly want an accord with Germany with the goal of integrating into the European community.

"I can no longer position myself against Germany as a loyal Frenchman and Anglophobe. So I am going to place myself at the disposal of the German authority.

"Please do not blame me for not betraying my French friends. I will do nothing against France."

On another day, he wrote:

"I'll explain to you the reasons for my attitude; I want to be useful to France, with all my strength, just as I have done for the past thirty-five years, and now that France is aligned with Germany, if Germany falls, France too will lose."

Wiegand, who interrogated him relentlessly, would report the following to his superiors on October 23, 1943:

"Lemoine persists in his refusal to provide the names of French officers. He refers to the word of honor that was given to him in exchange for his release and his proposition of a voluntary collaboration…"

At the Hotel Continental, inhabited by senior staff members of the Wehrmacht, the Abwehr had taken occupation of an entire floor. This was the Disciplinar Abteilung, where it provided "lodging" for a few French personalities who had had dealings with the Deuxième Bureau, shielded from the Gestapo. Apartment 159, where the couple lived from March 1, 1943, was comfortable and luxurious. Thus, the Lemoine couple, now confined in a more or less sincere religious mysticism, would meet in one of the upstairs bedrooms, Colonels Rea, a former military attaché in Berlin, and Rissler, a friend of Rivet, who was mobilized in 1939 to our Bureau.

Every day, at around 4 p.m., the changing of the guard took place in the inner courtyard of the building. The ritual was immutable, performed with an impressive rigor. The new guard positioned himself by the old guard. Upon the brash command of a mounted officer, honors were rendered in the striking of arms.

Captain Weichart and the adjutant Breuer, in charge of the Disciplinar Abteilung, were personally responsible for taking care of the Lemoine couple. Through the orderly who brought them food, the couple could request the purchase of anything they desired (including on the black market). Rex certainly didn't deny himself anything. Corrupt by nature, he was constantly greasing the palm of their attendant.

Everything was going well. The cozy atmosphere was welcoming. The same evening of their arrival, around 7 p.m., Oberst Rudolph came to greet his guests and thanked Lemoine for his excellent cooperation. The next day, March 2, 1943, the interrogations began. They would last nine months.

Wiegand, who led the questioning in the company of Frau Schmiedeler, his affable bilingual secretary, left Rex to speak at will; Rex staggered his revelations depending on his mood. At best he limited his questioning from time to time to the clarification of a detail. Referencing the files that he had committed to memory, he worked to gain the trust of his "friend." But his obsession, like that of his bosses, was to unravel the mystery of the Berlin leaks.

Sometimes hesitant to continue his odious work as an informant, Lemoine hid behind the responsibilities of his former assistant Drach. He spoke about Drach initially and at length:

"Believe me, Monsieur Wiegand, if I talk about him right now it's because he's working for our English enemies. This German Jew is a communist. He has a hatred of his homeland. Since 1933, he has denounced the work of the Third Reich. His book *Deutschland in Waffen* (*Germany under Arms*) is an accusation against the Reichswehr, whose secret weapons were in direct contradiction to the provisions laid out by the Treaty of Versailles."

Thus fully engaged, Rex masterfully pushed his collaborator forward, placed the man in front of him, as if to protect himself from some of his shameful initiatives. Wiegand and his secretary recorded his words, unflustered, listening to the endless stream of what the old man had to say:

"You will find Drach at the home of his mistress Nelly Goujat, on the first floor of 43, boulevard d'Arras in Marseilles. But be careful, he is concealing his identity under the name of Denis. It was Osvald, the director of police, who issued his false identity papers."

On March 5, 1943, before returning to the Hotel Continental, Wiegand summoned Henri Marette, a.k.a. Hubertus, to the Hotel Lutetia. He complimented him, gave him 10,000 francs as a thank you for his excellent work in Saillagouse, and assigned him to the Drach case.

"We need him as quickly as possible. Rush down to Marseilles, and do not hesitate to ask for assistance from our representatives and those of the S.D. if you deem it necessary."

With a new bonus of 10,000 francs, Hubertus would fulfill his mission within four months. On July 14, he discovered Drach hiding out in Nîmes.

With the help of the Avignon S.D., he had Drach arrested by the Feldgendarmerie on the afternoon of July 15, 1943. It was an eventful arrest. Drach decided to fight tooth and nail and opposed the Germans with fierce resistance. Taken initially to Nîmes prison, his body was found there the next day, July 16.

That day at 2:10 p.m., a telegram from the Marseilles Abwehr post informed Wiegand that Drach had committed suicide by hanging in his cell on July 16, 1943 at 4 a.m.

It was a strange end to a man of character who knew too much. His death would be concealed from Rex. Drach was quite knowledgeable about H.E.'s unique intelligence resources, their exceptional origin, and the quality and extent of the information provided. I am inclined to believe that he was driven to suicide or even murdered.

By July 1943, the Schmidt scandal had been causing commotion for over three months, traumatizing the highest German institutions and indeed Hitler himself. Even more than the Sorge case, the H.E. affair revealed an unprecedented attack on the security of the Reich. By discrediting its defense mechanism, by dishonoring the army, it could strike at the very core of a nation already shaken by the setbacks of the Wehrmacht. It was necessary at all costs to avoid such a disastrous outcome.

It took Wiegand, Protze, and occasionally Rudolph, fifteen days of interrogation, each one employing either a persuasive or threatening approach to force Rex to reveal the unimaginable. Between March 17 and 20, 1943, Rex would finally discard the last remnant of his scruples and reveal his ultimate and darkest secret.

It took a monumental set of documents seized from the Police Department and the National Security Bureau, evidence of trips to Switzerland and an extraordinary amount of funds deposited into an account in Basel, noted in his personal logbook, for Lemoine to have an excuse to reveal what he knew about H.E.

Everything was then exposed in an abundance of detail, from the meeting in Verviers when a needy Schmidt had been eager to monetize the secrets of the Chiffrierstelle, to the extraordinary delivery of intelligence and documents on the Enigma machine, the O.K.W., the Abwehr, and the Forschungsamt.

He told everything he knew of H.E.'s personal life, his relationship with his brother, his ability to evade the authorities, surveillance, his membership of the N.S.D.A.P., and his skill at concealing the origin of the considerable resources generated from his espionage activities.

Scheduled breaks allowed for a pause in the endless confessions. The old man took advantage of the opportunity to clear his guilty conscience and to try and justify his position in the eyes of the Germans, who were stunned by the magnitude of the case.

"H.E.'s greed and venality are such that having severed all contact with us since 1939,[244] I fear that he has sought out new resources by working for the Soviets…"

Late on the night of March 19, Rudolph joined Wiegand at the Hotel Continental. Now aware of all Rex's revelations he took stock of the extent of the disaster: the secrets leaked from the Chiffrierstelle, the Reich Chancellery, the O.K.W., the Forschungsamt, the R.S.H.A., senior officials, dignitaries of all kinds, of senior officers and generals who were compromised, either directly or indirectly, and especially the traitor's systematic looting over ten years of the thoughts and archives of his own brother and one of the greatest leaders of the Wehrmacht, General Rudolf Schmidt.

All the revelations previously made by Lemoine seemed unimportant. Yet one was nonetheless able to find among the jumbled dozens of agents or upstanding correspondents whom he had recruited and contracted such famous names as the former Ambassador von Hoesch, the former Reich Chancellor Wirth, the brother of aviation General Milch, Otto Hartmann, Friedrich Wegener, the Count Strachwitz, the nephew of Weltchek, the German ambassador in Paris…

Choking with emotion, Rudolph said: "Do not tell anyone of this new deal. Hear me well Wiegand, I say no one, including our colleagues at the Hotel Lutetia, including your direct superior Lieutenant Colonel Reile. Complete your report. Insist that Lemoine clarifies the nature of the intelligence that was supplied by Schmidt. He must give to you his particulars, his mailboxes, addresses. It is essential that there isn't any doubt about the person in question and his relationship with General Rudolf Schmidt. Hand the documents over to me tomorrow before 5 p.m. I will carry them to Berlin myself."

On March 21, 1943 at 10 a.m., Rudolph entered the Tirpitz-Ufer. Canaris, having already been secretly alerted to the situation, was waiting for him, alone, impatient, and anxious. For hours, the two men, isolated in the office of the head of the Abwehr, examined the numerous aspects of this huge revelation, and the considerable impact it might cause if it got out.

Canaris had a close friendship with General Schmidt. He knew all too well the respect Hitler had for him:

"The Führer's confidence in this great soldier is absolute. He entrusted to him on November 15, 1941 before Moscow, the command of our 2nd Army. A month later, on December 25, 1941 he then called him to the head of the 2nd Panzer Army to replace Guderian, who had been 'sacked'. Today he is confronting the Soviet offensive in the Orel region. What a spectacle! Do you realize our responsibility, and what a scandal this will provoke if this gets out into the public? We must at all costs keep Lemoine close to you and in the strictest of secrecy, especially vis-à-vis the R.S.H.A. Later, we will advise him on his future. Now that the origin of so many leaks has been established, we cannot allow the traitor to continue his dirty work for another moment..."

Canaris reflected for a moment. Perhaps he thought that this astounding revelation was likely to overshadow the suspicion that weighed on his friend and collaborator Oster. In fact, this would not be referred to again until another round of leaks was announced.[245]

He decided to pay Goering a visit and seek his advice. The plan was to locate and immediately arrest Hans-Thilo Schmidt, a plan which came to fruition on March 22, 1943. Goering, deeply surprised and shocked, asked Canaris to inform him of the results of the operation before reporting them to the Führer.

The investigation would be entrusted to Section III.F of the Abwehr with the assistance of the police from the G.F.P., chosen by Rohleder. It would initially take place outside of the R.S.H.A., in the greatest secrecy.

They were able to identify the traitor almost immediately. The Forschungsamt's organizational plan stated his official function: "Leiter (chief) of the Templin Forschungsstelle." His private home was listed in the phone book: Ketchendorf near Fürstenwald on the Spree.

For many months, Hans-Thilo Schmidt had been aware of the threats that were piling up against him. With complete lucidity he recorded each of them: the discovery in Warsaw of the work being conducted on the reproduction of the Enigma machine, the capture in La Charité-sur-Loire of the archives from the French General Headquarters and its Deuxième Bureau, which everyone in the Berlin military and police circles had taken pleasure in mocking, the abandoned French archives which the Abwehr, the S.D. and the Gestapo were all exploring… and above all the uncertain fate of Lemoine and the French S.R. officers he had met with on so many occasions. Finally, there was the formal system-wide survey on the staff of the Forschungsamt coming out of the Chiffrierstelle that had occurred in 1941. His phone was being tapped. His correspondence was being monitored. In the street he found himself constantly looking over his shoulder. He believed he was being watched. The constant uncertainty about his future had within two years destroyed all of his joie de vivre. H.E. was filled with anxiety.

His brother, overwhelmed with responsibilities and honors, didn't have much faith either; his letters from the Eastern Front were depressing, devastating for the Führer and the regime. He was overwhelmed with doubts. What was the point of taking so much? What was the point of having given to the French so many arguments and ways to bring a halt to Hitler's criminal madness? What was the point of all this tainted luxury, to end up miserable and unhappy? During the pre-war years he had been the rogue, the bon vivant, the jolly fellow, but now he had lost his insatiable thirst for money and adventure. Withdrawn into the monotony of a position that had become uninteresting and absent of any perks, his morale sank to new lows. His health was deteriorating.

One day, consumed with worry, harassed by somber thoughts, he slipped into the fold of his truss, which he never took off, a few cyanide pills.

At 6 a.m. on March 1943, the fatal climax arrived. The henchmen of the Abwehr finally cornered him. His house, the annexes, his office—everything was turned upside down and searched thoroughly. Everything was seized. Tightly handcuffed and surrounded, he was dragged to the fate he had long feared but never attempted to escape.

*

Here begins the mystery. For years I have tried to locate traces of his hypothetical trial. With assistance from official authorities of the

French, the Allies, and the Germans, I have searched throughout Germany and elsewhere. I wanted to know what his attitude was like, what he was able to reveal, what happened to him. Yet his name is not in any police or court records that I could find.

One could infer that interviewers, judges, friends, family, in short all his compatriots who had any knowledge about the existence and death of Hans-Thilo Schmidt, were seized by the shame of his monumental betrayal and decided to conceal from history these shady pages and the end of a story that offended their concept of honor.

There has been complete silence since March 23, 1943.

Could it be that the scandal, perhaps buried in the rubble of Berlin, was so unbearable that no one in Germany would ever be willing to take the risk of exhuming the memories of it?

The only testament to his downfall is the membership card declaring Hans-Thilo Schmidt's appurtenance to the Nazi Party. Marked with a diagonal line, it shows he was barred from the party.[246] On May 5, 1943 by Order Number 5.43/81 from the Brandenburg Kreisleiter, he was dismissed from the N.S.D.A.P.

In Berlin, in the offices of the administrative archives from the Tiergarten sector, Schmidt's death certificate, severely damaged by fire, was found. It was partially restored with great difficulty. His death was recorded on September 16, 1943 at 61 Lehrterstraße, the sinister street where the Moabit Prison, overseen by Himmler's S.S., was located.

Without any further data, I have had to resign myself to the conclusion that suicide (spontaneous or advised) was the most likely reason for his death. This responds most closely to what Navarre and I had thought about H.E. ever since the last meeting in Lugano. It coincides with writer-historian Gert Buchheit's affirmation:[247] "Hans-Thilo Schmidt was poisoned in his cell before the commencement of his trial at the Reichsgericht."

Like all my comrades, and Bertrand in particular, I had previously accepted that Schmidt had been shot in July 1943.[248] This hypothesis was primarily the result of statements from Rudolph and Wiegand. Their accounts, however, were not founded on any formal evidence.

Since March 23, 1943 a thick veil has hidden this event, which one could call the largest and most scandalous case of treason against Hitler's Germany.

The tragic fate of General Rudolf Schmidt

On April 11, 1943, on Hitler's personal orders, General Oberst Rudolf Schmidt, commander of the 2nd Panzer Army on the Eastern Front, was relieved of his command.

Due to the violence and uncertainty of combat, he was immediately replaced by General Heinrich Cloesner. There was no decision more serious, no punishment more degrading than the withdrawal of a combat leader—especially when his command was facing the enemy. When such a measure strikes down a great soldier whose notoriety gained on the battlefield has earned him esteem and respect, its resonance undermines the military hierarchy and develops into a state affair.

Goebbels[249] made no mistake about it. He noted in his journal on May 12, 1943:

"The Führer has gone over the heads of the generals. His main wish is to have nothing more to do with them. He carries over all of them a judgment that is overwhelming in its rigor, which is at times subjective and unfair. All told, he is relatively accurate. He explained why he no longer comes to lunch at the large table at the O.K.W. He is no longer able to see the generals! And it is not because he has become a misanthrope. Quite to the contrary. His old friends are welcome more than ever. But his colleagues as of recent times have simply not been able to win his heart and trust."

"'All of the generals are lying,' he said. 'All of the generals are infidels, all of the generals are against National Socialism, all of the generals are reactionaries.' This is obviously not absolutely true, but to a certain extent, our Führer is right.

"They are too often bitterly disappointed. On a certain level they are devoid of any spiritual and cultural sense and are thus incapable of finding anything in common with the Führer. They are infidels, they have no allegiance to him and a large part of them don't understand him.

"Thus, for example, an entire series of letters between General Oberst Rudolf Schmidt and his brother have just been found for which one had to arrest him for high treason.

"Very harsh judgments against the Führer appear in these letters. And moreover from a general of the highest rank in whom the Führer had placed all his trust. He has thus once again suffered a new and grave disappointment. He has suggested that no general could now ever offend him. This class of man has become totally foreign to him. Henceforth he will maintain a distance from them more than he ever has before…"

S.S. Reichsführer Himmler, with no reservations, sought to take command of the Wehrmacht. He clearly understood the Führer's mood with respect to the generals and the reasons for his bitter disappointment in Rudolf Schmidt. To achieve his military ambitions,[250] he needed the support of competent and disciplined leaders. Curiously enough he was referred by Hitler for this case; he would either plead the case himself or oversee the defense of Rudolf Schmidt against the Führer. He knew that this poor soul was the innocent victim of his brother's actions. He would obtain for him on July 10, 1943 an assignment with a command reserve. He would have no power, though, to avoid on September 30, 1943, two weeks after the death of H.E., his final dismissal based on the opinion of the Reichskriegsgericht.[251]

This was the supreme body of military law established by Hitler to handle this case and to determine the general's responsibility. In the evidence presented during the trial that brought about his disgrace, no allusion to his brother's betrayal was presented. Rudolf Schmidt was only blamed for his severe and open criticism of the Führer's war policy.

Kept informed by Canaris and the Oberreichskriegsanwalt[252] about the progress of the investigation into the activities of Hans-Thilo Schmidt, the Führer, after realizing he had lost Rudolf Schmidt's respect, measured the severity and extent of the secrets confided in his brother. Secrets and indiscretions had undoubtedly been made in good faith, but with a recklessness that made Rudolf appear especially guilty in his eyes, particularly since his responsibilities were great and a high degree of trust had been given to him.

On April 9, 1943 Keitel received the head of the 2nd Panzer Army at his command post at Hitler's headquarters in the Rastenburg Forest, in East Prussia. Very pale, deeply moved, the head of O.K.W. revealed to his distraught subordinate his brother's betrayal.

"The day after tomorrow you will send your necessary orders to Cloesner. You will then retire to your home in Weimar. There you will wait quietly for the Führer's final decision.

"I pity you. This case places your character in question as much as it does our most secret services. It would be dangerous for the morale of the army and the nation for the extent of this betrayal and scandal to be revealed."

General Rudolf Schmidt's ordeal was not over yet. It is characteristic that his peers, as well as historians of the Third Reich, have had the decency never to discuss his suffering. The silence should have buried the miserable end of his career. It took the Nuremberg trials for his character to be publicly questioned for a completely different set of motives that were infinitely painful and disturbing. I remember the facts. On September 30, 1941, after the Wehrmacht's lightning breach into the Ukraine, the Führer had decided to achieve a prestigious success by capturing Moscow. In late October, the German army arrived at the gates of the city, whose evacuation was underway.

Suddenly, the torrential rains of November transformed the ground into swamps, roads into quagmires. The offensive was brought to a halt. On the other side Zhukov finally received the reinforcements he had requested. Intelligence from Sorge, the Soviet agent in Tokyo, reassured Stalin about the Japanese threat and released Soviet troops being held in Siberia.

The cold weather set in, brutal, harsh: -20°C, -30°C... The Wehrmacht, paralyzed, stamped about on the icy fringes of the capital. The petrol was frozen, the engines wouldn't run, 100,000 people were evacuated in a matter of a few weeks for dysentery, frostbite, pulmonary disorders and so on. It was a complete disaster.

On December 5, 1941, along the thousand-kilometer front, Zhukov's counteroffensive transformed the retreat into a mad panic. Von Bock's army was dismantled, shaken up, and reduced to fleeing in complete disorder toward the Polish border.

Hitler suddenly appeared, shook up command, and replaced Bock with von Kluge, and Guderian with Rudolf Schmidt.

There was an orderly and restrained retreat, followed by a stampede. The Führer's orders were terrible: "… There, where the Russians have succeeded in breaching the front with the intent to reoccupy the surrounding villages, they find there nothing but ruins…"

A sinister order for which Rudolf Schmidt would pay the consequences, having done everything he could to combat it.

On February 22, 1946 General Raginsky, Soviet deputy chief prosecutor in Nuremberg, took the bench and made the following accusation:[253]

> In their insane hatred born out of defeat, the Nazis and the commander of the 2nd Panzer Army, General Oberst Rudolf Schmidt, created task forces to destroy cities, towns, and collective farms of the Orel region. Bands of looters destroyed monuments, burned towns and razed villages. Women, children and the elderly were murdered.

Raginsky cited the testimony of the Soviet Professor Bourdenko of the Academy of Medicine: "'… The spectacle I witnessed was beyond imagination. The survivors I met had an expression of mental stupor, indifferent to life, indifferent to death…'"

The professor completed his impressive testimony of February 13, 1946 with the following:

"In the Orel prison, it was the mass murder of prisoners of war: over 3,000 dead from lack of food. All in all, 200 grams of bread made with a mixture of sawdust, a liter of soup made from beans and moldy flour a day […] The survivors, gnawed on by vermin, living in groups of eighty in spaces no bigger than 20 sq m without heating, devastated by famine and exhausted by hard labor…"

It seems that such accusations hurled in a torrential flood from those who were condemning the major war criminals did not arouse the curiosity of the court. The former commander of the 2nd Panzer Army was not called to testify, which was perhaps justifiable.

In his Weimar retreat, peace returned. Isolated, abandoned, Rudolf Schmidt did not know about this new twist of fate when, a year later, in 1947, the Soviet justice system learned of his location, apprehended him and transferred him to Russia.

On January 10, 1955, weakened and exhausted, he was released on medical leave through the intervention of Chancellor Konrad Adenauer. Evacuated to the Krefeld hospital in the Federal Republic of Germany, he found his wife Frieda, and without great resources, they settled into a small, modest apartment on Bismarckstrasse.

Two years later, on April 7, 1957 at 4:55 p.m., General Oberst Rudolf Schmidt died at the Krefeld hospital.

I did not want to know any more.

Ultra-Enigma safe and sound in the storm

In April 1943, the Saillagouse gendarmerie contacted me in Algiers, where I had taken on the leadership of Military Security and Counterintelligence Services, to tell me that Lemoine had been arrested in late February. The circumstances led us to believe he was collaborating with the Abwehr.

This was serious. I informed Rivet, who was once again the official head of military intelligence services following his escape from France in November 1942. We decided to inform Gustave Bertrand, who had retreated to Théoule (Alpes-Maritimes), and who was preparing to take on leadership of our clandestine intelligence network "Kléber."

His answer was immediate. He confirmed Rex's arrest and his transfer to Paris. Even more worryingly, Bertrand announced the arrests on March 13, 1943 of Lieutenant Colonel Langer, Major Ciezki, Palluth, and two other colleagues from the Polish Cipher Bureau. Keen to reach London through Spain, but alas left to their own devices[254] for reasons that made no sense, these poor unfortunates had had to resort to travelling through a sector of the Pyrenean border that was controlled by the enemy. Incarcerated in the prison of Perpignan, then interned at Frontstalag 122 in Compiègne, they would be deported to Czechoslovakia on September 9, 1943.

What a horrible, devastating blow! More distressing still was that the Poles now in the hands of the enemy were outstanding specialists in cryptology. Unlike Lemoine and Schmidt, they were aware of the ultra-secret conditions under which Enigma messages were received, decoded and operated. Wouldn't the smallest revelation provoke significant changes in the transmitting Enigma machine, as well as its operational instructions? As the Allies prepared to set foot on the European continent in Italy, they were in need of reliable and accurate intelligence more than ever. The questioning of assumptions made at Bletchley, the ruin of so many years of work to break the encrypted transmissions of the Wehrmacht, would represent a veritable disaster.

General Menzies, notified of the arrests of the Polish technicians, was now aware of the whole situation. Unaware of their fate, what could the English do, other than increase their efforts to overcome any new cryptographic challenges and enhance the security measures surrounding the work of Bletchley? Their rigor was such that the few survivors of Bertrand's Polish team were kept separate from the moment of their arrival in England in late March 1943. This was particularly the case for Rejewski, the best of the Warsaw cryptologists, who would not be permitted to participate in the work of deciphering alongside the British scientists until the end of the war.

In Paris, the S.D. and the Gestapo eventually learned about the Abwehr's considerable successes. The S.S. claimed their piece of pie: on 5 May 1943, through Memo IV E12, the head of the R.S.H.A. in France asked Rudolph "on what date Lemoine and his wife will be available to be transferred to Berlin." They were unaware of the instructions given by Canaris to keep Rex in strict secrecy at the Hotel Continental.

Wiegand's response Number 135 clearly expressed the intransigent position of the Abwehr: "Transfer has not yet been planned. [Lemoine] must be used to obtain very important military intelligence."

Two days later, Lemoine noted that the name "Alison," mentioned several times in his address book, referred to Colonel André Perruche, the former head of the S.R. Research Division.

Perruche had a brother who was a pharmacist on rue du Cherche-Midi in Paris, not far from the Hotel Lutetia. It was easy for Wiegand to monitor this pharmacy. In less than two weeks, Perruche was spotted. Arrested on June 1, 1943 by the Abwehr, he was incarcerated in Fresnes. This was another blow. He too knew how successful the Allies had been with their decoding program. Would he talk?

Threats were starting to pile up against Bletchley's secrets—and it was not over yet. An ultimate blow: on January 5, 1944 at 8:40 a.m., Bertrand himself was arrested inside the Basilica of the Sacred Heart at Montmartre by a team of Wiegand's V.M.s led by Masuy.[255] Originally, it had nothing to do with the accusations against Lemoine and the Enigma case.

As head of our Kléber intelligence network, Bertrand had come to Paris seeking radio equipment made available by London. The intermediary responsible for handing the equipment over had been made known to the Abwehr. Instead of arriving at his meeting scheduled with Bertrand on January 5, the latter was apprehended. The false papers he had on him did not stand up to scrutiny. Masuy, who was interrogating him, quickly made him confess his true identity.

From that point on, his treatment changed completely. From avenue Foch, where a round of waterboarding might have been awaiting him (the satanic invention of the Gestapo and adopted by Masuy), he was transported to the Hotel Continental and placed in a comfortable room. Reference was made to the places frequented by the famous and generous Lemoine. The same Feldwebel official from the Disciplinar Abteilung wasted no time in alluding to the many services he could provide—for payment, of course. Unfortunately for him, Bertrand did not possess Rex's level of "comprehension," or the same financial means.

Having just arrived at the Hotel Continental, Wiegand, obsequious, greeted the French officer and chatted with him. He knew through Lemoine the positions Bertrand had held in the Cipher Service and at the S.R. Rudolph, stylishly dressed in civilian clothes, joined him a few hours later. He politely assured him that he'd have his turn to tell his side of the story. He suggested that "everything can still get better." A slight allusion to Asché: "… A real nasty affair where its Berlin supplier, finally unmasked, had to confess everything before being shot…" [256]

Nothing was said about Enigma, just a long diatribe about the communist threat and finally the proposal that Bertrand had seen coming for some time:

"You should help the country in its fight against the common enemy. Would you be willing to cooperate loyally with us? It would be understood that you would be asked to do nothing against your country… Your expertise would assist us with the double radio game with the British, who are your worst enemies…"

"Okay," replied Bertrand, who had his own ideas. "But I must be free. Nothing should arouse suspicion on the part of my friends with whom I have meetings in Vichy."

And so the agreement was made. In his book *Enigma*,[257] Bertrand offers an in-depth account of the conditions in which, on January 13, 1944, about eight days after his arrest, he managed to slip away from the Abwehr after alerting its network.

"… With my honor now safe, I disappeared and went into hiding…"

The Abwehr had a different idea about the concept of honor. On January 28, 1944 a search warrant was published with the following indication: "*Cdt B. ist sofort nach Ankunft in Clermont-Ferrand geflohen—hat Ehrenwort gebrochen.*" (Commander Bertrand has fled immediately after his arrival in Clermont-Ferrand—he failed to keep his word of honor.)

Both Algiers and London were advised of this feat, and combined efforts to evacuate our friend by air to England. It would take months to achieve. On June 3, 1944 at sunrise, Bertrand and his wife finally landed near Cambridge.

*

I had been in England since May 8, 1944, engaged in difficult negotiations with General Eisenhower's secret service. It concerned the finalization of an agreement with Allied Special Services about our relationships and mutual responsibilities in the liberated French territories. I absolutely had to obtain respect for our national sovereignty in terms of counterespionage activity.

Upon my arrival, I was presented by General Menzies himself to General Bedell Smith, Chief of Staff for the commander-in-chief and with the various heads of offices of the S.H.A.E.F.[258]

I still feel gratified at how they took me into their confidence and, before General de Gaulle had even been informed, revealed to me the outline of Operation "Overlord" and its launch scheduled for the first half of June 1944.

Bertrand's arrival—after his mysterious escape from France and having landed a few days prior to the date we had been told to expect him—had raised a few questions. Menzies knew that our comrade was familiar with the mechanisms of the Enigma ciphers and Bletchley's expertise. Was he brought here to reveal what he knew? For what price had he purchased his freedom?

After Lemoine, after Schmidt,[259] after the Polish technicians, after Perruche, had Bertrand, who was even more engaged at the heart of the matter than anyone else, broken his silence? Would the enemy, if he knew about the British prowess with Ultra-Enigma, continue his usual mechanical encryption to deceive the S.I.S.? Would he once again turn everything upside down? Would he again render their radio transmissions impenetrable? Just hours before the decisive offensive, would Allied Command be deprived of its "most valuable source of intelligence"?[260]

Two days before Bertrand's return, Menzies asked me to join him in his office. Affable, as usual, but anxious, he entrusted me with a number of serious security problems that were bombarding him:

"We have a twofold and terrible responsibility: to ensure the absolute secrecy of the landing operations in Normandy, and to ensure the success of the deception plan."

The chief of the S.I.S. knew that my staff were involved in the deception of the enemy within the framework of "Force A."[261] According to the S.H.A.E.F. guidelines, we were also responsible for using our agents embedded in the Abwehr to weight the assessment of the threats of landings in France away from the coast of Normandy. Without knowing the details of what my British and American comrades were doing, I was unaware of the vast operation of subterfuge being undertaken to convince the Wehrmacht to maintain the distribution of its forces from the Belgian border all the way to Brittany. It was the famous Operation "Fortitude,"[262] implemented over a long period by agents who had infiltrated the enemy and by the creation of a fictional U.S. Army, under orders from Patton, which was to be concentrated in the east of England, threatening the Pas-de-Calais.

"We have to rely on the interception and deciphering of messages by Bletchley to monitor the impact of Operation 'Fortitude,'" continued Menzies. "So far everything looks normal. But we wouldn't want to be victims of any decoys or tricks if our friends were to be arrested and forced to reveal the reality of 'Ultra-Enigma.' Our landing troops could risk falling into a German trap and come up against powerful reinforcements. The disaster would be irreparable."

This was the first time that the chief of the S.I.S. had elaborated on the brilliant work of British cryptologists with such frankness and detail, as well as the benefits he was expecting from Operation "Fortitude." Undoubtedly he had decided to share these secrets in order to stress the importance of the mission he was entrusting to me, and motivate me to complete it.

"Bertrand is your comrade, your friend. He is a great Frenchman. It is up to you, it is your duty, to get the whole truth from him, in order to ensure the security and quality of work at Bletchley Park. The outcome of the war may very well depend on this."

A thankless and tricky mission if ever there was one. I feared the shady character and the susceptibility of my old comrade, though I had no doubts about his courage or his loyalty. Certainly the circumstances of his escape were still unclear and posed some serious problems. It was thus due to me that on June 3, 1944, as soon as he arrived in London, the S.I.S. summoned Bertrand.

We were alone. Straightaway, I was immensely relieved. The spontaneous, unrestrained joy that Bertrand displayed as soon as he saw me was shocking. His look was sharp, blunt, familiar, like old times. For hours, alone together, we talked. I met him again the following day. Without hesitation, without omitting the smallest detail, sometimes with mystical impulses that surprised me, Bertrand told me about his adventurous life since our separation in November 1942. He answered my questions, happy to tell his story. My beliefs were confirmed: the Abwehr had been masterfully played.

If Rudolph or Wiegand spoke about Lemoine or Schmidt, at no time did they ever make reference to the arrest of the Poles or to Perruche in Fresnes. Never was there any question of Enigma, of any methods of deciphering, any results obtained by the Allies...

It was amazing! This incredible deficiency of the Abwehr remains for me a lesson. That Lemoine and Schmidt never offered a single revelation pertaining to technical issues is understandable. They were always kept out of the scientific achievements of Polish and English. On the other hand, I am bewildered that the Polish technicians, nor Perruche, nor Bertrand were never asked to explain the results of the exploitation of the Enigma machines that had been either reproduced or captured in 1940.

Certainly, the disruption of the Abwehr staff, a prelude to their dissolution in February 1944, could possibly explain Rudolph's attitude at the time of Perruche's arrest and especially that of Bertrand. But how should one understand the lack of insight with respect to the Polish scientists who were captured in March 1943? Everyone, I repeat, everyone, especially Langer, had been fully aware, down to the most minute detail, of the issues pertaining to the deciphering of Enigma messages. A simple examination of the situation would have revealed their expertise, the importance of their role and most likely the extraordinary exploits achieved at Bletchley.

Several explanations of this monumental oversight by the German intelligence services come to mind. One relates to their organization, and could serve as a lesson to all intelligence services throughout the world: an absence of a unified sense of direction and lack of a centralized filing system; the rivalry between the Abwehr and the R.S.H.A.;[263] a lack of coordination among law enforcement bodies; and perhaps also the mediocre quality of the personnel recruited in haste by Canaris and Himmler in 1935. The unshakable confidence that the Wehrmacht had in the reliability of its mechanical cipher systems might be another reason. As ludicrous as it may seem today, the Germans never seriously accepted that the Allies could break their codes using scientific methods. It was solely a matter of routine precaution that led to the Wehrmacht Command banning the use of radio transmissions in December 1944, in order to ensure the secrecy of its ultimate Ardennes offensive.[264] British surveillance fell silent for several days and were not able to supply Bletchley with the necessary intelligence. The Allies were taken completely off guard.

Such absolute confidence by the Germans regarding the privacy of their Enigma transmissions, along with their ignorance of the possibility that the Allies could decipher their codes, was confirmed by the conclusions reached at the international symposium organized around the subject from November 15 to 18, 1978 in Bonn and Stuttgart by professors Jurgen Rohwer and Eberhard Jaeckel.

German, British, American and Polish experts and historians all admitted to this fundamental flaw in the Reich's understanding of the scientific achievements made by the Polish and Bletchley.

Not a single French author was involved in the remarkable papers presented in a book published in 1979.[265] It is not surprising that the critical role of our Bureau was barely mentioned. Undoubtedly, we are the incorrigible ones absent in many areas of history.

The conclusion reached at the symposium, which was led by Professor Rohwer, can be summarized thus: "The Allied victory was certain. With Ultra-Enigma it was achieved more quickly and saved many human lives."

From the Abwehr to the Gestapo: Rex's tribulations

While at Torgau[266] under the leadership of the Attorney General, the war tribunal continued its investigation of the Schmidt case and its aftermath; in Paris, Lemoine remained the main attraction of Section III.F, the Abwehrleitstelle.

For nine months, Rudolph, Wiegand, and his secretary, with the slowness of all governments throughout the world and the meticulousness that characterized the German bureaucracy, listened to Rex.

Inexhaustible, the old man spilled his memories, condemning his best agents. The extent and quality of activities that he revealed left his interlocutors smugly satisfied with their accomplishment. Their attentive reactions, surprised, sometimes even enthusiastic, flattered the pride of the "prisoner of honor" and encouraged further confessions.

Every now and then, arrests were successful—not always convincing, sometimes annoying. Such as that of Bodo. This great agent of the S.R., of Austrian origin, had been recruited by Lemoine when he was a colleague of the Austrian ambassador in Paris. After the Anschluss, Bodo continued his diplomatic career at the German embassy. He was one of our most valuable informants in Paris.

From time to time, the interrogation, or, rather, I should say the hearing, paused.

One day, Rex was bedridden, victim for the first time of a serious case of hemoptysis. There was complete panic in the Disciplinar Abteilung: a succession of nurses, doctors, specialists, Rudolph and his subordinates, came to his bedside. The Feldwebel assigned to him saw to his every need, more dedicated and better paid than ever.

In April and June 1943, Lemoine, accompanied by Wiegand, took a few short trips to Berlin. The central office of the Abwehr and the Oberreichskriegsanwalt questioned him politely and requested a few details about his meetings with Schmidt, details supplied by H.E., his relationship with his brother, his payments… They never demanded from him details about the nature of the intelligence provided about the Enigma machine or its utilization. At no point did a cipher expert join the investigators.

This leads one to believe that they felt it was unnecessary due to the reliability of their encryption. I do not propose a hypothesis that Canaris deliberately downplayed this aspect of Schmidt's case in order to serve the Allied cause, because I know that Canaris showed unquestionable loyalty to his homeland.

Sometimes, the supreme leaders of the Abwehr, the Oberreich-skriegsanwalt himself and his deputy came to "interrogate" Lemoine at the Hotel Continental. A perfect excuse and opportunity to visit Paris. Only once, during a round of questioning that was more intense than usual, did the "Doctor" from Torgau want to know who, after Schmidt's departure from the Chiffrierstelle, continued through his intermediary to deliver intelligence to the French about this department of the Kriegsministerium. Faced with Rex's inability to satisfy his curiosity, Wiegand, full of zeal, once slipped up and threatened him—it was a short-lived incident.

Finally, on November 17, 1943, Rudolph, with permission from Canaris, decided to assign his guest to the S.D. and the Gestapo, who had been claiming him with hue and cry. After five and a half months of silence, the H.E. scandal seemed to be stifled. General Schmidt's fate was resolved without too much noise in September, and Hans-Thilo had died... discreetly.

The Abwehr "had nothing more to learn from Lemoine" and his collaboration as an agent no longer seemed useful or convenient. Rudolph had discussed the possibility with Rex, but Rex replied: "It's too late. You've burned me. I am too old, I just want to be in peace..." And peace he would have. He would also have his freedom, and it would be the Gestapo who gave him both.

On November 18, 1943 Lemoine and his wife were transferred from the five-star Continental to a residence in the four-star Hotel Louvois,[267] 1, rue Lulli in the heart of Paris. Their comfort would not be affected. Quite to the contrary.

They were welcomed by a smiling Kriminalkommissar Kieffer:

"Dear Monsieur Lemoine, the special commission created by the Berlin R.S.H.A. to deal with important matters such as yours has placed you at my disposal. I have carte blanche. I know it is no longer possible to consider your outside employment. The Abwehr has stupidly 'grilled' you. We have kept you too long making use of you. I invite you to help me. We will study together a few matters, nothing against France. Your advice will be valuable to me."

An agreement between the two men was reached. In reality, Rex's work would remain symbolic. Meanwhile he was able to observe the villainous games played by Kieffer's devoted team of henchmen. They were foreigners for the most part, a few French supervised by the S.S. of the Gestapo: Commissioners Sommer, Bock, Müller, Müssig. Everyone was armed to the teeth, possessed police identity cards and had a wide range of powers. The raids, based mainly on accusations, took place throughout France against patriots, Communists and especially against wealthier Jews. Jewelers were prime targets. The booty was what supported the gang. The remainder was (apparently) sent to the R.S.H.A. in Berlin.

It was like a wedding party at the Hotel Louvois after each mission. Keeping company with Kieffer's henchmen, Lemoine led a merry life at the hotel. Sincerely or not, everyone invited one another over to their homes. Champagne and money flowed freely. They frequented the good restaurants located between the Opera and Richelieu. The new year of 1944 earned Lemoine a pleasant surprise. Kieffer, to wish him happy Christmas and a New Year's gift, offered him his freedom:

"The only thing I ask of you is not to go far away. Continue to live here and to take at least one meal a day in our cafeteria."

A grateful Rex doubled his generosity: nightclubs, jewelry, perfumes to ladies, good bottles of alcohol to the gentlemen. Unsurprisingly his funds ran out. He himself admitted to having spent more than a million francs in a few weeks. He asked one of his sons to visit. Rex whispered into his ear that he was to go and retrieve the gold buried in the cellar of the small house in Saillagouse. It was the remaining gold, worth 170,000 marks, bequeathed by his father, a former jeweler in Berlin.

And so the good life continued, occasionally interrupted by handsomely paid interventions as a favor to friends having difficulties with the occupying authorities. But it did not last.

The Allied troops were approaching. On August 17, 1944 he had to leave.

"The last time I met with Lemoine," Wiegand later wrote, "was on August 18, 1944. It was at Châlons-sur-Marne. He was with his wife in a hotel with his friends from the S.D."

From one comfortable place to another, always paid for by Rex, the group arrived at Frankfurt an der Oder on September 1, 1944. The Lemoine household, virtually unmonitored, lodged at the Hotel Prinz von Preusse. With the assistance of the hotel manager, a staunch Nazi, Lemoine killed time by selling anything he could find in the Frankfurt of 1944 on the black market: meats, butter, American cigarettes, stockings, etc.

On February 9, 1945, under threat from Soviet troops, Berlin was undergoing a catastrophic upheaval. After a few days at the Hotel Albrecht the couple, who were now totally free, sought refuge with Lemoine's great-niece, who lived alone on 22 Wundstrasse.

The guns were getting closer. Stoically, not without courage, Lemoine endured the bombings in Berlin, always replenishing his stores in unexpected ways and methods: sometimes with the assistance of the Wehrmacht or the police, sometimes through the black market.

A few days after the armistice of May 8, 1945, a French repatriation office was opened on 96, Kurfürstendam in Berlin. It took the form of a strange French liberation committee led by Lemoine and a few Frenchmen who had come to the Reich capital in 1942 and 1943 either under the guise of "relief"[268] or with the S.T.O.[269] Established on May 1, 1945, on the eve of the General Weidling's capitulation, the last defender of the city, the committee was immediately made available to the Red Army "to help find or expose Nazis or enemies of the Allies."

Rex had a prominent position in the new organization. His knowledge of Berlin, of the German language, his intuition, and his people skills were of the greatest help. He knew how to paint a heroic picture of his past. His affiliation with the Deuxième Bureau, which he didn't hesitate to make known, brought him consideration and respect. In the disorder and confusion that reigned throughout the recently liberated capital, he took back his complete freedom without any discussion. He participated in the screening of the French, eliminated suspects, gave relief in the form of gold to French prisoners repatriated from Russia and in transit. He was a one-man band. Everything was easy and simple, including the resupplying of the small troop who, thanks to him, found unexpected resources on the black market or in the cellars of S.S.

However, the occupation of Germany was underway. My staff, who were searching everywhere, were finally able to track him down in Berlin. On October 27, 1945, to his amazement, he was arrested and flown to Wildbad in the Black Forest. This was the interrogation center of the French Counterespionage Bureau led by Colonel Paul Gerar-Dubot and his adjutant Captain Maurice Dumont. These were two of the best experts in my Bureau. In October 1944, I asked them to prepare to undertake in Germany, in conjunction with our allies, an extensive purging mission. They completed their mission perfectly.[270]

In this case, it was appropriate to determine the extent to which Rex, in the hands of the Germans, could be detrimental to our services and the interests of France. It was necessary to evaluate his share of responsibility for the terrible consequences of his "arrest." A difficult task.

In 1945, my comrades were far from possessing all the intelligence I now have today in order to write this book. The report they wrote in 1946 about Lemoine's hearings reflects their disappointment:

> … Preceded by an amazing reputation, even among our opponents, we had the greatest hopes for this opportunity to question Rodolphe Lemoine.
>
> Unfortunately, if his life had been so filled with excitement to the point of characterizing him as a hero in a true adventure story, nothing was left of this figure of international intrigue, of the man searching for gold in Guyana, of the high society corrupter, of the most famous intelligence agent of our time, other than an old man plagued by illness, sinking into the mysticism of his past life, sometimes having no memory of the events that created this character in the first place.

His interrogation was unintelligible.

In consideration of the services he had previously rendered, despite serious suspicions against him, he benefited from being a French citizen; due to his age and physical condition he received preferential treatment.

He was able to obtain from the outside what he needed in terms of medication, coffee, sugar, butter, brandy, etc. [...]

He was free to move about. He especially took advantage of this liberty by participating in certain discreet speculative operations for which he had particular taste...

The end for Rex

At the end of September 1946, I was in Baden, commanding a post of French occupation troops, having left my previous post a few months before.

General Koenig, commander-in-chief in Germany, and General Navarre, who became his chief of staff on July 7, 1945, invited me on a few hunting trips in the Black Forest. My friend Andre Poniatowski was a great master of such hunts. The program he had arranged for me allowed me to go from time to time to Wildbad. There I had the absolute joy of seeing my former subordinates. Their center was in full operation.

I could not resist the desire to see Lemoine.

"He still continues to recount stories from his past," said the boss, Colonel-Dubot Gerar. "He is incapable of breaking the habits of his former shady life. He is in the Carola house,[271] where you will find him in poor condition. He tried to buy a young N.C.O., believing that the boy could free him. I had to punish the one and increase surveillance on the other."

I interrupted my comrade to express my surprise: "How is he able to behave in such a corrupt manner at his age, with no money and no assets?"

"Lemoine is never short of resources, even with one foot in the grave. When this boy assured him that he could, through his contacts, gain his release, he gave him a glimpse of the substantial reward he could offer. He took his razor and carefully ripped the seam of the left shoulder of his heavy coat. From it he pulled out four gold coins. He gave them to the boy promising that the day he was free, he would find much more in the right shoulder... Dazzled, the soldier continued to make him promises but when Rex saw no return, he asked the lad to return the gold. When he refused, he turned him in! It wasn't pretty..."

In his modest room at the austere Carola house, Lemoine was sitting on his bed in his pyjamas. Unrecognizable, skeletal, unshaven, his eyes bright with fever; a bottle of cognac sat half empty on a wobbly night table. When I entered, he tried to get up. He recognized me. I invited him to sit. His voice was low.

I asked him about his health. Slowly, I encouraged him to tell me about his detention, his stay in occupied Berlin.

My presence seemed to please him and awakened in him memories of our pre-war meetings. Gradually, his speech became clearer, easier. He then spoke a lot, moving from one subject to another without any difficulty; he whispered to me about his accusations, the full extent of which I had never really known. I mentioned Schmidt's name. Without any emotion, he said that the Germans knew about his betrayal. Venomously, he sneered: "His greed is what brought him down. I am sure he must have gotten caught working for the Russians..."

With senile stubbornness, he kept returning to the influence he had had over the people at the Abwehr and even more over those at the Gestapo.

A question was burning on my lips. Finally, I asked:

"But, Monsieur Lemoine, how do you explain the freedom that you've been able to enjoy, while so many of our compatriots, who have caused much less harm to Germany than you, have suffered the worst hardships?"

He stared at me for a long time. Before responding, he clasped his emaciated hands and raised them in a gesture of offering:

"You will understand, my commander (he had remembered what grade I was during our last meeting). Over my thirty years serving the Bureau, I paid off ministers, ambassadors, military officers, policemen, civil servants. With 50,000 or 100,000 francs, sometimes with less, these people risked their freedom, their lives."

"Is it so incomprehensible that there were in the Gestapo in 1943 and 1944 S.S. commissioners who were willing to share 1,170,000 francs in return for granting me favors that cost them nothing and for which they would not even receive any punishment?"

His hands had fallen back onto his knees. He spoke no more, he appeared defeated. I left in silence. I never saw him again.

A few days later, on October 2, 1946, he did not get up. He told his attending officer, who visited the center at 8.45 p.m., that he was sick. He was coughing up blood. As soon as the officer alerted the military doctor, Lemoine was transferred to the hospital. At 11.30 a.m. on October 3, he succumbed to a violent attack of hemoptysis.

I felt this miserable end as the end of an era. One in which I myself had spent ten of the best years of my life as a soldier.

It was a period when intelligence research was achieved more or less through the singular resources of the reputable individuals involved in the project.

A "Belle Epoque" which inspired the spy novels of Charles Robert Dumas and Peter North. That of the Deuxième Bureau, of Captain Benedict…

Though unknown to the public, Rex and his super-product H.E. were the most effective intelligence agents of this secret war, providing modern espionage with the infinite resources of a science in which they had complete confidence.

They depended on nothing other than their exceptional capabilities and knew well that their rich and abundant harvests could not have been any better exploited through their efforts.

The fruits of their adventurous lives—and this is the very heart of the matter—contributed more than the efforts of any other agents to the successful outcome of World War II.

APPENDIX I

The *Wehrmacht* Enigma Machine

To facilitate an understanding of the problems faced by the Allies when deciphering mechanically encrypted messages by the German army, it seems useful to provide a few technical points regarding the Enigma machine used by the Wehrmacht during World War II.

Its mechanical complexity—as well as its rules of operation—explains its reliability and the enormous difficulties faced by the Allies when attempting to penetrate its secrets.

Externally the *Wehrmacht* Enigma looks like a portable typewriter topped with a display, including a keyboard and 26 lights, one for each letter of the alphabet.

The technician modifies the machine according to the key for a specific day. He types on the keyboard the letters of the message to be transmitted by the sensors.[272] For each letter typed on the keyboard, the substituted letter appears through the corresponding lights on the display.

The decoder[273] is in possession of a similar machine set with the same parameters. He types on the keyboard the coded message just as he received it from the radio station. The process of ciphering a code thus takes place in reverse. The plain text appears through the lights of the screen, under the principle of reversibility that is the primary characteristic of Enigma.

We know that decoders[274] can manage to penetrate the secrets of intercepted messages because they have a large number of messages that have been encrypted with the same key.

Military technicians of the Chiffrierstelle (Cipher Bureau of the German Ministry of War) sought to make it impossible for anyone to decipher the message unless they were in possession of the exact replica of the code originating from the Enigma machine emitting the message. They are oriented toward an electromechanical design allowing for the encryption of the same message with the greatest possible number of keys. Starting from a 1923 commercial version of the Enigma cipher machine, imagined by engineer Arthur Scherbius, the problem was gradually solved. In 1926 the first mechanically encrypted messages by the German Navy appeared. They were impenetrable. In 1928 it was the Army who then adopted a derivative of the commercial Enigma. Perfected in 1930, this modified derivative led in 1937 to the *Wehrmacht* Enigma cipher machine, which allowed for the creation of an infinite number of substituted combinations.

A description of the encryption "journey" of the letter O, for example, reveals the complexity and multiplicity of combinations allowed for that single letter, which, if repeatedly struck by the encryptor on his keyboard, would never give the same numerical result.

The basic device consists primarily of three electronically interconnected interchangeable and movable rotors (or drums).[275] On both sides, each rotor has an equal number of plugs (26) corresponding to the letters of the alphabet. They are connected two by two, according to an internal wiring permanently set within the construction of the apparatus.

The encryptor types the letter "O." This triggers an electrical impulse. The current enters into the first rotor through the plug corresponding to the letter C. The appropriate wiring for this rotor assures that the current goes from the letter C to the output plug corresponding to the letter I. This plug is in contact with the input plug of the second rotor corresponding to the letter connected to the output of the letter Q. The current enters into the third rotor through the letter K, which is output with W. The circuit is then reversed through a return drum which acts as a mirror. New substitution combinations based on the same principles as the outward process returns the current into the first rotor with the output of the letter X. This is the letter that lights up on the corresponding screen.

The second strike of a letter on the keyboard determines the shifting of one notch of the first rotor.

When the first rotor has completed a full rotation, the second rotor and the third rotor rotate in turn.

It is understood that several strikes of the same letter O may never result in the same letter of substitution.

This simplified—if not simplistic—description of the operation of the apparatus shows that variations in its setting can be determined simultaneously or successively by the number and the positioning of the rotors in service. This is the configuration of the machine. A few months before World War II, the Germans were up to five usable rotors, always in groups of three.

The deciphering of messages encrypted by Enigma required the following:
1. A machine to receive the message analogous to the one used for encryption;
2. The constant control of settings according to the daily configuration and keys of the machine emitting the encrypted message.

A twofold and formidable problem.

The reproduction of the military Enigma machine produced in 1933 by the Poles, thanks to the technical intelligence provided by the French S.R., was a decisive factor.

It was then necessary to determine the functional and constant alterations made to the keys on a daily basis, as well as the modifications made by the Germans to the basic machine.

What a headache.

That was the challenge for the high-level mathematicians, first the Polish, then British, to solve with the documents provided by Asché, including monthly tables providing the daily settings that were in use.[276]

If, on occasion, errors or omissions by the encryptors, along with the seizure, during the course of the conflict, of documents and Enigma materials facilitated the mathematicians' research, they had the science and perseverance to locate and improve the state-of-the-art material and scientific methods[277] which allowed the decoding and strategic exploitation of messages en masse within a reasonable amount of time.

For however great the merits and services rendered by the French S.R. and the Allied technicians, it would be wrong to imagine that their work resulted in reading all the internal communications of the Germans like an open book.

Apart from the fact that the decoding of Enigma messages was met with failures, the enemy in many cases used transmission methods that could not be intercepted: teletype, telephone, telegram, written and verbal messages.

In the above explanations and for sake of clarity, a very important change made by the German army to the original design of the commercial Enigma machine was not mentioned.

This concerned the addition to the machine's entry point of a wiring panel that, with the help of movable sheets, permitted the machine to increase the combinations of the daily settings.

And so the daily setting (the configuration) of the machine, as prescribed by the secret monthly table distributed to users includes the following operations:

1. Establishment of three movable drums[278] in a prescribed order;
2. Positioning the respective plugs of the three drums in relation to one another;
3. Organization of the movable plugs on the wiring panel.

The last complication: each message included a specific key. It was incorporated by the issuer at the beginning of the text to be encrypted. It forced a particular modification before the coding of each message of the positioning of the mobile drums on both the emitting and receiving machines.

Excerpt from a 1974 memorandum by Colonel S. A. Mayer, former head of Polish Intelligence

The French phase of the Enigma problem[279]

On October 1, 1939, Lieutenant Colonel Langer arrived in Paris. He had been invited by the French S.R. in order to continue his efforts on the cryptographic work with his Polish team. The Polish authorities—the new government in exile—gave him authorization to continue the research, given the impossibility of organizing an independent Polish service to conduct radio surveillance: an authorization upon which their cryptographic work depended.

On October 20, 1939 Langer and his group were incorporated into P.C. Bruno, located at the Château de Vignolles, some thirty-five kilometers to the southeast of Paris. The offices of P.C. Bruno were dependent upon the Cinquième Bureau (S.R.) of the French General Staff. Commander Bertrand (later lieutenant colonel) was in charge of P.C. Bruno. Langer was there as a representative of the Polish Army. Captain MacFarlane, a British representative from the British Cipher Service, was also present.

At P.C. Bruno in addition to Lieutenant Colonel Langer there were fourteen members of the Polish group, including cryptographic experts from the German section: Major Ciezki, W. Michalowski, Lieutenant Pazkowski, Lieutenant A. Palluth, civil employees M. Rejewski, J. Rozicki, R. Zygaslki, S. Palluth, K. Gaca, R. Krayewski, L. Fokczynski, and cryptologists from the Russian section, Captain Gralinski, Lieutenant S. Szachno, and the civil employee Smolenski.

Ten French officers were assigned to essential positions at P.C. Bruno. However, according to Lieutenant Colonel Langer's impressions, which I found among his papers, the French officers did not play an important role in the cryptographic work. In terms of the cryptographic work, the state that Lieutenant Colonel Langer found it in upon his arrival at P.C. Bruno was not especially brilliant. The French cryptologists were not using their reproduction of the Enigma machine to conduct new studies; they were only concerned about keeping the machine in good working order. The situation was completely different on the British side. In December 1939, Lieutenant Colonel Langer paid a visit to London and learned that an amount of 12,000 pounds had been allocated for the construction of new reproductions of the

Enigma machine. The research conducted on the Enigma was being actively encouraged.

P.C. Bruno had at its disposal three reproductions of the Enigma, constructed by the Polish. One was a copy given by the Polish to the French in August 1939; the two others were brought by Lieutenant Colonel Langer and produced from parts produced by the Polish. Everything else had to be destroyed after the 1939 defeat. Lieutenant Palluth would dismantle one of the machines so he could truly understand the technical design, thus allowing for the creation of other Enigma reproductions. Unfortunately, the new copies ordered by Commander Bertrand were not delivered before July 1941—in other words, too late. And so, only two machines were available at P.C. Bruno for the experts to use in their cryptographic research during the critical period of the Battle of France.

P.C. Bruno was in operation until June 23, 1940. The encrypted messages that were deciphered covered the period from July 6, 1939 to June 18, 1940. More precisely, messages relative to 110 days during this period were deciphered; thus 126 daily keys had to be discovered: for certain days, messages intercepted belonged to groups who were using different keys. The British participation in the discovery of keys was crucial: it represented 83 percent. The reason for such a high percentage is partially due to an agreement on the division of work: P.C. Bruno had to focus on the research, while the British were essentially responsible for performing the technical work and daily exploitation of the intercepted messages. It is clear that during this period the British were better prepared with respect to the interception of German radio messages and their deciphering, for they had more technical equipment. On occasion, P.C. Bruno received daily keys from the English for which it did not yet have the relevant intercepted messages.

The total number of telegrams delivered by radio that were read during the period between October 20, 1939 and June 23, 1940 by the Polish team at P.C. Bruno came to 8,440. Out of this number, 1,151 messages concerned the Norway campaign, 5,084 the France campaign, 287 were clandestine communications from the Germans with their agents[280] and 1,085 were messages coming in from the Russian sector. The 833 remaining messages came from a variety of sources (mostly Swiss). Among the messages concerning the French campaign, a few were of exceptional operational importance. They provided intelligence of great value on the movements and the order of battle of German units; such intelligence became available just in time to order countermeasures.

On June 26, 1940, P.C. Bruno ceased to exist. Its Polish personnel, under the direction of Lieutenant Colonel Langer, were evacuated by air near Oran and then to Algiers. Lieutenant Colonel Langer attempted to get in touch with the Polish authorities and to evacuate his group to England in order to rejoin with what remained of the Polish troops; he did not receive the necessary assistance from his French bosses.

At the end of September 1940, Lieutenant Colonel Langer was persuaded by Colonel Bertrand to return to France with his group—to the Château de Fouzes near Uzès. He once again received authorization from the Polish authorities to work in contact with the French, but this time, under Post number 300 of the Polish Secret Service (Exspozytura 300). According to intelligence contained in Langer's papers, the name of Post 300 was "Cadix"; the Algiers post of the Polish Secret Service which existed from August 1941 to January 1942, under the Polish code name of P01, and the French code name of "Post Z".

Throughout 1941, the work accomplished by Post 300 consisted of the decoding of 4,150 German radio messages and 2,435 Russian radio messages. Found among the German messages were interesting facts from the Luftwaffe network during the Balkan campaigns, which had been mechanically encrypted. Beginning in September 1941, the messages that were intercepted had the character of routine exercises. A few rare messages were intercepted coming from the Russian front.

The Russian telegraph messages encrypted with codes of two, three and four characters offered little useful intelligence. It was obvious that the discipline of radio communications had been reinforced: examples of irresponsible carelessness had become rare—code names were used more frequently for leaders, units, and locations. Nowhere in Lieutenant Colonel Langer's papers can be found evidence of detailed intelligence on Post 300's work in 1942. He simply mentions that the results were similar to those from 1941.

Other than the cryptographic work, which constituted the primary task of Post 300, there were secondary (though still extremely important) responsibilities. From March 7, 1941, the post had a direct radio connection with the Central Intelligence Bureau of the Polish Secret Services operating in London and in close contact with "Commander" Dunderdale from the British S.I.S. This radio connection was used as a link between Lieutenant Colonel Bertrand (Bolk) and Commander Dunderdale.

The role performed by Post 300 as an intermediary between the Algiers post of the Intelligence Bureau of the Polish Secret Service ("Rygor" station) and the central headquarters in London was no less important. Rygor's mission was to gather together intelligence that would serve as the organizational basis of the future Operation "Torch."[281]

APPENDIX III

Clarification from General Bertrand regarding the subject of the Enigma equipment and Anglo-Polish-French relations

On April 15, 1976, a few weeks before his death, General Bertrand sent me a "point of clarification" intended to enlighten me and my comrades on his role in the "Enigma" affair, a role which he claimed was "massacred" [sic] by certain British authors.

Here is the essence of that communication:

In the presence of counter-truths which are spreading about the origin and arrival in Great Britain of the Enigma coding machine, I owe it to myself to restore the truth such that I personally experienced from 1931 to 1939 during the course of the following:

- Eighteen special missions abroad to contact a German agent who was on staff at the Chiffrierstelle[282] and to photograph in my hotel room the documents he had brought to me.
- Twelve technical liaisons in Warsaw in order to deliver the results of each meeting to the Polish Cipher Bureau and to prepare with them the questions for the following meeting according to the progress of the research on the mechanically encoded messages that had been intercepted by each of our organizations.

I declare on my honor the following:

All of the documents and intelligence (Asché) were communicated to the Polish Bureau, who relentlessly continued its research and knew how to magnificently make use of the intelligence.

As for the British Bureau, it maintained no relation with Warsaw, for neither party trusted one another… it was difficult to place them in contact with one another.

Despite this, London was kept up to date about the existence of certain documents. It did not appear to be too interested judging by the German threat, which it deemed uncertain and not urgent. In reality they had absolutely no knowledge about the Enigma machine. We'll see later how this turned out.

After the Anschluss (March 1938), London realized that danger was approaching and that the machine had a role to play if they could focus their efforts on it. My connection thus allowed me to understand that they were indeed completely in the dark regarding the Enigma matter, for the documents that I brought caused quite a stir and left them wanting more.

I alerted Warsaw myself and accepted to eventually collaborate with London. This is why, one day in January 1939, a meeting between Polish and British cryptologists was organized in Paris to clarify the matter: no light was shed on the issue, with neither of the parties wanting to admit [what they knew], but a hope was born out of it (especially on the part of the Polish).

A friendly luncheon took place at Drouant on January 10, 1939 to… get to know one another better, at which the following were present:

- From the Polish side: Lieutenant Colonel Langer and Major Ciezki.
- From the British side: Commander Denniston, Monsieurs Knox and Foss.

It was in July 1939 that the big event took place: I had succeeded at acquiring an invitation for those from London to Warsaw […] where there was something new awaiting them.

Indeed so, I went there with Captain Braquenié (our only expert on the subject) and London sent Commander Denniston, Monsieur Knox, and Commander Sanswith (head of the Interception Bureau of the Admiralty […] who gave the impression of being on a temporary posting!). The British delegation stayed at the Hotel Bristol and we stayed at the Hotel Polonia…

On the morning of July 26, everyone was driven to the 'Forest Station' (Piry) where the actual meetings were to take place.

The Wehrmacht Enigma, entirely reproduced by the Polish Bureau (thanks to all of the documentation received by us and our super-brains), was presented to everyone: this was a stunning moment for Denniston and Knox […] and it was there that, for perhaps the first time, the pride of the British technicians succumbed to the results that the Polish experts had been able to obtain. They recognized, however, that Great Britain was able freely to take advantage of an eight-year-long Franco-Polish friendship, forged at the cost of a dozen or so connections from both sides, maintained in mutual confidence.

Finally, they couldn't believe their ears when we were told that two copies of the machine were destined for us, one for Paris and one for London, which would be delivered to me before our departure, I would then clear my arrangements with London, since I had crafted the affair.

A grand lunch followed at the restaurant of the Hotel Bristol, at which were the following:

- From the Polish side: Colonel Mayer, Head of Polish Intelligence, Lieutenant Colonel Langer, head of the Cipher Bureau, Major Ciezki, his adjutant.
- From the British side: the delegation.
- From the French side: the delegation.

On the next day, each one returned to their countries. The two machines were delivered by diplomatic valise to Paris. You know the rest…

General Bertrand concluded his report by sending me the text of the long citation awarding him the DSO on July 25.[283] It reported:

1. *Bertrand's trusting relationship with the S.I.S. and the supplying top secret intelligence on Germany prior to the war.*
2. *The clandestine pursuit of connections with the S.I.S. beginning in 1940 and the quality of intelligence delivered henceforth.*
3. *Bertrand's arrest and escape in 1944.*
4. *The importance of services rendered to the British Intelligence Bureau and to her allies.*

Note on the conference in the Reich Chancellery, 4.15 p.m.–8.30 p.m. November 5, 1937 [284]

In attendance: The Führer and Chancellor of the Reich Adolf Hitler, Field Marshal and War Minister von Blomberg, Army Commander-in-Chief Colonel General Baron von Fritsch, Navy Commander-in-Chief Admiral Dr. h.c. Raeder, Luftwaffe Commander-in-Chief Colonel General Göring, Reich Foreign Minister Baron von Neurath, Colonel Hossbach.

The Führer first declared that the subject of this day's conference was of such importance that its discussion would certainly be a matter for full Cabinet meetings in other countries, but the Führer himself had decided not to discuss the issue before the wider circle of the Reich Cabinet, simply because of the importance of the matter. His following declarations were the result of thorough deliberation and the experiences of his four and a half years of power. He wished to explain to those present his fundamental ideas concerning the opportunities and necessities for the development of our foreign policy, in the interests of a long-term policy. He requested that his declarations be considered, in the event of his death, as his last will and testament.

The Führer then declared:

The aim of German policy is the security and the preservation of the nation—and its expansion. It was therefore a matter of space.

The German nation comprises more than eighty-five million people and, because of their number and the density of inhabitable space, forms a homogenous racial corpus that no other country could equal, and as such implies the right to a greater living space greater than that of any other nation. If there exists no resulting political policy to respond to the need of this racial corpus for a vital living space, which was a result of centuries of historical development, and if such political conditions continued, it would present the greatest danger to the preservation of the German nation (*Volksturm*). Instead of an increase, there would be stagnation, and in consequence, tensions of a social character would arise within a certain number of years, because political and ideological ideas are of a permanent nature as long as they are capable of providing a basis for the realization of the vital demands for the Volksturm. Germany's future was therefore wholly conditional upon the need for vital living space. Such a solution could be sought, of course, only for a limited period of about one to three generations.

Before tackling the question concerning a solution to the problem of vital living space, one must decide whether a solution of the German perspective, which has a chance for success in the future, could be attained by means of either self-sufficiency, or by means of an increased participation in the world industrial economy.

Self-sufficiency: Its implementation would only be possible in the case of a National Socialist policy, which is the basis for self-sufficiency; and if one admits that this can be accomplished, the results would be as follows:

A. In the domain of raw materials, with only a limited rather than total self-sufficiency, the following could be achieved:

1. When it is possible to use coal as a source of raw materials, self-sufficiency is possible.
2. In the case of minerals, the position is much more difficult. The demands for iron and light metals can be sourced domestically, however, this is not the case with copper and tin.
3. Synthetic textiles can be supplied domestically, as long as one has access to timber supplies. A permanent solution is impossible.
4. Edible fat. Possible.

B. In the case of food supplies, the option of self-sufficiency must be completely avoided.

With the general rise in the standard of living compared with that of thirty or forty years ago, there has been a simultaneous increase in demand and an increased personal consumption, even on the part of the producers. The fruits of the increased agricultural production were intended to respond to the increased demand, and so do not represent an absolute increase in production. A greater augmentation in production, by making greater demands on the soil, is not possible, because it is already showing signs of depletion, due to the use of artificial fertilizers; it is therefore certain that even with a maximum increase in production, participation in the world market would be unavoidable. The considerable expenditure of foreign exchange to order to insure food supplies through imports, even when harvests are good, would grow to catastrophic proportions when the harvests are really bad. The possibility of such a disaster grows in proportion to the increase in population, and an annual of birth rate over 560,000 would lead to a further increase in bread consumption, since a child is a greater consumer of bread than an adult.

Confronted with long-term difficulties of maintaining food supplies, lowering the standard of living and rationing would be impossible on a continent enjoying a practically common standard of living. Just as the solution of the heating problem proved that the ability to consume would deplete resources, while a few minor modifications in our domestic agricultural production would be possible, they would not represent a complete transformation of the standard of food consumption. Thus self-sufficiency would become impossible particularly with respect to food supplies, but also in general.

Participation in the world economy: there are limitations with this which we are unable to escape. The fluctuation of the market would be an obstacle to the secure establishment of Germany's position; international commercial treaties would offer no guarantee for a practical implementation. One must consider, in theory, that since the Great War from 1914 to 1918, industrialization has been established in countries which had formerly been food exporters. We are living in an age of economic empires in which the tendency to colonize can be compared with the original impulses that drove man to colonization in the first place; in Japan and Italy, economic motives underlie their desire to expand, and it is this economic need that will equally push Germany to do likewise. Countries outside the great economic empires have unique difficulties for economic expansion.

The growth trend in the world economy caused by the effects of rearmament could never form the basis of a sound economy over a long period, and the latter was also hindered by an economic collapse caused by Bolshevism. There was a distinct military weakness in those states which based their existence on foreign trade.

As our exports and imports are carried out over the sea routes dominated by Britain, it is more a question of transport security than one of foreign exchange, which explains the major weakness of our food situation in wartime. The only remedy, which might appear fanciful, lays in the acquisition of a larger vital living space—an effort which has at all times been the origin of the formation of states and the migration of nations. Such a motivation was met with no interest in Geneva, nor in any state whose daily needs were being satisfied. If the security of our food situation must be our principal concern, the space necessary to insure it can only be sought in Europe, not, as in the liberal-capitalist view, in the exploitation of colonies. It is not a matter of conquering a population, but it is a matter of conquering usable space from an agricultural point of view. It would be equally advantageous in our view to search for areas producing raw materials in Europe and in immediate proximity to the Reich, and not overseas; the solution should be implemented for one or two generations. The development of great universal bodies is naturally a slow process and the German people, with its strong racial roots, for this purpose, has the most favorable prerequisites in the very heart of the European continent. The history of all ages—the Roman Empire, the British Empire—has proved that each territorial expansion can only be carried out by breaking down resistance and taking risks. Setbacks are inevitable; neither in the past nor today has the search for space been achieved without having to deal with someone who already possessed it. The attacker always comes up against the owner.

The issue for Germany is to obtain the largest conquest at the lowest cost. German policy has to contend with two enemies, Britain and France, for whom a German colossus in the center of Europe would be intolerable. Both of these countries would be opposed to any further strengthening of Germany either in Europe or overseas; in support of this opposition they would have the support of all their allies. Both countries would consider the establishment of German military bases overseas as a threat to their overseas communications, as a safeguarding of German commerce, and, as a consequence, a strengthening of Germany's position in Europe.

England is not in a state to yield to us any of its colonial possessions, given the resistance that it was up against in its dominions. After England's loss of prestige due to the transfer of Abyssinia to Italy, a return of East Africa could no longer be expected. Whatever type of resistance that would come from the British would at best be represented in an offer to satisfy our colonial demands by the appropriation of colonies which are at the moment not in British hands, for example Angola. French concessions would probably be of a similar nature.

A serious discussion concerning the return of colonies could only be considered at a moment when Britain was in a critical situation and the German Reich was well armed. The Führer does not share the opinion that the British Empire is unshakable. Opposition against the Empire was to be found less in the conquered territories than among its competitors. The British Empire and the Roman Empire cannot be compared in terms of their duration. After the Punic Wars the latter did not have a single serious powerful political rival. It was only the disintegrating effects of Christianity, and the signs of age that appear in every nation, which made possible the submission of ancient Rome to the ancient Germans.

With the British Empire, there exist today a certain number of nations stronger than her. The British motherland was only able to protect her colonial possessions only in alliance with other states, and not through her own power. How, for instance, could Britain alone defend Canada against attack from America, or her Far Eastern interests against attack from Japan.

The choice of the British Crown as the symbol of the unity of the Empire is in itself already admission that the Empire can not be maintained in the long run through a policy of power. The following points provide significant evidence of this:

A. Ireland's struggle for independence.
B. The constitutional struggles in India, where Britain's half measures left the door open for the Hindus to use the nonfulfillment of her constitutional promises as a weapon against Britain.
C. The weakening of Britain's position in the Far East by Japan.
D. The opposition in the Mediterranean to Italy who, due to her history, and pushed either out of necessity or under a spell, was expanding her position of power, and thus as a result has encroached more and more on British interests. The outcome of the Abyssinian War is a loss of prestige for Britain, which Italy strives to increase by stirring up trouble in the Mohammedan world.

One must establish in conclusion that the Empire could not be maintained through a policy of power by 45 million British, in spite of the solidity of its ideals. The ratio of the population of the Empire to that of the motherland is 9:1, and this should be a warning to us: the foundation constituted by the numerical strength of our own people must not be allowed to become too weak in our territorial expansion.

France's position is more favorable than that of Britain. The French Empire is better placed geographically; the population of her colonial possessions represented a supplement to her military strength. But France is confronting her own internal political difficulties. For the moment only approximately 10 percent of nations have parliamentary governments, whereas 90 percent have totalitarian governments. Be that as it may, we must take into consideration the following nations as political powers: Britain, France, Russia, and the smaller adjacent countries.

Germany's issue can only be solved by a show of force, which is never without risk. The battles of Frederick the Great for Silesia and Bismarck's wars against Austria and France involved immense risk, and the swiftness of Prussian action in 1870 had kept Austria from entering the war. If we accept the following explanations, the decision to resort to force with the risk that comes with this, then it remains for us to respond to the following questions: when and how? With regard to this we have three different cases to consider:

Case 1: Period from 1943–1945

After this we can only expect a change for the worse.

The rearmament of the army, navy, and the Luftwaffe, as well as the formation of the officer corps, is practically complete. Our equipment and weapons are modern; if we delay, the danger increases that they will become obsolete, in particular the secrecy of "special weapons" cannot be preserved forever. The mobilization of reserves would be limited to current recruitment by age group and an addition of older groups for whom training would no longer be possible.

We would lose our relative power in comparison with the rearmament which will have been carried out at this time by the other nations. Given the absence of reserves, if we do not act by 1943–1945, each year could only lead to a food crisis and we would have to address the issue without the necessary foreign exchange. This must be regarded as a weak point in the regime. And besides, the world will expect our attack and increase its countermeasures each year; while other nations are isolating themselves in defense, we are forced to take the offensive.

No one today knows what the actual position will be in 1943–1945. However, it is certain that we are not able to wait any longer.

On one hand, the powerful armed forces and the necessity to meet their needs, the aging of the Nazi Party and their leaders; on the other hand, the prospect of a diminished standard of living and of a decrease in the birth rate, which leaves us no choice but to act. If the Führer is still alive, his decision will certainly be irrevocable to resolve the problem of vital living space before 1943–1945.

The necessity for action before 1943–45 will be elaborated in cases 2 and 3.

Case 2:

If social tensions in France were to lead to a domestic political crisis so crucial that it would completely absorb the French army and render it incapable of participating in a war against Germany, then the time for action against the Czechs will have come.

Case 3:

It will be equally possible to act against Czechoslovakia if France is so engaged in a war with another country that she would be unable to act against Germany.

For the improvement of our politico-military position, our first objective, in the event of our being embroiled in war, must be to overthrow Czechoslovakia and Austria simultaneously in order to minimize any threat to our flanks, in the case of a possible advance to the west. In case of a conflict with France, it would be unlikely that Czechoslovakia would declare war on us on the very same day as France. However, Czechoslovakia's desire to join in the war would increase in proportion to any weakening on our part. Her actual participation could clearly take the form of an attack on Silesia, either to the north or to the west.

Once Czechoslovakia is overthrown and a common German–Hungarian border is obtained, a neutral attitude on the part of Poland with regards to a German–French conflict could be more easily conceived. Our agreements with Poland remain valid for as long as Germany's strength remains unshaken. If Germany were to encounter any setbacks, an attack from Poland against East Prussia, and possibly against Pomerania and Silesia as well, must be taken into consideration.

Summarizing a development of the situation which would lead to a systematic attack on our part in 1943–45, the conduct of France, Britain, Italy, Poland, and Russia should probably be judged in the following manner:

The Führer personally believes that almost certainly Britain, and probably France as well, have already silently written off Czechoslovakia, and that they have become reconciled to the idea that this matter would be cleared up in due course by Germany. The difficulties of the British Empire and the prospect of being pulled into another long European war are decisive factors in Britain's desire not to participate in a war against Germany. Britain's attitude would certainly not be without influence from France. An attack by France without British support is unlikely, presuming that its offensive would be brought to a standstill along the western fortifications. Without Britain's assistance, it would no longer be necessary to envisage an attack from France in Belgium and in Holland, and nor would we have to consider it in case of a conflict with France, given that in every case, the consequence would entail the hostility of Britain. In any case, we will have to close our borders during our attack against Czechoslovakia and Austria. One must equally take into consideration that the Czechoslovakian defenses will grow in strength from year to year, and that the internal strength of the Austrian Army will also increase over the course of time. Even though the Czech population is not weak, the incorporation of Czechoslovakia and Austria would nevertheless constitute an increase in food requirements for five to six million people, provided there is a compulsory emigration of Czechoslovakians along with one million people from Austria. The annexation of these two countries into Germany means, from a politico-military point of view, a substantial advantage because it would mean better and shorter frontiers, the freeing of forces for other purposes, and the possibility of creating new units up to a level of about twelve divisions, that is, one new division per million inhabitants.

No opposition against the elimination of Czechoslovakia is expected from Italy, however, one cannot be sure today what its attitude would be regarding Austria, that would largely depend upon whether il Duce was still alive or not.

The degree and swiftness of our action will determine Poland's attitude.

Poland will have little inclination to engage in war against a victorious Germany—with Russia behind her.

One must confront Russia's military intervention by the swiftness of our operations. It was a matter of knowing if this has to be taken into consideration, given Japan's attitude.

Should Case 2 arise (the crippling of France by a civil war) the situation should thus be seized, regardless of the time, to launch operations against Czechoslovakia, given that Germany's most dangerous enemy would have been eliminated.

The Führer sees Case 3 approaching; it could emerge because of the present tensions that exist in the Mediterranean, and if it occurs, the Führer is resolved to make use of it regardless of the year, even if it is as early as 1938.

In the light of recent experiences during the Spanish War, the Führer does not see any early end to the hostilities in that country. Considering the length of time that Franco's offensives would demand, it is possible that the war could last for three years. On the other hand, from the German perspective, total victory for Franco was not desirable either. We are no longer interested in a continuation of the war and preserving the tensions in the Mediterranean. If Franco were the sole possessor of the Spanish Peninsula, this would signify the end of any intervention from Italy, and Italy's presence in the Balearic Islands.

Given that our interests are focused on the prolongation of the war in Spain, the goal of our future policy must be to strengthen Italy in order to take hold of the Balearic Islands. However, any reinforcement by the Italians on the Balearics would be intolerable both to France and Britain, and might lead to a war by France and England against Italy, in which case Spain, should she be entirely in the hands of the Whites, might take sides with Italy's enemies. Italy's defeat in such a war appears to be unlikely. Raw materials could be brought into Italy through German routes. The Führer believes that the Italian military strategy would be to remain on the defensive against France on the Western Front and to take against France in Libya, against France's North African possessions.

Given that a landing by French troops on the Italian coast could be eliminated, and given that a French offensive over the Alps toward northern Italy would be very difficult and would probably come to a halt before the powerful Italian fortifications, the French lines of communication threatened by the Italian fleet will cripple to a large extent the transportation of combat personnel from North Africa toward France, to such an extent that France will only have troops from the mainland at its disposal on its borders with Italy and Germany.

If Germany takes advantage of this war while resolving the Czech and Austrian problems, one has to presume that Britain, herself at war with Italy, would not launch a war against Germany. Without assistance from Britain, an attack from France against Germany should not be expected.

The date of our attack against Czechoslovakia and Austria must be independent of the progress of the Anglo-French-Italian war, and would not necessarily coincide with the commencement of military operations by these three states. Nor was the Führer thinking about military agreements with Italy but, taking advantage of this favorable occasion and in complete independence, commencing operations against Czechoslovakia. The attack against Czechoslovakia will take place at lightning speed (*Blitzartigschnell*).

Field Marshal von Blomberg and Colonel General von Fritsch, giving their appraisal of the situation, repeatedly emphasized that Britain and France must not appear as our enemies, and declared that the war with Italy would not commit the French Army to such an extent that it would not be in a position to unleash operations on our Western Front with superior forces.

Colonel General von Fritsch estimated that the French forces which would be dispatched to the Alpine border against Italy would consist of twenty divisions, with the result that a strong French superiority would still remain on our western borders, which, according to the German view, will attempt to invade the Rhineland; moreover, one must take into account and consider the advanced progress of French mobilization; this renders the four motorized divisions destined to the west more or less mobile, in view of the minimal value of the old positions of our fortifications—which was indicated especially by Field Marshal von Blomberg. In terms of our offensive toward the southeast, Field Marshal von Blomberg drew particular attention to the strength of the Czechoslovakian fortifications, the construction of which had become like the Maginot Line, and which would be difficult to attack.

Colonel General von Fritsch mentioned that this was the purpose of a study which he was conducting this winter, which was to examine the possibility of conducting operations against Czechoslovakia with special consideration given to conquering the system of Czechoslovakian fortifications. The Colonel General also expressed his opinion that due to existing circumstances he must delay his personal leave to go abroad, which was due to begin on November 10; the Führer gave him a counter-order due to the fact that the possibility was not imminent. In response to declarations made by General Field Marshal von Blomberg and Colonel General von Fritsch concerning France and Britain's position, the Führer repeated his previous declarations and stated that he was convinced by Britain's non-participation, and as a result did not think France would take military action against Germany. If the Mediterranean conflict mentioned above were to lead to a general mobilization in Europe, it would then be necessary to launch operations against Czechoslovakia. If, on the other hand, the Allied powers who were not participating in the war were to declare that they themselves were no longer interested in the matter, Germany, for the time being would adopt the same attitude.

Given the intelligence provided by the Führer, Colonel General Goering considered that it was imperative to think about a reduction or an abandonment of our military intervention in Spain. The Führer was of the same opinion provided that such a decision could be delayed to a more opportune date.

The second part of the conference dealt with matters of armament.[285]

Signed: HOSSBACH

Appendix V

Conference with Admiral Canaris on December 9, 1937

STATE SECRET

December 10, 1937

The following were in attendance at the conference that began at 3.00 p.m. and ended at 4.20 p.m.:

Head of the Abwehr, Admiral Canaris, Lieutenant Colonel Bamler, Abwehr III, Lieutenant Colonel Oster, Abwehr III C,[286] Captain Protze, Abwehr III F,[287] Permanent Secretary Doctor Best, Ministry of the Interior (S.I.P.O.[288]), R.R.[289] Doctor Kurzbach—Forschungsamt (F.A.).

The conference began with a long presentation from the admiral whose obvious goal was to bring Doctor Best up to date about what has occurred.

He stated the following: a meeting of the heads of the three military branches, including Field Marshal von Blomberg, took place at the Führer's private apartment on November 5, 1937. During the conference, the matter of the distribution of steel among the three branches was discussed. Against the desire of the others, the Führer decided that the navy should receive 20,000 tons. A number of superior officers in the anterooms were discussing, at times vehemently, this issue of distribution. Thus a veritable debate commenced between Secretary of State Körner (F.A.) and an admiral. Orderlies and servers offered port and we wore out the telephone.

As it came from a confidential memorandum of the Forschungsamt, François-Poncet wrote up a proper report of this meeting the very next day. Statements made prior to the meeting thus confirmed that François-Poncet had at his disposal excellent sources of intelligence.

Canaris informed General Field Marshal von Blomberg about this and with his agreement, the question was posed to all present in order to discover if they had any idea of the origin of such an indiscretion.

Their responses were negative.

But in a general manner their responses brought attention to the intensity of discussions taking place in the anterooms, and that this aspect of the matter must be taken into consideration.

As far as he was concerned, Canaris, through his role, was obliged not to trust anyone, including the most senior officers, and to follow any lead, this being even more the case for Major Kaupisch, brother of the general of aviation, who has a close and suspicious relationship with François-Poncet, as well as with a questionable Italian who was suspected of espionage. In a strange incident, François-Poncet visited Kaupisch in a munitions factory he owned in southern Germany.

Major Kaupisch and his brother the general could not be held responsible. Neither of them had any more knowledge than Canaris himself about this meeting.

It is possible, however, that the officers present, who went to the Hunter's Ball immediately following the conference, which François-Poncet was also attending, continued discussions between them, possibly in the presence of their wives.

Furthermore, it is worth noting that the last sentence of François-Poncet's report, which General Beck brought to Canaris' attention, expressed the opinion that the question regarding the distribution of steel to the navy was secondary and was not the only reason for a meeting at the Chancellery with so many general officers present.

General Beck's opinion was that François-Poncet knew that his diplomatic code had been deciphered. His last sentence indicates that he knew much more about the situation and that he would deliver his intelligence through a separate courier.

In fact, the "war plans" were discussed throughout the meeting.

And thus the Rhineland operation in 1936 had not been kept secret. Hoffman, from the Czechoslovakian legation, knew about it the day before. By chance, he had spoken about it with one of our agents who had reassured him and thus avoided a failure of the operation.

With everyone present at Hitler's meeting having responded negatively, Colonel General Goering wrote to Canaris that he had already located the source of the indiscretion. Lieutenant General Bamler further explained that he had observed Goering launch an inquiry (through the F.A.) and had discovered the possible source. Canaris clarified that the matter was very sensitive, for in this case it concerned the Chancellery and the Führer's apartment. Colonel Hossbach confided that the Führer would not tolerate an investigation on the personnel of his cabinet. Bamler elucidated that for such an investigation to take place, the Führer would have to provide authorization.

Canaris met with Goering, who drew his attention to Lescrenier and to the report he wrote for the Forschungsamt. The admiral received a copy of it and shared it with the other officers present.

Doctor Best expressed his surprise that Captain Wiedemann[290] was in contact with a character as shady as Lescrenier: he knew him personally and had quite an unfavorable opinion of him. Canaris responded that the Abwehr had much respect for Wiedemann. He had the intelligence curse like others who are avid devotees of Canaris and wanted to penetrate the secrets of the French intelligence services.

Canaris recalled that the purpose of the meeting was essentially to locate at all costs François-Poncet's source of intelligence. Such an achievement would require an unparalleled level of collaboration. He was directing this particularly to Doctor Best, whom he considered a dear and good friend, as well as to the signatory of the present C.R., expressing his hope that he could count on the complete collaboration of the F.A. Occasionally there would be misunderstandings among the staff members, such as the Kampmann case. In this matter the F.A. disagreed with the Abwehr. The signatory not being up to date minimized the importance of this incident and affirmed that the F.A. was completely cooperative and friendly.

Canaris, without responding to this affirmation, claimed to have been annoyed and that he would agree to forget the matter, which had never been fully clarified. He emphasized that the indiscretion of the Chancellery was raised by him and that its progress should necessarily be centralized through the Abwehr.

Doctor Best responded neither positively nor negatively.

Canaris proposed:

1. "a close surveillance of the French Embassy, of Lescrenier and of 'The Tavern' restaurant." To this end, a long discussion on a reciprocal agreement between the agents of the Abwehr and the Gestapo achieved no clear conclusion. The details would have to be the subject of a meeting between Doctor Fischer from the Gestapo (Schambacher had been let go by Canaris) and Lieutenant Colonel Oster.
2. "Swift and complete communication by the F.A. of the results of the French Embassy surveillance." Concerning this latter point, the admiral observed that the F.A. offered an opinion without submitting any original documents to the Abwehr. The signatory responded that the intercepted conversations were often only in fragments and

of little interest, however, the essential points were fully reproduced in the analyses provided by the F.A. He hoped that, henceforth, the Abwehr would receive the entirety of the reports and quickly. He offered the opinion that the common mission of the Abwehr and the Gestapo would oblige the F.A. to disseminate its interceptions to both departments. Canaris responded that the work of circulating the intelligence gathered by the F.A. did not fall under his jurisdiction. The signatory observed that communication via telex would only be possible at the beginning of the afternoon, which the other attendees confirm. He then added that transmission is only available to the Gestapo in case of emergency and he would request Doctor Best to assign transmission of the K. K. Wipper to Doctor Fischer. He requested that the F.A. be kept informed of the results of the surveillances by agents from the Abwehr and the Gestapo and be invited to future meetings. Doctor Best approved and Canaris offered no objection. Oster is in agreement, provided his telephone number and requested to be in close contact with him.

Canaris asked if the F.A. had any further propositions. The signatory called attention to the obligation to alert the head of the government, in order to obtain authorization from the Führer if the sources of indiscretion led to the Chancellery, and if the F.A. were to decide to tap its lines and to put forth false intelligence in order to detect the origins of the leak and to adjust the surveillance from the Abwehr and the Gestapo. The proposal was approved. Canaris asked whether the Chancellery was currently being monitored by wiretapping. The signatory showed his surprise by such a question; he clarified that such interceptions would require preliminary authorization from the head of the government and that the latter had no reason up to now to propose to the Führer surveillance of his own Chancellery. Canaris concluded that if this hypothesis were to become reality, it would be advisable to alert Goering.

In summary:

Intensive surveillance over the French Embassy, Lescrenier, and his entourage.

Embedding an agent into "The Tavern" restaurant.

The distribution of labor to be determined between the Gestapo and the Abwehr.

The F.A. to communicate Lescrenier's telephone conversations via telex to the Abwehr and the Gestapo.

The creation of a list of every German in contact with any members of the French Embassy.

Transmission via telex of all meetings by members of the French Embassy with any Germans or with anyone under suspicion.

Canaris remained after all the other attendees left, with Doctor Best, in order to discuss two other matters.

Signed: Doctor Kurzbach
December 10, 1937

Appendix VI

Excerpts of declarations signed by Lemoine (Rex) for the Abwehr

After having given as much detail as possible on Schmidt's recruitment and work with the French S.R., during the previous days, Lemoine concluded his deposition on this subject on March 20, 1943:

… His involvement with the German intelligence services lasted around ten years. He left the Chiffrierstelle two years before the war.[291] It was not because of any sort of reprimand or punishment; I was trying to persuade him to win his brother over to our side. He stated that this was absolutely impossible. If the latter had the slightest suspicion on the "work" he was doing, he would have immediately put a stop to it. […] His wife did not know about his connections with Intelligence […] Schmidt always needed money. I have the impression that our remunerations were no longer enough for him during the later years. He was in touch with another foreign power—I have no doubt about that. And for that very reason, I would consider this man to be very dangerous. I still have to add that after having left the Chiffrierstelle, Schmidt, upon my recommendation, continued to stay in contact with his friends from the War Ministry […] He took advantage of his brother's friendship to learn about the activities of his General Staff and to get us even more interesting intelligence on its armaments, the formation of new units, the motorization of the Wehrmacht, as well as political intelligence on military locations, on the strategy and tactics of the Reich, on the general situation, and so on.

April 27, 1943:
I declare that for the 25 years I was involved with the Deuxième Bureau, I dealt with a thousand other matters outside of the ones for which I have been interrogated and about which I have voluntarily spoken to you.

I am prepared to inform you about other cases, but I have a failing memory. I am 73 years old. I need time to reflect. […] My principal activities were directed against Germany. My specialty consisted in the trafficking of codes. This was my greatest success.

Thanks to my suppliers, I established for myself a global network of connections. I am fully prepared to resume certain relations for the greater interest of the Reich [...] I can seek out contacts in southern France with organizations supported by the British. The trustworthiness of the contact[292] with whom I will collaborate is certain. We will have the opportunity to penetrate the escape routes of British and American prisoners and to control the flow of British currency between Spain and France.

July 8, 1943:
...I had no need to go in search of people to spy against Germany. The majority of them instinctively sought me out [...] In the files of the National Security Bureau or the police department which you have presented to me, which are all marked with the stamp "Counter espionage," I can tell you that they are about persons working for the Deuxième Bureau. The proof is in my own file, which has the same stamp. This is how I was able to intervene with the National Security Bureau, and on behalf of the Deuxième Bureau, in order to obtain residency cards, passports, etc. [...]

Ever since I have been in contact with the Deuxième Bureau, I have been prohibited from working against the United States. It was the same for Britain.

Appendix VII

Excerpts from the journal of General of Infantry Schmund, head of the Personnel Service of the Army High Command

July 10, 1943: Colonel General Schmidt, commander of the Second Panzer Army, was placed in the army command reserve.

This decision followed charges of high treason against his brother due to his espionage activity for the Deuxième Bureau.

During the examination of his correspondence, letters from General Schmidt to his brother were discovered, where he was giving his opinion on policies that created an environment in which it was impossible for him to continue his position. In particular, he criticized the High Command and accused it of having committed mistakes that led to harsh consequences. The Reichsführer S.S. was informed about his comments.

August 22, 1943: Colonel General Schmidt sent a letter to the Reichsführer S.S. arguing for his reinstatement.

The Reichsführer S.S. responded that it could only advise him to supply the Führer with proof of his good faith. The war could still provide this opportunity in such a way that reinstatement wouldn't be entirely impossible.

September 2, 1944: At the request of the Reichsführer S.S., General Burgdorf once again sought benevolence from the Führer in favor of General Schmidt. The Führer categorically refuses to reinstate him.

September 13, 1944: General Burgdorf intervened yet again with the Führer pleading on behalf of the Reichsführer S.S. to obtain the reinstatement of General Schmidt in the active army. The Führer's refusal is definitive.

Notes

1 Paul Paillole, *Services Spéciaux, 1935–1945*, Paris, Éditions Robert Laffont, 1975.

2 On this initial period, see Simon Kitson's study, *Vichy et la chasse aux espions Nazis*, Paris, Autrement, 2005.

3 On the Bureau of Anti-National Activities (B.M.A.) and on the Rural Works Program (TR), see the works of François Delalez, Olivier Zajec, and Gauderic Vannier, who wrote the first monographs during their time at the Saint-Cyr Military Academy, Coëquidan. See also Olivier Forcade, "Services spéciaux militaires, 1940–1944," "Travaux ruraux: le contre-espionnage clandestin, 1940–1944," "Renseignement et résistance," in François Marcot, Christine Levisse-Touzé, Franois Leroux (director), *Dictionnaire de la Résistance*, Paris, Robert Laffont, collection "Bouquins," 2006, pp. 211–213, 216–217, 755–756.

4 On the role of Marseille, see Simon Kitson, The Marseille Police in their context from Popular Front to Liberation, Doctoral Thesis, University of Sussex, 1995.

5 On North Africa, see Christine Levisse-Touzé, *L'Afrique du Nord dans la Guerre 1939–1945*, Paris, Albin Michel, 1998.

6 We are not the first to discuss this end period of the war during which the "fusion" of various services provoked a violent clash regarding the question of political legitimacy of secret action led by one or another. This question is noted by Sébastien Laurent in Olivier Forcade, Georges-Henri Soutou, Jacques Frémeaux (director), *L'Exploitation du renseignement*, Paris, Economica, 2001. On the B.C.R.A., see Sébastien Albertelli, *Les Services secrets du général de Gaulle*, Paris, Perrin, 2009, and, more generally, the groundbreaking work by Louis Crémieux-Brilhac, *La France libre. De l'appel du 18 juin à la Libération*, Paris, Gallimard, 1996.

7 Gustave Bertrand, *Enigma ou la plus grande enigma de la guerre, 1939–1945*, Paris, Plon, 1973.

8 Archives of Colonel Paillole, SHD 1 K 545.

9 Sophie Cœuré, *La Mémoire spoliée: les archives français, butin de guerre nazi puis soviétique*, Paris, Payot, 2007.

10 David Kahn, *The Code-Breakers, the Comprehensive History of Secret Communication from Ancient Times to the Internet*, New York, Scribner, 1996. Even if the question of Enigma represents only a small part of David Kahn's seminal work of over 1,180 pages, the author retains an important position here due to his work with the journal *Cryptologia*, and his extensive articles on topic. Among these see David Kahn, *Seizing the Enigma, The race to break the German U-Boat Codes, 1939–1943*, New York, Barnes and Noble Books, 2001.

11 Gustave Bertrand, *Enigma ou la plus grande énigme de la guerre 1939–1945*, Plon, 1973.

12 Gordon Welchman, *The Hut Six Story, Breaking the enigma codes*, London, Allen Lane, 1982.

13 Sir Francis Harry Hinsley (director), *British Intelligence in the Second World War*, London, HMSO, 1979–1990, 4 volumes.

14 Władysław Kozaczuk, *Enigma: How the German Machine Cipher Was Broken, and How It Was Read by the Allies in World War Two*, University Publications of America, 1984.

15 In 2011, *Cryptologia* published its 35th volume, with the number 2/2011, for a total of 134 editions published.

16 Among the numerous articles, of note is the bibliography offered by David Kahn, "The Biggest Bibliography," *Cryptologia* 1/1977, pp. 27–44; Kahn, "The Forschungsamt: Nazi Germany's most secret Communications Intelligence Agency," *Cryptologia* 1/1978, pp. 12–19; and more recently, David Alvarez, "Wilhelm Fenner and the Development of German Cipher Bureau, 1922–1939," *Cryptologia* 2/2007, pp. 152–163. One should also mention a review of the recent book by Mavis Batey, *Dilly—The Man who broke Enigmas* (Biteback Publishing, 2009), not only dedicated to Marian Rejewski but also to Dilly Knox, who placed a central role in the work on the Enigma machine at Bletchley Park.

17 Note for example the English version of an article by Gilbert Bloch, who had been in regular contact with Paul Paillole: "The French Contribution to the Breaking of Enigma," *The Enigma Bulletin*, 1/1990, pp. 3–15.

18 *Intelligence and National Security,* Great Britain, Routledge.

19 *The Journal of Intelligence History,* Germany, The International Intelligence History Association, since 1933.

20 Hugh Sebag-Montefiore, *Enigma, The Battle for the code*, London, Weidenfeld & Nicolson, 2000. It includes an excellent index and a very good bibliography which includes a number of unedited documents.

21 Christopher Andrew, Vassili Mitrokine, *Le KGB contre l'Ouest, 1917–1991, Les archives Mitrokhine*, Paris, Fayard, 2000.

22 *Ibid.*, p. 82.

23 *Ibid.*, p. 83. Note 36 clarifies: "Paillole, *Notre espion chez Hitler*, p. 132. The meaning of the negotiations is rarely very clear. But according to Mitrokhine's notes 'Orel' (Bertrand) passed to Reiss a new Italian cipher on November 1933."

24 "1905–2005, W Stulecie urodzin Marian Rejewskiego" (On the 100th Anniversary of Marian Rejewski's Birth), *Przegl d Historyczno-Wojskowy*, Rok VI (LVII) NR specjany 5 (2010), Warszawa, 2005.

25 Władysław Kozaczuk, *W Kr gu Enigmy (In the Orbit of Enigma)*, Warsaw, 1979; Kozaczuk, *Enigma, How the German Cipher Machine Was Broken,* University Publications of America; Władysław Kozaczuk, Jerzy Straszak, *Enigma, How the Poles broke the Nazi code*, New York, Hippocrene Books, 2004.

26 Jean Medrala, *Les Réseau de renseignements franco-polonais, 1940–1944*, Paris, L'Harmattan, 2005.

27 Olivier Forcade, *La Républic secrete. Histoire des services spéciaux français de 1918 à 1939*, Paris, Nouveau Monde editions, 2008.

28 Peter Jackson, *France and the Nazi menace. Intelligence and Policy making, 1933–1939*, Oxford, Oxford University Press, 2000; R. Gerald Hughes, Len Scott, *Exploring Intelligence archives. Enquiries into the secrete State*, New York, Routledge, 2008; Forcade, *La République secrete*, pp. 311–318 (beginning with the Moscow archives).

29 General Louis Rivet, *Carnets du chef des services secrets, 1936–1944*, annotated and

presented by Olivier Forcade and Sébastien Laurent, Paris, Nouveau Monde editions, 2010.

30 External Documentation and Counterespionage Service. General Lacze is the former Army Chief of Staff.

31 Alias of the German Hans-Thilo Schmidt.

32 The position of the mobile elements of the machine which are set each day by a secret monthly rubric distributed among its operators.

33 It is estimated that there were approximately 70,000 Enigma machines at the beginning of 1940.

34 The settings for this specific secret being analyzed are referred to under the name of "Ultra."

35 Special service created by Goering for interceptions, wiretapping, and decoding.

36 Head of the Intelligence Bureau.

37 Head of the Deuxième Bureau of the Army General Staff.

38 General Colson, Army Chief of Staff.

39 Japanese Secret Service.

40 Baron Alexandre Schenck, living near Brussels, a personal friend of Lemoine.

41 Reichswehrministerium.

42 Approximately 800 French francs in 1985.

43 Oschmann later became commander of the 338th Grenadier Division in the Vosges and was killed on November 14, 1944, engaged in combat against the French 1st Army when he took control of the Belfort breach. Having been the "victim" of the French Intelligence Bureau in 1931 and 1932, Oschmann this time fell "victim" to a deception created by our Counterespionage Bureau directed by General de Lattre. General Schlesser, who was one of Schmidt's officers, participated in the groundwork of this operation, which was fatal for the 338th Division and its chief.

44 Roughly equivalent to 5,700 French francs in 1985.

45 Schmidt himself chose the alias of Asché a little later, which means "ashes," prophetic intuition of his fate or phonetic translation of two letters from our alphabet?

46 75 rue de l'Université was in 1931 an inconspicuous annex of the War Ministry used by the military's Special Services, which was officially known as the Intelligence Section (S.R.) or the Central Intelligence Section (S.C.R.).

47 Address of the French embassy in Berlin.

48 Colonel Laurent, one of Colonel Rivet's predecessors at the head of the military special services (S.R. and C.E.).

49 Bertrand used this alias, which was expressly chosen by Schmidt, whereas Rivet, Perruche, his collaborators and I referred to the informant by the initials H.E.

50 Around 500 meters from 2bis, near the metro stop "École Militaire."

51 Lemoine was in the habit of playing music on his portable radio whenever he had a confidential rendezvous. He believed that this would prevent anyone from overhearing his conversation.

52 Concerning a secret document meant for the daily settings of the machine, in other words the configuration for both the transmitting and receiving Enigma machines.

53 Approximately 100,000 French francs in 1985.

54 Head of the Lille Intelligence Office, in frequent contact with the Central Intelligence Office in Paris due to his particular knowledge about Germany.

55 Assault sections (*Sturmabteilung*) of the N.S.D.A.P.

56 An intelligence officer since 1920, Rivet was a German specialist. After having directed the S.R. in Germany, Belfort, and Lille, he was called to Paris to take up the position of adjutant to the head of military Special Services of the Deuxième Bureau (S.R.-S.C.R.). He would be the supreme leader of these services from 1936 to 1944.

57 Notably, Maurice Dejean would be the French ambassador to Prague from 1945 to 1949, and to Moscow in 1955.

58 General von Schleicher, Reichswehr Minister.

59 The report, closely read by the author, insisted on the fact that of these 100,000 men, the Reichswehr claimed that 74,644 of them were non-commissioned officers or corporals on July 1, 1932.

60 Future leader of the Abwehr (Intelligence and Counterespionage Bureau of the Army).

61 Such as the key settings being prepared for October 1932.

62 Cipher Bureau.

63 Falling in two trimesters, it allowed one to determine the trimestrial setting for the order of the drums. The H.E.'s previous intelligence had not yet offered the possibility to make such an observation.

64 Organization of the National Socialist Party in the business sector.

65 Military academy.

66 State of mind.

67 *Land* (plural *Länder*) is a state within the German federal structure.

68 *Schutzstaffeln*: elite troops of the Nazi Party and Hitler's private guard under orders from the S.S. Reichsführer Heinrich Himmler.

69 Himmler and Heydrich lived in Munich, the first seat of the N.S.D.A.P.

70 Roehm would be assassinated under orders from Hitler on 1 July 1934, on the same night as other S.A. leaders (The Night of the Long Knives).

71 The creation of the Forschungsamt was ordered on April 10, 1933, that of the Gestapo on April 26, 1933.

72 Paul Körner would be nominated Secretary of State to the Prussian Ministry of the Interior on November 30, 1933, and would remain in this position until 1942.

73 "… Confronting a disarmed Germany, disarmament is a moral obligation. Confronting a German who is rearming herself, disarmament […] becomes a necessity for the defense and peace of a nation," Jacques Kayser, *La République*, August 3, 1933.

74 In his book *Le 2e Bureau au Travail*, Édition Amiot-Dumont, p. 122, General Gauché sees it in these terms: "The Deuxième Bureau, thanks to the vigilance of the Intelligence Bureau (S.R.), has been able to extract the essentials from this effort and penetrate the meaning and destination of new messages as they eventually come to surface."

75 Ministry of Aviation.

76 H.E. handed over the Heeres M. documents. The contents only dealt with the daily settings of the Enigma in service in the Army.

77 Chief and Deputy Chief of the Forschungsamt.

78 Accomplished on April 20, 1934.

79 Accomplished on April 22, 1934.

80 Accomplished on April 24, 1934.

81 In less than a month, H.E. would respond by letter using invisible ink.

82 Excerpt from notes and letters of appreciation given annually by the Chief of Staff to his colleagues.

83 Testimony of General Gauché, head of the Deuxième Bureau of the Army General Staff.

84 Colonel Rudolf Schmidt was still the head of the Kriegsakademie (War Academy).

85 This is the prefiguration of the doctrine for the use of Panzerdivisionen illustrated by Guderian. Rudolf Schmidt's lesson would earn him the name "Panzer-Schmidt": "*Als 'Panzer-Schmidt' in die Heeresgeschichte eingegangen.*"

86 Head of the S.D.

87 Future head of the S.D. in occupied France.

88 Future head of special S.S. missions.

89 Lacking his current address and not having been able to obtain his agreement, I do not feel authorized to give his name.

90 Schlesser effectively had to fulfill a certain amount of time commanding a cavalry regiment beginning on January 1, 1935. He would return to the Bureau to take charge of Counterespionage (S.C.R.) with me as his adjutant.

91 Cf. Rivet's regimental diary from June 28, 1934.

92 H.E. was alluding to the tentative failure of the Nazi invasion which would cost the life of Chancellor Dollfuss and would provoke the massing of some 60,000 Italians on the Brenner Pass.

93 In actuality the brother of General Milich would deliver the construction plan (*Aufstellungsplan*) for German aviation to Rex in the first months of 1935 (cf. Rivet's Journal).

94 Law (announced by Schmidt) punishing treason or attacks against the regime.

95 Headquarters of Goering's Ministry of Aviation.

96 Rivet, Schlesser, Perruche, Bertrand.

97 Königsberg, Breslau, Stettin, Dresden, Nuremberg, Nordhausen, Munich, Stuttgart, Frankfurt, Cologne, Hamburg, and Berlin.

98 Former Reich chancellor from December 3, 1932 until Hitler's rise to power.

99 Head of the N.S.D.A.P. and second in command of the party until 1932.

100 The prosecutor Justice Jackson didn't even make reference to the primary responsibilities of the Forschungsamt: wiretapping and radio decoding.

101 Reichssicherheitshauptamt, Central Office of Reich Security created by Himmler and led by Heydrich (1939–42), then by Kaltenbrünner (1943–45).

102 On February 18, 1935, Benita von Falkenhayn and Renata von Natzmer were beheaded in the Plötzensee prison in Berlin.

103 It would take place on March 7, 1936.

104 Oberquartiermeister III (Organization—technical matters).

105 Announced to High Command by Rivet upon Perruche's return from Basel and confirmed by various other intelligence sources.

106 Allusion to the pro-German position of this publication.

107 High Command of the Army.

108 Daily newspaper of the National Socialist Party.

109 General von Fritsch.

110 Admiral Raeder.

111 General Goering.

112 Thus how our diplomatic telegrams were read and the codes of our internal military liaisons were breached, including those of the Navy. Heinze Bonatz, former officer to the Cipher Bureau of the German Navy, confirms this fact in his book *Seekrieg im Äther*, Verlag E.S. Mittler and Sohn-Herford, p. 45.

113 Headquarters of the War Ministry and the Army General Staff.

114 Ministry of the Interior.

115 General Gauché, *Le 2ᵉ Bureau au travail*, Éditions Amiot-Dumont, p. 34.

116 In his book, pages 48 and 49, General Gauché reproduces a sketch furnished below by H.E.

117 Organization responsible for preparing governmental decisions regarding matters of defense. Presided over by the Minister of National Defense and War (Daladier), in included the Ministers of the Navy (Campinchi), the Air Force (Pierre Cot), Marshal Pétain, and the principal leaders of the Army.

118 See in Appendices the official translation of the secret minutes, a copy of which had been located in Berlin in 1945 by the Allies.

119 Head of Section III (Counterespionage) of the Abwehr.

120 "Calm down!"

121 Goering, the supreme leader of the Forschungsamt, Minister of the Air Force and still President of Prussia.

122 His name was Lescrenier.

123 Cf. Rivet's journal.

124 I don't have authorization to reveal his name.

125 High Command of the Army (similar to the Army, Navy, and Air Force General Staffs).

126 On Goering's order, these conversations were recorded by the Forschungsamt. Recovered by the Allies in 1945, these recordings were examined by the prosecution during the war crimes trial in Nuremberg.

127 Future head of the R.S.H.A. Condemned to death by the Nuremberg trials.

128 On March 12, 1938 Rivet notes in his journal: "Summoned by the War Cabinet (which transmits current affairs) to explain 'the inconceivable suddenness' of this operation!!!"

129 It was recommended to Schmidt to never post multiple letters at a time in the same mailbox—or in mailboxes under the same jurisdiction of the same post office—when sending his messages to our Bureau.

130 Section specializing in counterespionage in France.

131 What Lemoine asserted was correct (cf. Paul Paillole, *Services Spéciaux, 1935–1945*, Éditions Robert Laffont, p. 91).

132 Ministry of Foreign Affairs.

133 Head of the Czech S.R.

134 During the course of June, the Forschungsamt, succeeded at intercepting telephone conversations between Paris and Prague (source: H.E.).

135 The French diplomatic service sought to evade application of the treaty of assistance by invoking the right of self-determination.

136 Incidents were increasing between the Czechs and the Sudeten population encouraged by Henlein who was seeking incorporation with Germany. Blood was flowing.

137 At the Nuremberg Conference on September 12, the Führer denounced the "aggression" against Czechoslovakia and affirmed that he would address the situation.

138 However, the operation of two additional moving drums (rotors) in December 1938 was not announced by H.E.

139 The armored division now comprised a brigade of 400 tanks, one infantry regiment, two civil artillery groups, a signal battalion, and a reconnaissance detachment, all of it motorized.

140 Future commander-in-chief in Indochina in 1953, Navarre directed our military Secret Service in occupied France from 1943 to 1944.

141 Perruche temporarily left the S.R. to carry out in turn a (brief) period of command in the troops—circumstances required him to return to the Bureau periodically to deal with a few sensitive matters, notably the H.E. affair in May and August 1938.

142 The Forschungsamt raided documents archived by the Austrian Cipher Bureau led by Figl in Vienna during the Anschluss.

143 Aubert was condemned to death on January 10, 1939 and executed (cf. Paul Paillole, *Services Spéciaux, 1935–1945*, Éditions Robert Laffont, pp. 118ff).

144 Head of the Naval Deuxième Bureau.

145 Pz Kw II and III tanks (cf. testimony from General Gauché, head of the Deuxième Bureau of the Army General Staff).

146 City and territory on the Niemen formerly German and incorporated in 1924 with Lithuania by the League of Nations.

147 Schmidt's vague intelligence has no connection with the Enigma machine. I have not been able to find any technical details on these "decoding machines." It appears that they were destroyed either through heavy bombing which wiped out Schillerstrasse in 1944 and Templin in 1945, or by the Germans themselves.

148 Arrested in Rome in August 1944 by our military Secret Services, Boccabella confessed without hesitation his membership in the S.I.M. (cf. Paul Paillole, *Services Spéciaux, 1935–1945*, Éditions Robert Laffont, p. 134).

149 Fall Weiss (White Plan), was the conventional name of the project.

150 General Gauché, *Le 2ᵉ Bureau au travail*, p. 100.

151 Minutes taken from meeting of August 23, 1939.

152 The French government had adopted the same attitude toward assistance as the British government (March 31, 1939).

153 See the propaganda pamphlet spread by the Nazis.

154 Boulevard Saint-Germain in Paris, thanks to the generous understanding of its patron Moutailler, supplied our Bureau with radio equipment.

155 British ambassador in Berlin.

156 Actually, the R.S.H.A. would be formally established a few weeks later and placed under the orders of Heydrich.

157 Henri Navarre, *Le Service de renseignements*, Plon, p. 81.

158 This is the day that the German-Soviet pact of non-aggression was signed in Moscow.

159 General Gauché, *Le 2ᵉ Bureau au travail*.

160 Ibid.

161 Ibid.

162 "The Spy who most affected World War II" in *Kahn on Codes*, MacMillan Publishing Company, New York, 1984, pp. 76–88.

163 Winterbotham, *Ultra*, Éditions Robert Laffont. Colonel Winterbotham of the S.I.S. was responsible for the exploitation of deciphered codes.

164 *Die Funkaufklärung und ihre rolle im 2 Weltkrieg—Rohwer et Jackel*, Motorbuch Verlag, Stuttgart, p. 84.

165 F. H. Hinsley, *British intelligence in the Second World War*, London H.M.S.O, vol. I, p. 494.

166 Or "*Gebrauchsanleitung*" (term utilized in early 1937).

167 Or "*Schlüsselmachine*," Enigma for the Navy.

168 Cf. testimony offered to the author by Bertrand and Lemoine.

169 He had left the Chiffrierstelle two months before.

170 Two Polish experts (including Langer), three British experts (including Denniston), two French experts from the Cipher Service of the Army General Staff, and Bertrand.

171 Gathered in Munich, Chamberlain, Daladier, and Mussolini signed with Hitler an agreement on the division of Czechoslovakia. Germany annexed the Sudetenland; Hungary, a part of Slovakia; and Poland, the region of Teschen.

172 Allusion to the use of two supplemental rotors by the German cryptologists since December 15, 1938.

173 Tom Green, known as Uncle Tom: 1.95m tall and about 120kg.

174 Deputy chief of the S.I.S. He would become chief two months later.

175 The construction of certain elements had been dispersed and entrusted to several reputable firms. The assembly of the various parts had to be undertaken by technicians from our Special Services.

176 General Georges was assigned to La Ferté-sous-Jouarre and later became head of the Deuxième Bureau. The man responsible for intelligence analysis was the future and remarkable General Baril.

177 Enigma prototype, perforated cards and especially the "Bomba."

178 It would be the future General Guy d'Alès, seasoned S.R. officer, former head of our post at The Hague.

179 Henri Navarre, *Le Service de renseignements*, éditions Plon.

180 General Bertrand was the mayor of Théole.

181 The theory was admitted a few weeks later, I was myself responsible for the exchange of some of the prisoners (cf. Paul Paillole, *Services spéciaux, 1935–1945*, Éditions Robert Laffont, p. 201ff).

182 Italian Intelligence Bureau.

183 Future marshal, head of the German expeditionary corps in Libya, then commander of the Army Group responsible in 1944 for the defense of the banks between the Loire and Belgium.

184 British Expeditionary Corps, 1st, 7th, and 9th French Army.

185 Commander-in-chief of the northeast theatre of operations.

186 Mussolini's son-in-law, Minister of Foreign Affairs.

187 These were the French forces for the French mainland and the British Expeditionary Corps.

188 To the best of my knowledge, our major operational units never provided evidence of mechanical use of decoding machines. It is certain that, contrary to the Abwehr, our intelligence services always had to make do with encryption systems that were traditional and archaic in nature, which explained our difficulties: the F.A. were able to breach our radio messages rapidly.

189 Such evaluations would come to light later in great precision.

190 It would be unleashed on May 10, 1940.

191 Deuxième Bureau of the Army, the head of which was General Vuillemin.

192 On June 2, 1940 the Enigma messages from the Luftwaffe could not be read.

193 Commander-in-chief of the Army (O.K.H.).

194 This is the case with the posts at The Hague, Brussels, Lille, Metz, and Belfort. Our

contacts with our posts in neutral countries were never disrupted, notably our remarkable posts in Basel and Bucharest.

195 Paul Paillole, *Services Spéciaux, 1935–1945*, Éditions Robert Laffont, *1935–1945*.

196 Parisian transport system: Regie autonome des transport parisiens.

197 Military airport near Bordeaux.

198 It had just been signed with Italy.

199 Winston Churchill, speech of June 18, 1940 to the House of Commons.

200 Winston Churchill, speech of June 18, 1940 to the House of Commons.

201 Central Office of Intelligence and Action.

202 Royal Air Force.

203 The Navy had at its disposal a unique Enigma model and specific keys that the Polish and British decoders would not be able to breach until much later.

204 Cheadle and Kingsdown for the RAF, Flowerdown and Scarborough for the Navy, Chatham for the Army.

205 Ultra-secret process of broadcasting intelligence thanks to messages deciphered by Bletchley.

206 Conclusion reached by Professor J. Rohwer, director of the Institute of History at the University of Stuttgart, following the Stuttgart International Symposium (15–18 November 1978), on the role of Ultra-Enigma during the Second World War.

207 In March 1944, the constitution of the D.G.S.S. (General Direction of the Special Services), overseen by Jacques Soustelle had forced Rivet to leave his position as head of the Special Services.

208 They would be officially recognized as such under the title of Force Françaises Combattantes (F.C.C.).

209 Camouflaged as a project of the Rural Works (T.R.).

210 My childhood friends. It was Doctor Recordier who would welcome Jean Moulin and would be one of Henry Frenay's colleagues in the group "Combat."

211 The Marseilles S.R. post led by Colonel Barbaro with his C.E. specialist Henri Guiraud and his Nice outpost, where Colonel Gallizia would earn distinction, demonstrated an exceptional level of competence and patriotic ardor.

212 It is necessary to state that the intelligence research on our fortifications was facilitated by the Service Technique du Génie's insistence on using foreign personnel, which even included the German company Siemens for the electrical installations.

213 Abwehrleitstelle (post director) having authority over establishing the Abwehrstellen in France.

214 Oskar Reile, Treff Lutetia Paris, Verlag Welsermühl, Munich.

215 General Dentz, the last French military commander of Paris, left the city on the 13th.

216 Oskar Reile was in contact with me until his death on April 27, 1983 in Mölln (R.F.A.).

217 Lieutenant Post, war minister at The Hague.

218 In code, 200 signifies invasion—10 indicates the date of the current month, thus May 10.

219 Major (commander).

220 Hauptmann (captain).

221 Among his roles at the Abwehr, Oster had been responsible for overseeing liaisons with foreign military attachés.

222 In June 1940, a Wehrmacht unit discovered two sealed train cars abandoned in a train

yard. Inside were the archives of the French General Headquarters (including those of the Deuxième Bureau). For a long time it was wrongly believed that they were the archives from the Cinquième Bureau (S.R. and C.E.).

223 Headquarters for the National Security Bureau and Territorial Surveillance Bureau.

224 Rivet's journal: "On July 24 at 15.00 a Reich commissioner accompanied by an officer from the Abwehr searched the house of the chief of staff in Paris." It was likewise for my own apartment and the apartments of my friends such as Schlesser, Navarre, Bonnefous, Bertrand, etc.

225 Vertrauen Männer: Secret agents.

226 Under the leadership of Obert, supreme S.S. leader of the police and the S.D. in France, the R.S.H.A. did not have the same scruples. He ordered in January 1943 that the central archives of the National Security Bureau be transferred to Berlin, 34 Wilhelmstrasse. The primary file related to the individuals who was being held and examined by the R.S.H.A., IV c/ 2, concerning associations, political parties, societies, etc… being under the responsibility of the R.S.H.A. D/4 (group IV of the R.S.H.A. is the Gestapo).

227 Head of the 5th Section of General Intelligence of the police department, responsible for the C.E. in Paris in connection with the authorities of the Army General Staff.

228 Mention of this conference appears in a study from 1951 on the Forschungsamt prepared for the records of the Institute of the History of National Socialism (Deutschen Instituts für Geschichte der Nationalsozialistischen Zeit), as well as in Reile's testimony to the author.

229 From September 1940 to June 1941, approximately 100 arrests of German agents were made in the free zone and in North Africa. Several death sentences were issued by military tribunals in the so-called free zone. (See Paul Paillole, *Services Spéciaux*, Éditions Robert Laffont).

230 Ordered by Goering to proceed with the purchase of metals. Roechling had met Marang before the war.

231 I left Marseilles in May 1942 (see Paul Paillole, *Services Spéciaux, 1935–1945*, Éditions Robert Laffont) to oversee the entire Counterespionage Bureau (S.S.M./T.R. network and covert military security).

232 Cf. the minutes from the hearings at the interrogation office of the French C.E. in Wildbad (October 1945 to October 1946).

233 Admiral Dupré and General Delmotte.

234 See Paul Paillole, *Services Spéciaux*, Éditions Robert Laffont, p. 380ff.

235 Ibid., p. 435ff.

236 Incarcerated in Marseilles—sort of held hostage—Lemoine's son would be freed in March 1943 after the arrest of his father.

237 End of November 1942.

238 Underlined in the original text.

239 Our S.R. had managed to intercept the line from April 1942 to Christmas 1942.

240 Cf. Lemoine dossier from the interrogation office of the French Counterespionage Bureau in Wildbad.

241 Today it is the Hotel Intercontinental (luxury five-star hotel) on rue de Castiglione.

242 Questioning of Protze by the French CE authorities from October to December 1947.

243 Cf. Lemoine's interrogation dossier from the Abwehr in Paris.

244 Lemoine never knew about the final meeting between Navarre and H.E. in Lugano in 1940.

245 Oster, just like Canaris, would be arrested following the assassination attempt against Hitler on July 20, 1944, and executed on April 9, 1945.

246 See Paul Paillole.

247 *Revue Politische Welt*, October 1967, p. 12.

248 Cf. Paul Paillole, *Services Spéciaux*, Éditions Robert Laffont, p. 64.

249 Ministry of Propaganda for the Reich.

250 After the assassination attempt of July 20, 1944 against Hitler, he would succeed in taking command of the State Army, then on the Eastern Front.

251 The Reich war tribunal.

252 Attorney General to the war tribunal.

253 Cf. the minutes in extenso of the Nuremberg International Military Tribunal.

254 This was a grave mistake by our Bureau which had access to the network of passages into Spain.

255 Defrasne a.k.a. Masuy, of Belgian origin, was recruited by the Abwehr in 1941. Sentenced to death in July 1947 by the court of justice in Paris, he was executed with three of his accomplices on October 1, 1947.

256 This was the story spread throughout the Abwehr to explain the disappearance of Hans-Thilo Schmidt.

257 Gustave Bertrand, *"Enigma" ou la plus grande énigme de la guerre, 1939–1945*, Éditions Plon.

258 Allied General Headquarters.

259 Bertrand, after his liberation, was able to inform us about the sad fate of H.E.

260 Expression from Winston Churchill apropos the Ultra-Enigma intelligence.

261 The entirety of the special measures taken by the Americans, English, and French intended to mislead the enemy. They were initiated under orders from General Dudley Clark who reported to the Allied Supreme Command (S.H.A.E.F.). See Paul Paillole, *Services Spéciaux*, Éditions Robert Laffont, p. 479ff.

262 Masterfully described by Larry Collins in his book *Fortitude*, Éditions Robert Laffont.

263 In other words: rivalry between military and civil intelligence services.

264 "Any use of the radio will be seen as high treason"—*"Funken ist Landesverrat*," possibly stated by General Fellgiebel, the big boss of Wehrmacht transmissions.

265 *Die Funkaufklärung und ihre Rolle im 2. Weltkrieg*, Stuttgart, Motorbuch Verlag 1979.

266 Old Prussian fortress in the district of Leipzig. It contained an important military prison. It was in Torgau that, in April 1945, Soviet and American troops joined forces.

267 Today it is the Hotel des Impôts in the 2nd arrondissement of Paris.

268 Hypocritical behavior imagined by the German and Vichy authorities in order to recruit laborers in exchange for the liberation of a few prisoners of war (one prisoner for every three trained laborers).

269 Obligatory Work Service.

270 It was their team—with, in particular Captain Bruel, Lieutenants Gandolphe, Loisel, Witheway, and the Commissioner Bibes—that, by its expertise and confidence in knowing how to inspire the Allies, were able to find in 1946 the "gestapiste" (Gestapo) trail of Lyon Klaus Barbie, employed by the O.S.S. in Italy. It was thus later able to proceed in the American zone with its interrogation by commission from the investigating judge of the military tribunal, Paris (Hardy affair).

271 House reserved for the lodging of those (Abwehr, R.S.H.A., etc.) under interrogation by the French C.E.

272 The message, once encrypted, is delivered to the transmission department responsible for expediting it to the recipient.

273 Operator responsible for translating into plain text an encrypted message for which the code is known.

274 Operators responsible for translating into plain text encrypted messages for which the code is not known.

275 Flat cylinders numbered 1, 2, and 3 placed in a different order set each day by the key (example: 2 June: 2, 3, and 1; 3 June: 3, 1, and 2 etc...)

276 A "day" is a twenty-four-hour period commencing at noon. Beginning in 1942 the duration of the settings will move from twenty-four to eight hours, thus three times the number of complications.

277 Such as the "Bomba" then the "Colossus," which were truly the ancestors of today's computers.

278 Beginning on December 15, 1938, the choice of three drums for one to use would be part of a set of five drums.

279 Unedited document. It contains a few errors in dates, notably those in relation to the period when P.C. Bruno was in operation.

280 Messages from the Abwehr, the majority of which were controlled by services from our C.E. (embedded agents).

281 Allied landing in North Africa (November 8, 1942).

282 Note that Bertrand did not give Hans-Thilo Schmidt's personal name. He would maintain such discretion with respect to his former agent until his death.

283 Distinguished Service Order.

284 One will note that Colonel Hossbach, the Führer's aide-de-camp, and friend of General Rudolf Schmidt, took five days to prepare the minutes of the secret conference from November 5, 1937. The accused, notably Goering and Reitel, who were present at this conference, did not discuss the authenticity of this document during the course of hearings at the Nuremberg Military Tribunal. (N.d.A.)

285 It was during this second part of the discussion that covered the distribution of steel, the protocol of which was reported (hereinafter) at the conference organized on December 9, 1937 by Admiral Canaris. (N.d.A)

286 C.E. in the Ministry of the Interior and in other civil administrations.

287 Lieutenant Commander Protz—embedded in the enemy S.R.s.

288 Chief of the Security Police.

289 Regierungsrat (R.R.).

290 Hitler's aide-de-camp (N.d.l.R)

291 This was so that he could enter the Forschungsamt as head of the Templin post. (N.d.A.)

292 Lemoine is alluding here to Drach, whom he had already denounced and whom he didn't know had been arrested by the Abwehr.